MAKING MONSTERS

What do we as artists do if not make monsters like Dr Frankenstein? Only instead of using cadavers, we graft flesh-like materials onto people who bring those creatures to life.

And who are we as people, if not the Monster himself? Not evil, world-dominating forces, but anxious, misunderstood and incapable, sometimes, of relating to normal people.

John Wrightson

Yes, I made people suffer. Bent their heads back for hours, drowning them in blood. Poured maggots on their faces till they screamed. All that ever mattered, though, was the effect. Pain's temporary, you know? Film is forever.

Tom Savini

People say, "Oh, it was so gruesome! I covered my eyes."

I've always thought that's a little weird. I'd rather have you lean forward and look at the effect I spent three months on.

Gabe Bartalos

DEDICATIONS

Howard
This book is dedicated to my parents, Kenneth and Susan Berger, who let me destroy my bedroom, their oven, and let me obsess over monsters and monster movies my entire childhood. Thanks for always lifting me up and supporting this weird little kid who grew up to be a weird big kid.

Marshall
The Ann Darrow to my Kong, Kay Lawrence to my Gill-Man and Buffy Summers to my Angel, this book is for my love, my life, the wind beneath my bat wings… my wonderful wife Ruta.

Text copyright © 2025 Howard Berger and Marshall Julius

The right of Howard Berger and Marshall Julius to be identified as the Authors of the Work has been asserted by them in accordance with the Copyright, Designs and Patents Act 1988.

Published by Welbeck Illustrated
An Imprint of HEADLINE PUBLISHING GROUP LIMITED

1

Apart from any use permitted under UK copyright law, this publication may only be reproduced, stored, or transmitted, in any form, or by any means, with prior permission in writing of the publishers or, in the case of reprographic production, in accordance with the terms of licences issued by the Copyright Licensing Agency.

Cataloguing in Publication Data is available from the British Library

ISBN 978-1-80279-845-6

Editorial: Ross Hamilton
Design: Russell Knowles, Bobby Birchall, Howard Berger and Marshall Julius
Production: Marion Storz

Printed and bound in China.

Headline's policy is to use papers that are natural, renewable and recyclable products and made from wood grown in well-managed forests and other controlled sources. The logging and manufacturing processes are expected to conform to the environmental regulations of the country of origin.

HEADLINE PUBLISHING GROUP LIMITED
An Hachette UK Company
Carmelite House
50 Victoria Embankment
London EC4Y 0DZ

The authorised representative in the EEA is Hachette Ireland,
8 Castlecourt Centre, Dublin 15, D15 XTP3, Ireland (email: info@hbgi.ie)

www.headline.co.uk
www.hachette.co.uk

MAKING MONSTERS

INSIDE STORIES FROM THE CREATORS OF HOLLYWOOD'S MOST ICONIC CREATURES

HOWARD BERGER & MARSHALL JULIUS

FOREWORD BY
ROBERT ENGLUND

AFTERWORD BY
ALEX WINTER

WELBECK

CONTENTS

INTRODUCTIONS / HOWARD BERGER – 6 / MARSHALL JULIUS – 8
FOREWORD – 10

 SIMPLY THE BEAST
12

 MARCH OF THE MONSTER KIDS
38

 WEIRD SCIENCE
66

 STOMP AND CIRCUMSTANCE
76

 FANGS FOR SHARING
94

 INFERNAL AFFAIRS
108

 FROM THE LAND BEYOND BEYOND
124

 SLICE 'N' QUEASY
136

 GROWLING PAINS
166

 TO SCARE IS HUMAN
182

 DO THE RIGHT THING
196

 CREEPY, CRABBY CRITTERS
224

 IT'S ALIVE!
250

 TOO GHOUL FOR SCHOOL
260

 BOO STORIES
288

 MAKING A MONSTER
296

AFTERWORD – 308
FILMOGRAPHIES – 310
INDEX – 314
ACKNOWLEDGEMENTS – 317
CREDITS – 318
AUTHOR BIOGRAPHIES – 320

INTRODUCTION

by Howard Berger

One night, when I was small, my father woke me up. "Howard, get out of bed. There's a movie on television I have to show you."

Rubbing my eyes, I shuffled groggily downstairs. The black-and-white TV cast a flicker in our living room, and as I walked in, my dad said, "Come sit down and watch this. It's one of the best films you'll ever see."

I was transfixed from frame one. The film was George A. Romero's *Night of the Living Dead* (1968) and it was my introduction to the world of zombies in all their greyscale, gory glory! Why my father thought it was OK to show a six-year-old such an intense horror movie is still beyond me, but then he never held back from sharing his love of monsters, sneaking me issues of *Famous Monsters of Filmland* and still unit photos he would get as gifts for me from studio film distributors.

That was the beginning of my love affair with monsters and monster movies. It was a habit my father fed with great enthusiasm: Universal monster classics, especially 1954's *Creature from the Black Lagoon*; Godzilla movies, with 1968's *Destroy All Monsters* being my favourite until 2023's *Godzilla Minus One*; *King Kong* (1933), of course; *The Thing with Two Heads* (1972), with Ray Milland, Rosey Grier and Rick Baker as the Two-Headed Gorilla at the start of the film; and *Dr Phibes Rises Again* (1972), the film that gave me intense, recurring nightmares of scorpions crawling on a human face, half-buried in the sand. Every night I'd wake up screaming and my mother would barrel in, yelling, "YOU'LL NEVER SEE ANOTHER HORROR FILM AS LONG AS YOU LIVE."

Obviously that didn't happen!

I don't know exactly what it is about monsters and monster movies that fascinates me, or why it's an obsession so many of us share. Pretty much everyone I meet – no matter who they are, what they do, or where they're from – loves monsters. I remember I was working on a film titled *The Way of the Gun* (2000) with Benicio Del Toro, and one day I happened to be wearing a *Creature from the Black Lagoon* t-shirt. I walked past Benicio and heard, "…that's my favourite monster."

I doubled back and we started talking about OUR favourite Universal Monster of all time. I would have never expected that and was so pleased that such a great actor shared my delight of the Gill-man, as well as my overall love of monsters. I worked with Tom Hanks on *The Green Mile* (1999), and he told me one of his greatest joys was awarding Ray Harryhausen with his Honorary Lifetime Achievement Academy Award! Another great, iconic movie star who loves the magic of monsters!

I could go on and on about why I – and so many others like me – love monsters and what drove me to become a monster maker, but you'll learn all about that, and a lot more besides, in the pages ahead.

Monsters are a part of our DNA, the fabric of what makes us who we are. They share our humanity, our curiosity; we share their pathos and love of frightening others... Insert evil laugh here: BWA HA HA HA!

What can I say? I LOVE MONSTERS! At 60 years old, that will never change. Once a monster lover, always a monster lover! Enjoy the read and MONSTERS RULE FOREVER!

Best, Howard

INTRODUCTION

by Marshall Julius

I could bang on forever about why I love monsters. Rationalize my devotion to the Nth degree: the spectacle, the mystery, the appeal of the impossible; the pathos, of course, and sheer, giddy invention. Then there's how they make you feel: the rush of fear followed by the curious comfort of feeling safe on the sofa while some screen stranger comes a cropper at the paws or jaws of some nightmare beast.

All of that is true, but likewise, utter bollocks. Just me trying to put into words a feeling all monster kids already understand, if not in their heads, then certainly in their hearts. In the dark bits of our beings. It's what draws us together. It's how we find our friends.

Perhaps what I'm after's not a word, but a sound? Like, imagine "Wheeeee!" had a baby, but wasn't sure if the father was "Aaarrgh!" or "Ooh!". So they raised it as a throuple, and whatever their sound baby grew up to be, that's how I feel about monsters. That's clear, yeah? No? Fine, I'll try something else.

I'm a big fan of swearing, but not when I write. As a word monkey and professional appreciator, I strive to express myself without resorting to expletives. So I'm sorry for using the word bollocks two paragraphs earlier, and then again, seven words ago. It just felt right. Equally, I apologize for the line after this one, but honestly, I can't think of a plainer, more concise or more honest way to describe how I feel:

I JUST FUCKING LOVE MONSTERS.

To paraphrase a favourite line of mine from *Annie Hall* (1977), even love's too weak a word for what I feel. I luuurve them. I loave them. I luff them.

Moving on, then.

The book you now clutch in your claws is the offspring of eighty-odd sparkling conversations that Howard and I enjoyed with a succession of friendly, enthusiastic creatives from across a variety of disciplines: writers, directors, composers and actors, make-up and special effects wizards, artists, designers… All of them fans, all excited to chat about their favourite film fiends, the movies that made them, the filmmakers who inspired them, and the adventures they've had in the big, wide, wonderful world of professional monster making.

It was a joy to be privy to those fabulous chats, my duty to carve out the best and most memorable bits, and my pleasure to present them to you in the pages ahead.

A handful of contributors are doing so from beyond the grave. As an entertainment journalist I've zealously exploited every opportunity to meet my heroes, and their stories deserve remembering: my hero, Ray Harryhausen; iconic directors George A. Romero and Wes Craven; Bond legend Richard Kiel and my friend Christopher Tucker, whom I met when Howard and I interviewed him for our last book, *Masters of Make-Up Effects* (2022).

I hope you enjoy what everyone has to say, and luff the pictures they gave us to share with you. And come, let's talk about monsters sometime, ourselves. Honestly, it's my favourite thing to do.

Marshall

Opposite (top): A golden moment for 19-year-old Marshall Julius, thrilled to be standing for a snap beside his filmmaking hero, Ray Harryhausen.

Opposite (bottom): Authors Howard Berger and Marshall Julius being as sensible as usual.

FOREWORD

by Robert Englund

Howard Berger has spent more time probing the various crevices of my face than any ear, nose and throat specialist. Between the prosthetic glue in my ears, inserting contact lenses in my eyes, snapping discoloured dentures over my teeth and sticking straws up my nose so I could breathe during the facial mould process, we forged what could be called an intimate relationship.

Howard must have wished he could have glued my mouth shut, too, for I constantly chattered during those three-hour-plus sessions. The subject of all this distracting talk was our mutual love of horror, science-fiction and fantasy films, and our memories of our favourite monsters and effects. Those rich memories and images informed my subconscious from childhood right up until today.

In a roughly chronological timeline, those visual landmarks that seared themselves into my brain go something like this: flying monkeys on a black-and-white TV; King Kong's fight with the pterodactyl and Fay Wray's nipples on *The Late Late Show*; Karloff's brow and bolts; Igor hung on a hook; the monster's bride's electric-shock afro and erratic movements; the sucker welts on that hapless sailor's face from the giant squid's tentacles in *20,000 Leagues Under the Sea* (1954); the clacking beak of that same squid; the sound of the giant ants in *Them* (1954); the soundtrack and the animation FX of the saber-tooth tiger in *Forbidden Planet* (1956) contrasted with Anne Francis's futuristic miniskirt; Jean Marsh's destroyed robot face on my favourite episode of *The Twilight Zone* (1959-1964); culminating in the reveal of Norman Bates' mother at the drive-in movie.

Then began my adolescence and graduation into the saturated colour of Hammer Film monsters and eventually the work of Dick Smith, Rick Baker, Stan Winston and my future colleagues and friends. From the outset of our relationship, Wes Craven counselled me to cherish those early memories and respect the genre and its monster makers. And so I have, and so I do.

Thanks, Howard, for letting me share my love of the genre all those years ago in the make-up chair, and thanks for sharing yours now.

Robert
September 2025

SIMPLY THE BEAST

Devoting your life to monsters takes weapons-grade inspiration: Kong-sized, Thing-shaped wonders that dramatically rewire young brains for the better, laying waste to any notion of a sensible life. How grateful we are for their intervention!

Like a virus – only far more welcome – once monsters stomp into our systems, they're there forever. Here, then, are the classic creatures, formative features and fantastic filmmakers who transformed our initially ordinary contributors into Master Monster Kids.

As a monster kid growing up in a house of athletes, the way Forry Ackerman presented himself in *Famous Monsters* magazine was very important to me.

Forry was like, "You're not weird. You're fine. I'm an adult and I love this stuff. Ray Bradbury's an adult and he loves this stuff. You're great. Keep going."

That sustained me.

Dana Gould

Probably my favourite contribution to *The Book of Lists: Horror* (2008) came from an interview I did with fantasy author Ray Bradbury, when he listed the top five monster movies that influenced him as a boy.

Number one was the original, silent version of *The Hunchback of Notre Dame* (1923). Ray said he saw it when he was three years old and never forgot it. Number two was *The Phantom of the Opera* (1925), so two Lon Chaney classics in a row.

Number three was *The Lost World* (1925), with stop motion dinosaurs from a pre-Kong Willis O'Brien. Ray wrote a bunch of articles about that movie during his early career, one of which caught John Huston's eye, and led him to hire Ray to write the screenplay for *Moby Dick* (1956).

Number four was *King Kong* (1933), because Ray was in love with Fay Wray. Kong was also a favourite, of course, of one of Ray's best friends, Ray Harryhausen. And number five was *The Mummy* (1932). Ray was so captivated by Boris Karloff's performance in that, he wanted to be the Mummy himself. Same as he wanted to be the Hunchback after seeing the Chaney movie. Clearly, Ray often empathized with the so-called monsters.

Del Howison

I've always loved the silent *Phantom of the Opera* (1925), and the older I get, the more I appreciate it. The make-up, costumes and production design are all extraordinary, but nothing's more iconic than the Phantom in costume as the Masque of the Red Death.

Damien Leone

"THE OLDER I GET, THE MORE I APPRECIATE IT."

Preceding Spread: Transformed by a full moon - and make-up legend Roy Ashton, of course - a young Oliver Reed terrorized audiences in Hammer favourite, *The Curse of the Werewolf* (1961).

Opposite (top): Best known to his fans as "Forry", Forest J. Ackerman beams with due pride in a characteristically treasure-lined room in Horrorwood, Karloffornia's glorious Ackermansion.

Opposite (bottom): Ray Harryhausen and Dark Delicacies owner Del Howison enjoyed a decades-long friendship, with Ray often conducting signings in Del's magical store.

Below: Lon Chaney is the belle of the ball in a fetching, fearsome Masque of the Red Death ensemble from *Phantom of the Opera* (1925).

There's something about Bela Lugosi's Dracula. Those piercing eyes. His mesmerizing expressions. The elegance with which he carries himself. He's iconic.

Justin Raleigh

Especially for the time, Fredric March's transformations in *Dr. Jekyll and Mr. Hyde* (1931) were absolutely brilliant. I don't think anyone has surpassed that look for Hyde, and the way March played him, it's no wonder he won an Oscar. It's a scary film, and it stays with you.

Allan Apone

Above: "Never has a role so influenced and dominated an actor's life as has the role of Dracula," said charismatic Universal star Bela Lugosi of his batty alter ego. "Dracula has, at times, infused me with prosperity and, at other times, drained me of everything."

Right: Fredric March won his first Best Actor Oscar for playing both leading men in *Dr. Jekyll and Mr. Hyde* (1931), one of the first films to showcase an on-screen transformation, achieved by an artful combination of make-up, lighting and cinematography.

Opposite: Painted in the Gogos style by artist Maelo Cintron, *Famous Monsters* #140 saw Glenn Strange's not-so Jolly Green Giant glaring from the cover (and beyond the grave) as Universal's second most famous Frankenstein's Monster.

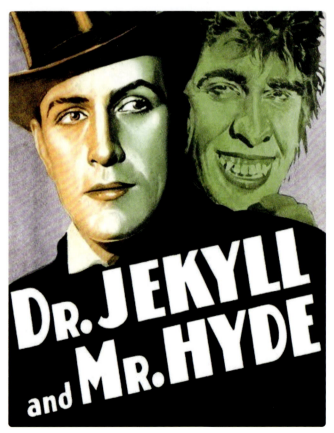

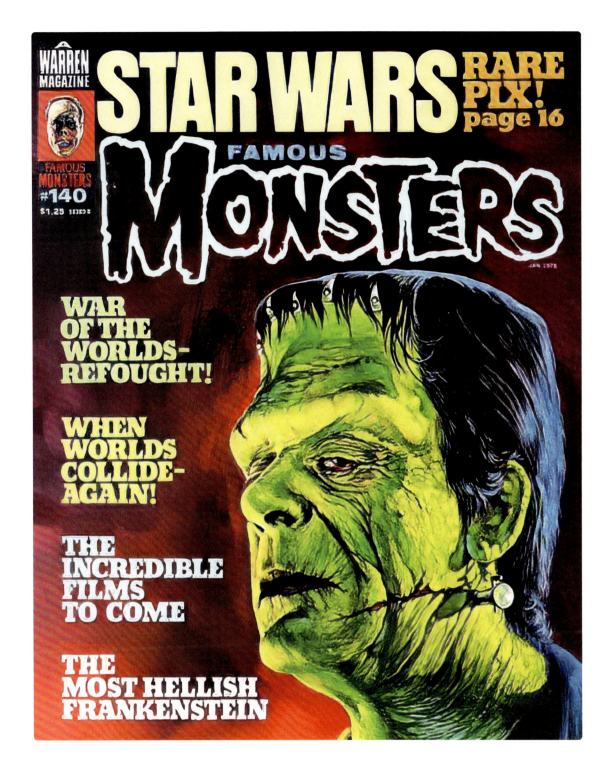

Working with Benicio Del Toro on *The Wolfman* (2009), we found we had lots in common. Specifically, monsters and monster movies, which I think he loves as much as I do. He'd buy old monster magazines and quiz me on stuff, show me pictures and test my trivia knowledge. I'd go, "That's Conrad Veidt from *The Man Who Laughs* (1928). That's who they based the Joker on."

We were doing great until he told me Glenn Strange was his favourite Frankenstein. I was like, "How can you say that? There's no doubt Karloff was the best."

Obviously I like Glenn Strange, especially in *Abbott and Costello Meet Frankenstein* (1948), but there's really no comparison. He was just a big guy, walking around. Karloff gave this amazing performance.

I don't think I changed Benicio's mind, but we didn't let it come between us. We made up!

Rick Baker

A lot of people say they can't do black and white, but I don't get that at all. The old Universal monster movies wouldn't have been nearly as impactful in colour. The way they play with light and shadow gives them a mythic quality that couldn't possibly be matched today. *Bride of Frankenstein* (1935) is easily my favourite. From the gothic horror and gallows humour to its eccentric cast of characters, it's inherently cinematic.

John Wrightson

Few designs are as striking as Elsa Lanchester's Bride of Frankenstein, but beneath the surface, her appeal is even more interesting. She's less a monster, I think, than a misunderstood being. She was created by men for a purpose, but that's not what she wanted. As a young girl, I identified with her struggle.

Tami Lane

When I was little, I wanted to be an archaeologist or a make-up artist. *The Mummy* (1932) ticked both those boxes and I loved it. Remember when there's a glimmer in his eye, and his hand starts to move? That freaked me out so bad! And Ardath Bey's mummified skin? So creepy!

Ve Neill

I wanted to meet Jack Pierce. I knew where he lived, out in the San Fernando Valley, so I cycled to his house with my brother one day. Without thinking to call ahead, we just knocked on his door and introduced ourselves. He invited us in and spent an hour telling us stories and showing us pictures of his old days at Universal. My Uncle Bud took his place there, so he could have been sore, but actually he couldn't have been nicer. I'm so happy I got to spend that time with him.

Michael Westmore

"WHEN I WAS LITTLE, I WANTED TO BE AN ARCHAEOLOGIST OR A MAKE-UP ARTIST."

Opposite: Here comes the *Bride of Frankenstein* (1935), all dressed in white, the immortal Elsa Lanchester sporting make-up from maestro Jack Pierce.

Below (left): Boris Karloff endured hours of painstaking make-up and costuming to create his iconic look for *The Mummy* (1932).

Below (right): The Uncanny Boris Karloff, simply chilling in Jack Pierce's Ardath Bey make-up for *The Mummy* (1932).

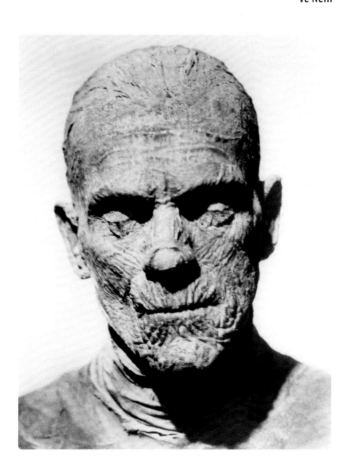

Creature from the Black Lagoon is so well designed, they've never been able to improve on it. Even Guillermo couldn't come up with a better version.

Joe Dante

Creature from the Black Lagoon (1954) excited me because, even as a kid, I had a sense of what looked good and what didn't. And the Creature looked great! Especially underwater, where an added layer of diffusion made it seem even more real. It can't have been easy to film those scenes, and I liked that it was difficult. I just enjoyed and appreciated the hell out of it.

Gabe Bartalos

The greatest creature suit ever made is the Gill-man from Creature from the Black Lagoon (1954). He's reptilian. He's amphibian. I love how he moves. I love how he swims. And through it all, that suit never buckles, wrinkles, or looks weird. The fact that they figured it out in the Fifties boggles my mind.

Howard Berger

"UNDERNEATH, I'M STILL THAT SAME PETRIFIED LITTLE KID."

Above: Better known as the Creature from the Black Lagoon (1954), the Gill-man's classic creature suit remains a best-in-class design.

Left: Though Ricou Browning played the Gill-man underwater in Creature from the Black Lagoon (1954), it was actor Ben Chapman (left) who played him on land. Here's Ben in Bud Westmore's (right) Universal Studios creature and make-up lab, inspecting the suits that transformed him into the iconic monster.

Opposite (above): Greg Nicotero, David Wogh, Michael Deak and Shannon Shea stand at the mouth of Bronson Canyon with their re-creation of Paul Blaisdell's Beula creature from Roger Corman's It Conquered the World (1956).

Opposite (below): Willis O'Brien's expressive stop motion model of King Kong (1933) was truly the 8th Wonder of the World.

I was four when I saw *It Came from Outer Space* (1953). This bizarre thing with a giant eyeball scared the shit out of me. I fell in love with it!

John Carpenter

My mom took me to see a re-release of *The Mummy* (1932) when I was very young. I was scared to death for the next six months. If I heard any sort of mysterious sound outside, like the wind blowing through the trees or an owl hooting, I'd sleep the whole night with my head under the covers. Everything about that film was real to me, and to this day, I can watch it and I love it, but underneath, I'm still that same petrified little kid.

Michael Westmore

Every Thanksgiving at our grandparents' house, it was a family tradition to watch *Mighty Joe Young* (1949) and *King Kong* (1933). Don't ask me why! Those films were my introduction to monsters having hearts and souls. To being characters in their own right, and not just creatures who kill and destroy.

Scott Stoddard

Paul Blaisdell and Bob Burns hail from that era of movies where they'd make monsters for little to no money, in five to six days. Quickly cut some foam together, slap some paint on it and you've got yourself a monster! Films like *It Conquered the World* (1955), *The She-Creature* (1957) and, of course, *Invasion of the Saucer Men* (1957). The designs are campy but memorable and still celebrated to this day.

What a fabulous Fifties' design those sci-fi Saucer Men were, with their big, veiny heads, bulbous eyes, eyeballs on the backs of their hands, and let's not forget their fingernail needles that injected you with alcohol. I mean, wait... What? It was all so weird!

Greg Nicotero

The invisible monster. The futuristic stylings. The electronic tonalities of Bebe and Louis Barron... I've always loved everything about *Forbidden Planet* (1956). It's the movie that inspired me to become a director, though to be honest, I've never really enjoyed directing.

On the special features for *Ghosts of Mars* (2001), there's a shot of me sitting in the recording studio, looking like a dead person. Directing is just so stressful and exhausting. But I do enjoy having directed. I like it when I'm done, and I can send my finished movie out into the world.

John Carpenter

Christopher Lee had a very unusual face: weird double cheekbones, a noble, flattened profile and, of course, that terrible graveyard of a mouth. His lower teeth were all over the place! Not Hollywood perfection, but those unique features worked in his favour.

He was a natural to play Dracula, and is by far my favourite actor to ever do so. A novel mix of aloof, aristocratic and fiery European. Cold and snobbish one moment, a snarling animal the next. Always a shocking transformation and amazing to watch.

Graham Humphreys

I've always had a soft spot for *The Blob* (1958), as it was the first horror movie I saw as a kid. This big, gooey, shapeless thing that oozes after you. I'd wrap myself in an old comforter and crawl around on the floor. Mom would be like, "Uh-oh, here comes the Blob!"

Terry Wolfinger

The Munsters (1964-66) was a cool TV show. It didn't matter how they looked, or how different they were. Yes, they were misfits – some Frankensteins, a vampire, a werekid – but aren't we all? Really they're just a family, muddling through. And such a nice, friendly way to introduce the classic monsters to kids.

Sarah Gower

For me, the real draw of Aurora model kits was James Bama's box art. The models themselves were rather disappointing. They fell short in likeness and certainly didn't live up to Bama's paintings.

His colour palettes made the greatest impression on me. Those rich purples and greens are so powerful! I learned so much from those covers about how colour can convey horror.

Say, for example, you're representing stonework, it doesn't have to be a natural colour. Just look at Bama's beautiful Dracula box art. The castle setting is purple, hardly the colour of stone, but still, you understand what it is. It's all about atmosphere.

Graham Humphreys

The Giant Claw (1957) is one of my favourite guilty pleasures. The monster looks like a giant turkey, and moves like a marionette, because that's exactly what it is! It's fake and hilarious and opened my eyes to so many other wonderful, terrible films about giant radioactive monsters.

Del Howison

Opposite: A glorious tribute to Christopher Lee by artist Graham Humphreys, referencing a handful of the actor's best-loved movies.

Above: James Bama's box art was typically more impressive than the model kits they adorned. His full-blooded box art for Aurora's take on Lugosi's Dracula was no exception.

Right: The perfect entry-level terrors for fledgling monster kids, Herman, Lily, Grandpa, Eddie and Marilyn were TV's frightful first family, *The Munsters* (1964-66).

Nothing spooked me more as a kid than monsters just out of sight. I'll take a threatening alien presence over a vampire or werewolf any day. *Quatermass and the Pit* (1967) was a real favourite. In the United States they called it *Five Million Years to Earth*. Martians are discovered in London and it's a real mind-bender. A Hammer adaptation of a Fifties' BBC series that seems to have inspired everyone from John Carpenter to Ridley Scott.

Gary Archer

I really admire the craftsmanship of *The Exorcist* (1973). Beyond and perhaps even above the make-up, the cinematography and sound elevate it into something truly haunting. To this day, Regan's demon voice scares the heck out of me.

Justin Raleigh

I saw *It's Alive* (1974) when I was way too young. That weird mutant baby scared me shitless. Its big veiny head, those crazy fangs and, more than anything, those huge three-fingered hands with the freaky claws. It's something I've never gotten out of my head, so thanks, Rick Baker!

Chad Coleman

"THAT WEIRD MUTANT BABY SCARED ME SHITLESS."

Above: Linda Blair as poor, possessed Regan was one of many enduring nightmares created by Dick Smith for *The Exorcist* (1973).

Left: A youthful Rick Baker refines his striking sculpture for Larry Cohen's baby monster masterpiece *It's Alive* (1974).

Opposite: Hammer's film poster for *The Curse of the Werewolf* (1961) promised fur and fang-fuelled frights and did not disappoint.

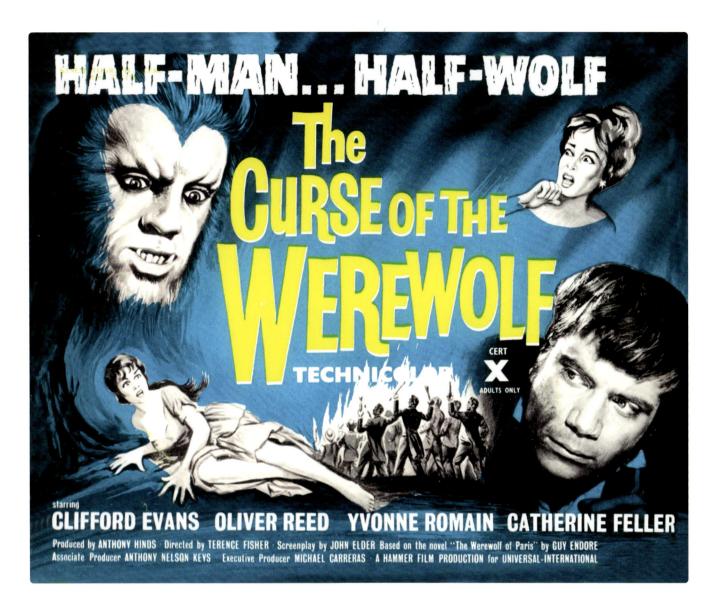

It might be sacrilege to say, and certainly it's the lesser known of the two, but I've always preferred *Legend of the Werewolf* (1975) to *Curse of the Werewolf* (1961). Freddie Francis directed it for Tyburn Films, and it felt very much like an old Hammer production, only with more of an edge. I loved the werewolf too, as it had a distinctive shock of white hair. A much better and more interesting make-up than Oliver Reed had in *Curse*.

Neill Gorton

Ever since I was a kid I've liked monsters. *The Fly* (1958), *The Blob* (1958), the Hydra from *Jason and the Argonauts* (1963)... They get you out of your head, out of your life, and take you somewhere new.

I grew up in the carnival business. My dad was a concessionaire who ran balloon dart and basketball games. I used to nap in boxes of stuffed animals under the counter! I took a lot of thrill rides, too, and scary movies give me the same sort of buzz, so maybe that's why I've always liked them. Still, I'm not easily fazed by freaky stuff, as I hung out in a lot of Curiosity Tents with wolf men, two-headed cows and babies in jars.

Trilogy of Terror (1975), though... The segment where Karen Black's hunted by a Zuni fetish doll. That scared me so much! Even today I have to check under the bed for that evil little critter.

Barbara Crampton

Star Wars (1977) isn't spoken of enough as a monster movie. Yes, it's this vast and mighty, buccaneering action adventure, but don't discount that cantina full of creatures. It's funny to think that's normal television now, but at the time, we'd never seen anything like it. Mad monsters everywhere. Joy! It was the first time in my life that I went to see a film twice. Such a happy memory.

Russell T. Davies

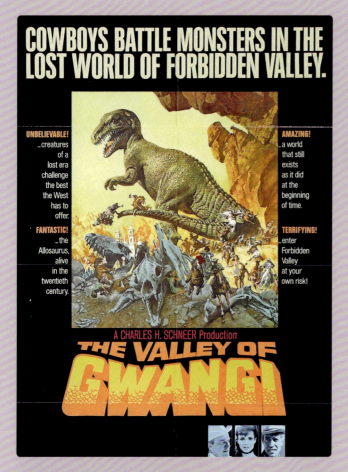

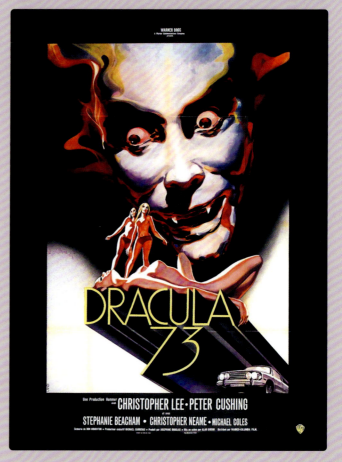

My five favourite monster movie posters? The first has to be *Jaws* (1975). A fiendishly simple piece of graphic design, and a beautiful painting as well. A classic example of less is more.

Next is *The Mummy* (1932). A lovely Art Deco poster with an exotic colour palette, capturing the fascination of the age with all things Egyptian.

A stunning, smoky headshot of Dracula dominates the very sexy, stylish French film poster for *Dracula 73* (1972) [a.k.a. *Dracula AD 1972*].

What more could you want from a horror movie poster than Vincent Price with a severed head, a skeleton dangling a corpse and a big, old, creepy house? *House on Haunted Hill* (1959) has it all!

From the colour palette to the dramatic composition and, of course, the massive dinosaur skulls in the foreground, Frank McCarthy's poster for *The Valley of Gwangi* (1969) instantly brings back the wonder and thrills I experienced watching the film as a child.

Graham Humphreys

Jaws (1975) was a staple of my childhood. The shark was great, of course. Easily one of the coolest-looking creatures ever created. But really it was the characters my family loved. My mum would talk about them, calling them by their first names, as if she knew them. Even at an early age it fascinated me that a movie could elicit such strong emotions from adults. I wanted to understand that power.

Damien Leone

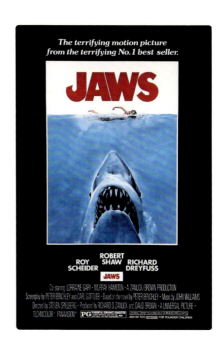

Opposite: A quartet of classic monster movie posters, as chosen by master of the art Graham Humphreys: *The Valley of Gwangi* (1969), *The Mummy* (1932), *House on Haunted Hill* (1959) and *Dracula 73* (1972).

Above: Graham Humphreys in his colourful studio, surrounded by posters from artists who helped inspire his signature style.

Right: Arguably the most iconic movie poster of all time, and top of Graham Humphreys' list, is Roger Kastel's gripping art for *Jaws* (1975).

Story-wise, there's almost nothing to *Alien* (1979). It's b-level stuff, but the simplicity works as it allows you to focus instead on the film's amazing attention to detail. The mood's just so tense and the textured, tactile nature of Giger's designs is genius. Clearly an incredible level of care went into it. It's dingy and scary and all the more believable for it.

Mark Tavares

There are a hundred things about *Alien* (1979) that make it perfect. Ridley Scott's stunning visuals. His decision to hire a crazy Swiss surrealist to design the monster. Jerry Goldsmith's score. It's one great decision after another, and every one of them is flawlessly executed.

When I worked on *Aliens* (1986) at Stan Winston's shop, Giger's original creature suit arrived in a crate. Boxed up for years, it was rank! Kluged together with macaroni and bottle caps, glued on and spray-painted black. Completely haphazard, but on screen, it worked beautifully.

Howard Berger

The best monster and the best monster movie, hands down, is *Alien* (1979). The discovery, the bizarreness, the freshness of it. From Ridley Scott's cinéma-vérité style of shooting to the inscrutable way Giger's creature continually changes shape, nothing will ever top it.

From a historical perspective, *Alien* changed everything about creature design. It introduced all the elements that every single designer of creatures in the world has used since. Yes, we're affected by *Star Wars* (1977), but *Alien* was just beyond, beyond, beyond. It introduced biomechanics. It introduced sexuality into design. It introduced the element of surprise: the idea that the mouth opens and something else comes out. All of these are now tricks in the creature designer's arsenal.

Jordu Schell

My father [Bernie Wrightson] was a big James Cameron fan, and watched *Aliens* (1986) more times than anyone could count. As much as he loved the movie, though, he found [H. R.] Giger's work unsettling and a little perverse. I'd tell him, "That's the point."

John Wrightson

Above: H.R. Giger's groundbreaking xenomorph from Ridley Scott's trailblazing *Alien* (1979).

Opposite: Peter Berg reacts with due horror in a scene from Wes Craven's *Shocker* (1989). It was Craven, in part, who inspired Berg to become a director, Berg's credits including *Lone Survivor* (2013), *Deepwater Horizon* (2016) and *American Primeval* (2025).

Wes Craven was honest with me about why he was making *Shocker* (1989). Soon after I was cast in the movie, he told me that back when he'd made *A Nightmare on Elm Street* (1984), he felt the studio, New Line, had ripped him off. He was never able to cash in on Freddy Krueger.

Shocker was his chance to reload, and Horace Pinker (Mitch Pileggi) was going to be his payday. Unfortunately the film didn't take off the way he'd hoped, but for me, watching Wes direct was an invaluable experience.

He was so kind and thoughtful. Such a sweet and intelligent guy. Not at all what you'd expect from the director of such terrifying films. I remember my first glimpse into his particular flavour of brilliance. Horace Pinker was about to be executed, and as I watched him explain to the crew how he visualized the horrifying scene ahead, his whole demeanour changed. It was like he entered some dark trance.

Before then, I couldn't line up in my mind that this mild-mannered guy was the horror master who'd freaked me out with *The Hills Have Eyes* (1977). But after I saw him shift into this intense, creative state, it all made sense. I feel privileged to have witnessed Wes at work, and often think of him when I'm directing. Like Wes, I try to shrug off everything but the scene at hand. To blot out the baggage of production and disappear into the headspace necessary to give the scene everything I've got.

Peter Berg

Before I met Wes [Craven] I had an image of him in my head, like maybe he was some sort of a Vincent Price-type character. But actually he was so sweet and soft spoken. More like a favourite professor, and I learned so much from him. Life stuff, like how he conducted himself, and how he treated people. And also when I was preparing to direct *The Tripper* (2006), he helped me with shot ideas and composition.

David Arquette

"HE WAS SO KIND AND THOUGHTFUL. SUCH A SWEET AND INTELLIGENT GUY. NOT AT ALL WHAT YOU'D EXPECT FROM THE DIRECTOR OF SUCH TERRIFYING FILMS."

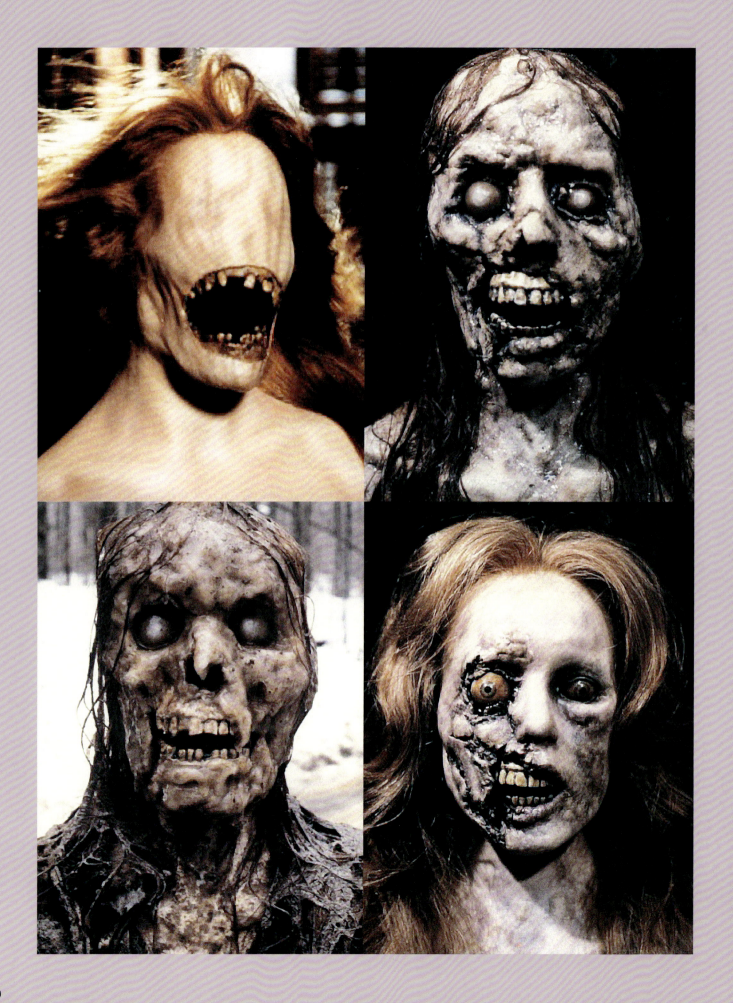

When I first saw *Dragonslayer* (1981), I was convinced Vermithrax Pejorative was real. It was so lifelike, the way it walked on its elbows like a bat. The design's just brilliant, and the animation's so smooth. All these years later, it's still the dragon to beat.

Howard Berger

For me, the greatest monster make-up of all time is Eva from *Ghost Story* (1981). Underneath all those layers of pain and decomposition, you can still see it's her. Dick Smith did a remarkable job as that's exactly what I expect a rotting ghost would look like.

Josh Turi

When I was small, I was obsessed with the octopus at the end of *Popeye* (1980). I knew it wasn't real, but that didn't stop me from being drawn into the magic. Even though it wasn't on screen for very long, I suspect it inspired my lifelong love of movies and otherworldly creatures.

Kerrin Jackson

I like weird, twisty, asymmetrical, mutated, bubbly stuff. That's why I love *The Thing* (1982).

Robert Kurtzman

When I first saw Rick Baker's transformation in *An American Werewolf in London* (1981) I was wowed. It was art in motion. Created with clever design progressions and stunningly well executed. It showed me that special make-up effects are truly artworks in their own right.

Gabe Bartalos

There was a moment, in my development as a Monster Kid, when I began to appreciate the artistry that went into creature creation. When I could trace the penmanship of a gifted creator like Rob Bottin.

Obviously there have been a lot of amazing make-up effects over the years, but still, I'd argue that Bottin's work in *The Thing* (1982) remains unparalleled. It's so inventive. It's so shocking. There's nothing quite like it.

Mike Mendez

"SPECIAL MAKE-UP EFFECTS ARE TRULY ARTWORKS IN THEIR OWN RIGHT."

Opposite: From the brilliant mind of Dick Smith sprang the many monstrous mugs of Alma Mobley (Alice Krige) from *Ghost Story* (1981).

Above: Phil Tippett's innovative go-motion dragon, Vermithrax Pejorative, dominates the sky in *Dragonslayer* (1981).

Jerry Goldsmith was brilliant. I did more pictures with him than any other director. Whenever something went wrong on set, we'd just say, "Don't worry. Jerry will fix it!"

He was a genius at figuring out where music should go, and where it didn't belong. And he always gave me exactly what the scene needed. Something different, and new.

It's exhausting making a movie, but attending Jerry's scoring sessions was reward enough for me. He loved his work, and that made all the difference.

Joe Dante

David Cronenberg is my favourite director to work with. Not only is he a genius, but also he respects and knows your work. I mean literally, you could probably train him to do your job in a few days.

He's sharp and attentive, but also very calm. His sets are the calmest I've ever been on. No big dramas ever. He's agreeable and understanding. If I go to him and say we need extra time to shoot a scene, to do a separate set-up away from the main unit, he's always like, "Yeah, good. Let's do that."

He's demanding, but he doesn't push you. More like, he pulls you to the limit.

Chris Walas

"EVERY TIME I THINK ABOUT CRONENBERG, I JUST GO CRAZY."

Jeff Goldblum's performance in *The Fly* (1986) is no less remarkable than the many amazing masks, suits and make-ups he wore for the movie. You really feel his pain as he endures every heart-breaking stage of that transformation.

Sean Sansom

David Cronenberg had the longest sustained run of genius horror cinema of anyone I can think of. Starting in the mid-Seventies with *Rabid* (1977) and going all the way up to the late Eighties with *Dead Ringers* (1988), he had a non-stop slew of films that were absolutely brilliant.

The vibe, mood and imagery, the writing, directing and sheer invention. Plus he's directed more actors to their greatest heights than any director other than maybe Martin Scorsese: Christopher Walken's greatest performance is undoubtedly in *The Dead Zone* (1983). Jeremy Irons' dual role in *Dead Ringers* (1988) is beyond accomplished. James Woods is incredible in *Videodrome* (1983), and Jeff Goldblum didn't show that kind of range either before or since *The Fly* (1986).

Every time I think about Cronenberg, I just go crazy.

Jordu Schell

You can make an argument for *The Fly* (1986) being the greatest monster movie ever made. There's no better way to seriously explore how a man might turn into a monster than by approaching it in the most realistic way possible. David Cronenberg delivered that on both a physical and emotional level, and knocked every facet of that story out of the park.

Damien Leone

My parents were very strict about what I could see on TV. I was only allowed to watch one thing a week, which had to be approved in advance. It was a complicated procedure. Every once in a while, though, I'd get a VHS from a friend and whenever my parents left the house, I'd sneak into their bedroom – the only place we had a VCR – and watch a little bit of something. My brother kept a lookout at the window and as soon as he saw them coming home, we'd stop the film and hide the tape.

That's how I first saw *The Fly* (1986), a few nervous minutes at a time, though somehow I managed to watch the last 30 minutes uninterrupted. The effects were so disgusting! I was grossed out, but at the same time, I couldn't stop crying because it mixed emotion with the scares in such a beautiful way.

Every time I go back to the movie, it feels like it's about something different. It could be about depression, or getting old, or getting sick. When you're a kid, it's about a man who turns into a bug, but it's so rich and layered, not only does it hold up really well, but also as you get older, it deepens with each viewing.

Axelle Carolyn

Opposite (left): Jerry Goldsmith conducts one of his many memorable movie scores, *Planet of the Apes* (1968), *Twilight Zone: The Movie* (1983) and *Gremlins* (1984) among them.

Opposite (right): A full-scale puppet designed by Chris Walas for director David Cronenberg's *The Fly* (1986), the acid-spewing Brundlefly had everyone reaching for the Raid.

Below: David Cronenberg surveys Chris Walas's handiwork on Jeff Goldblum on the set of *The Fly* (1986).

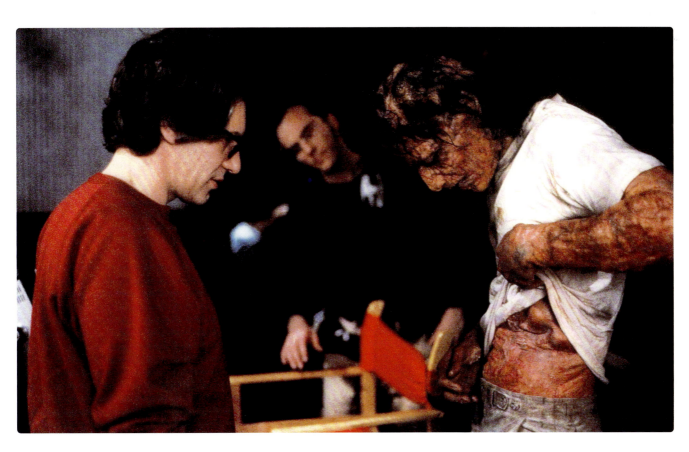

I've always enjoyed working with Sam [Raimi] because of his energy and sense of humour. He's like a big kid.

Robert Kurtzman

I was in high school when I saw *The Lost Boys* (1987). It was one of the most refreshing vampire movies I'd seen in a long time. It was accessible. It was funny. The soundtrack's fantastic and the boys were all really cute.

I just watched it again and I don't know why Jason Patric was so hell-bent on killing the vampires. They're lots of fun, make him part of the gang and yeah, they bite some people, but they're just cleaning up the boardwalk.

Silvi Knight

Every shot in *Evil Dead II* (1987) is a work of art. Whether it's a matte painting, a puppet, a miniature or stop motion, a make-up, a mask or flying eyeballs, there's always something special. That's incredibly rare.

Mike Mendez

"I DON'T KNOW WHY JASON PATRIC WAS SO HELL-BENT ON KILLING THE VAMPIRES."

It was always puppets with me: *Gremlins* (1984), *The Dark Crystal* (1982), *Critters* (1986)... Audrey II from *Little Shop of Horrors* (1986) is perfect, I think. Every size from the tiny guy up. Right from the start, when he was just lips and a few frills, it was a beautiful design. And he had so much character! Even at his largest, he moved so fluently, and you could tell it was really there.

Kevin Wasner

Stephen King had a part in *The Stand* (1994), so we hung out on set a lot. He always had a book in his hand, but when he wasn't reading, or writing, or singing Seventies' rock 'n' roll songs, he'd tell us stories. He was awesome.

I remember, there was this one scene where Mother Abagail (Ruby Dee) is in a cornfield, playing guitar. Her hands start bleeding from stigmata, and Stephen looks at me and goes, "You guys are gross!"

I said, "We're gross? You wrote it!"

Later, when we won Emmys for Best Make-Up, he sent me a giant bouquet of black flowers. Getting that from him was even cooler than winning the Emmy!

We worked together again on *The Shining* (1997). He was so excited to be playing a zombie in that, and rot on camera. They rigged him so his jaw would fall apart and he loved all that stuff. He's just a big, goofy kid!

Bill Corso

Opposite: Director Sam Raimi jokes around with a sassy, skeletal Deadite on the set of *Army of Darkness* (1991). Having created hordes of suits, make-ups, puppets and exploding skeletons for the film, every day the lads at KNB EFX would ask Raimi what he needed, and invariably he'd respond, "Give me everything ya got!"

Below: Ruby Dee in her Mother Abagail make-up, courtesy of artist Bill Corso, under the supervision of Steve Johnson's XFX for Mick Garris's *The Stand* (1994).

Bottom: On the Las Vegas set of *The Stand* (1994) with John Landis, Mick Garris, Stephen King, Bill Corso, Matt Frewer, Steve Johnson, and Joel Harlow.

I absolutely love Mick Garris. He's a wonderful director. Nice Guy Productions is so apropos of him. He's soft-spoken and personable with the kindest energy. You immediately feel you want to do your best for him.

Dirk Rogers

Rob Zombie is a great illustrator with an Ed "Big Daddy" Roth sensibility. When we started working together, at the beginning of every project he'd give us drawings to work from, way-out designs we'd just rein in a little to make them more believable.

Rob's a monster kid, like us, and could easily have become a make-up guy. He has the skills and the love for it that we do. He just wound up doing his own thing. It spoils you, really, when you're on the same wavelength as a director. When you have the same passions and references. You develop a shorthand, so you work faster, and have more fun too.

Wayne Toth

My favourite Godzilla is from *Godzilla Minus One* (2023). It's such an incredible design. There's something almost comedic about those little arms, but he's still so scary! And there's a Jaws-like quality to the way they use his fin that's just perfect.

Still, even with the most kick-ass monster, if I didn't give a shit about the characters, or there wasn't a story that compelled my heart, it wouldn't do it for me. Fortunately, *Godzilla Minus One* has both, and that's really why I love the film so much.

David Dastmalchian

The Godzilla from *GMK* (2001) really scares me. My other favourite Godzilla is from *Shin Godzilla* (2016), because it feels like a walking atomic mushroom cloud.

The character designer on *Shin Godzilla* was Takayuki Takeya, who was one year senior to me at art school, and one of the reasons I pursued visual effects and film directing. I'd planned on being a sculptor till I saw his work, but once I realized there are absolute geniuses living in the world, I decided to go in a different direction.

Takashi Yamazaki

I've always loved Godzilla. I just get great joy out of seeing a guy in a giant monster suit crushing miniatures. It's a beautiful thing.

Howard Berger

Opposite (top): Filmmaker Mick Garris and creature performer Dirk Rogers on the set of *Nightmare Cinema* (2018). Mick is one of the nicest human beings on Earth, hence the name of his production company, Nice Guy Productions.

Opposite (Bottom): Rob Zombie (left) with make-up genius Wayne Toth of Ex Mortis Studios. Wayne is also the proprietor of wondrous all-year Halloween emporium, Halloween Town.

Above: The King of the Monsters, Godzilla surveys his handiwork in Takashi Yamazaki's *Godzilla Minus One* (2023), the film that reinvigorated the real Godzilla franchise and finally, after 70 years, won the series an Academy Award for Best VFX.

MARCH OF THE MONSTER KIDS

Ignore the folks fleeing in terror from the thing with forty eyes, and focus instead on the monster kids racing towards it. They're the ones who traded solid sleep and sweet dreams for midnight movies and nightmares. The ones who related less to their classmates than they did to the creatures of the night. The ones whose mad bedroom labs, with their ruined, clay-embedded and plaster-speckled carpets, ran red with fake blood. Because it's this rare bunch whose origin stories we're proudly relating here.

Growing up in Australia in the Eighties, we had this TV series called *Great Mysteries of the World*, a repack of the American series, *In Search of...* (1977–82). The opening titles ended with a shot from *Nosferatu* (1922), of Count Orlok slowly looking towards the camera. The thing is, when I was a kid, no one told me it was from a movie, and in context of the show being about actual mysteries of the world like Stonehenge, the Bermuda Triangle and the Great Pyramid of Giza, I assumed that creepy, pale, bald figure with pointy teeth and fingernails was real as well. For years I just accepted him, until my teens, when I finally saw the movie!

Kerrin Jackson

I'm old enough that when I was old enough to go to the movies alone, they were showing reruns of the old Universal horror movies. I saw *Dracula* (1931) and *Frankenstein* (1931) on the big screen and I was in awe of them.

I just always loved the genre, and giggled at gore from an early age.

George A. Romero

"I GIGGLED AT GORE FROM AN EARLY AGE."

When I was five years old, I knocked out my front teeth, right up to the canines. To compensate, my mother made me a vampire cape, which I wore till my big teeth grew in. I'd go run through the neighbourhood and everyone would say, "Hey, Dracula!"

Howard Berger

I wondered how they made the actors look like monsters in the old Universal movies. When I was small I watched them all on TV with my stepdad. He told me they painted their faces with make-up.

At school, in art class, the paint we used was water-based, and somehow I figured out you could reactivate the paint in your paintings by adding water to them. So I'd always paint using colours I could use later on my face!

I painted myself as Dracula. I'd only ever seen him on a black and white TV, but in my mind, he was yellow, with blue around the eyes. I was curious from the start, eager to experiment with whatever I could find, and I guess that hasn't changed.

Mike Elizalde

"I WAS EASILY ALARMED AS A CHILD, BUT STUBBORNLY CURIOUS."

I was watching TV with my dad, flipping through the channels, and there was this show on Bigfoot. I thought maybe it was a made-up character, like Bugs Bunny or Mickey Mouse, but Dad assured me, "Bigfoot's real."

I was like, "How come no one's taking this seriously? Why aren't grown-ups hunting for him? We're going to get murdered!"

I was easily alarmed as a child, but stubbornly curious.

One night my sister was watching a movie in her bedroom. I wanted to watch it too, but she knew better. She told me, "It's *Salem's Lot* (1979) and you're much too young for it."

Later she left her room and I combat-crawled back in, peering at the TV over her water bed. At that very moment, Barlow sat up in his coffin and I ran out of the room, horrified, screaming, "I'm not old enough! I'm not old enough!"

Derek Mears

Preceding Spread: Artist Terry Wolfinger was born a monster kid. Here's a dastardly Dracula he drew as a young 'un.
Opposite: Count Orlok (Max Schreck) and a friend in F.W. Murnau's genre-defining vampire classic, *Nosferatu* (1922).
Above: Young Mike Elizalde in a monster make-up of his own creation.
Above (Right): Decades before playing DC's mighty Swamp Thing, Derek Mears socked crime on the nose as a pint-sized Batman.

At a very young age, I lived in a conservative household with a lot of conflict and fear. My parents' marriage was falling apart and they fought a lot. I didn't feel safe. I'd hide up in my attic room and every night when I fell asleep, I'd have these two recurring dreams.

In the first, a little Frankenstein's Monster came out of my closet and chased me down the stairs. It always turned to slow motion, and I'd feel like I was trying to run through syrup. In the second, a man desperately needed my help, a suicidal werewolf who'd throw himself into the fire, but then he would transform, and chase me.

I had this duality: a paradoxical love and dread of monsters.

Watching my cartoons one Saturday morning, I saw a teaser ad with this ghoulishly glorious, gorgeous woman with pale make-up, looking like a vampire and coming out of her coffin with bats dangling around her. She said, "Boils and ghouls, don't forget, Friday night at 10pm, come to *Crematia's Friday Nightmare* (1982–90)."

She was this incredible woman, a horror host called Crematia Mortem on KSHB 41 in Kansas City. She ran for, like, nine years, and they were the prime years of my adolescence.

I started sneaking downstairs every Friday night while my family was asleep. I'd hide under my blanket, hoping I wouldn't get caught in the basement, watching as she introduced me to, and shared historical titbits about, classic horror movies. She had this great, kid-friendly sense of humour, and the dread faded.

That was how my love affair with scary movies began. Films like Corman's *Little Shop of Horrors* (1960), *Horror Express* (1972), *The Last Man on Earth* (1964) and *Black Sabbath* (1963)... B stuff, Z stuff. RKO, Universal, Hammer... I became addicted.

Inspired by Crematia, I've developed a horror host character of my own: Dr Fearless. It's a great way to share my love of horror movies, and I have a lot of fun with him. Also, as there's no budget in comic book marketing, you'll often spot him on YouTube and social media promoting my comicbook series, *Count Crowley: Reluctant Midnight Monster Hunter*.

David Dastmalchian

Growing up, I felt like an outsider. I got bullied a lot, and often sympathized with monsters as they were the ones being picked on. Humans were usually to blame for victimizing and provoking what they didn't understand. Like, just leave Frankenstein's Monster alone, you know?

Chad Coleman

Top (left): Count Crowley to the rescue! David Dastmalchian's Reluctant Midnight Monster Hunter springs into action.
Above: Iconic horror host Svengoolie (Rich Koz) tucks David Dastmalchian in for the night.
Left: Though he loved all things monstrous, David Dastmalchian carefully hid his horror habit from his parents.

I was a huge fan of the Universal Monsters and drew monster art everywhere. Then at my first grade book fair I picked up a copy of Alan Ormsby's *Movie Monsters* (1975), a beautifully illustrated book of monster profiles with a guide to making yourself up like the monsters, then putting on monster plays with your friends. That was the start of my make-up trajectory.

My dad took me to see *Young Frankenstein* (1974), then I begged him to take me again, and again, as I was illustrating my own comicbook version from memory. I planned it out and sketched it all. Sadly I've no idea what became of it.

Bill Corso

Above: Make-up artist Bill Corso is flanked by painted revisions of two of his favourite films, *Young Frankenstein* (1974) and *Abbott & Costello Meet Frankenstein* (1948). Instead of purchasing the posters, Bill painted them himself, a testament to how truly talented he is.

Right: Alan Ormsby's *Movie Monsters* (1975) was the book that inspired Bill Corso to become a make-up artist.

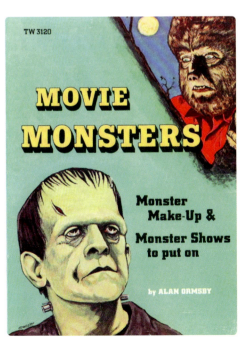

I was quite squeamish as a kid. A sensitive soul, God bless me. I hated blood and steered well clear of anything too modern that might offend my eyes with convincing gore and visual effects. So the cosiness of Universal's monster movies was a safe first foray into horror for me.

Not so much Lugosi's Dracula, as I'd heard he got staked at the end, and that made me nervous. But the visuals of Karloff's Frankenstein Creature, that square head and the neck bolts, fascinated me from the first time I ever saw it, which was a gaudy green sticker of his head on a toy shop cash desk. I stared at it for ages.

The night before I finally saw *Frankenstein* (1931), I remember worrying, not because I thought it was going to be scary, but because I knew it was going to be sad. But I was brave and watched it, and was really moved by Karloff's performance. The way he moved. The sounds he made. His Creature was tragic. Pathetic, even, but in the most beautiful way.

When I was older, and a bit braver, I found my way to Dracula. Not Bela Lugosi's, but Christopher Lee's suavely sexy version. There was no way I could resist all those heaving bosoms.

The first really scary film I forced myself to watch was *The Omen* (1976). I'd heard it was all very real, with this infamous decapitation. I was 13, maybe, but when my mum and dad went out they left me with a hot babysitter. A girl I'd had thoughts about, so I stayed up and watched it with her on the telly. She hid behind a pillow and I was like, "Don't worry. It'll be alright."

Real coming-of-age stuff!

Stephen Murphy

My mom found a bunch of drawings I did when I was five, of spaceships and skeletons and guys attacked by giant squids. Lots of red Crayola for blood!

For me, it all started with *King Kong* (1933) on TV, followed by *The 7th Voyage of Sinbad* (1958) at the movies. When the cyclops emerged from the cave, it was all over for me. I was totally hooked on the spectacle. That film always was and still is my inspiration.

Phil Tippett

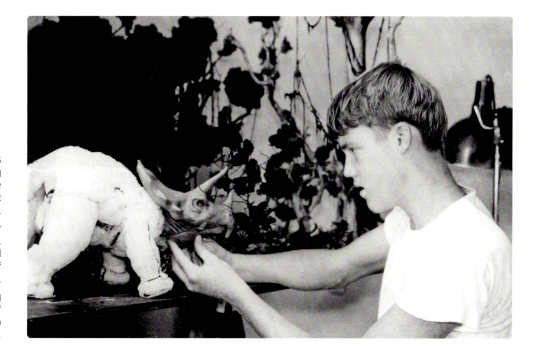

Opposite: Stephen Murphy began his monster-making journey by designing and applying make-ups inspired by the classics. Here he is in his out-of-the-kit Phantom of the Opera make-up.

Top: Phil Tippett with one of his Raptor armatures from *Jurassic Park* (1993). Phil's expertise in movement and physics proved crucial to the task of bringing digital dinosaurs to life.

Right: Phil Tippett was inspired by Ray Harryhausen and the magic of Dynamation to bring his own stop motion characters to life.

"JUST A BUNCH OF MONSTER KIDS DRESSING UP AND MAKING MOVIES. DOING WHAT CAME NATURALLY!"

All four of my older brothers were athletes. Mom's body was out of testosterone by the time I was born, so I was the runt of the litter. I wasn't into sports or hunting, so monsters became my thing from the jump.

Born into an Irish Catholic family, *The Wolf Man* (1941) was, for me, all about shame and being out of control. As a kid, you can't help but say and do things you feel bad about later, and that's Larry Talbot in a nutshell. I could relate.

I think maybe the reason Lon Chaney Jr was so great in the role was because of his alcoholism. I doubt Curt Siodmak meant it intentionally, but *The Wolf Man* does seem to be the story of an alcoholic. He's helpless. He can't control himself. He does terrible things and then feels horrible the next day about the wreckage he's caused. Kids and alcoholics have that in common, I guess.

I remember, my mother cut the collar off her fake-fur coat, and following *Dick Smith's Do-It-Yourself Monster Make-Up Handbook* (1985), I made a Wolf-Man mask. Likewise, my friend Rusty, who was lumbering, uncoordinated and really just too big for his body, dressed up as Frankenstein. Together we'd play *Frankenstein Meets the Wolf Man* (1943) in the cemetery at the end of my street.

Later, with my friend Alan, who had an 8mm camera, we made a Wolf Man comedy called *Howling Harry*. Just a bunch of monster kids dressing up and making movies. Doing what came naturally!

Dana Gould

Opposite: Writer, actor and comedian Dana Gould transforms into The Wolf Man in a scene from Greg Nicotero's short fan film, *The United Monster Talent Agency* (2010). Nicotero took painstaking efforts to ensure the process and make-ups for the movie were as close as possible to those created by Universal Monsters legend Jack Pierce.

The first make-up I ever did on myself was the Wolf Man, with the black nose, cheap fake fangs and the crepe wool glued to my face and hands. I then ran around my neighbourhood at Halloween scaring trick-or-treaters.

My dad was a World War 2 veteran, and really didn't understand why I wanted to fill my head with lurid, bloody monster stuff. He'd say, "If you keep reading about monsters, you'll become a monster."

Dad wanted to send me to military school. Make me straighten up and fly right. But my mom, who was a teacher and understanding said, "No, he's just creative."

She bought me clay and sculpting tools for Christmas, and always supported me, even after I destroyed our kitchen sink by mixing plaster in it. That's when I learned that plaster still hardens, even if it's very watery. Back then I didn't know what the hell I was doing. There weren't any books or classes on monster making, but thanks to my mom, I had the chance to learn.

Kirk Thatcher

Above: Carey Jones as Ted the Man-Thing sneaks up on Kirk Thatcher's Jovan the Monster Hunter behind the scenes on Michael Giacchino's scarifying *Werewolf by Night* (2022).
Opposite (top): Make-up artist-in-training Kevin Yagher always tested his creations on his actor brother Jeff.
Opposite (bottom): Jeff Yagher dons the headpiece of his brother Kevin's take on Jack Pierce's Wolf Man make-up.

As interested as I was in make-up effects, acting was always the goal for me, so whenever my brother Kevin and I made monster movies, I always played the monster. One time – I guess I was about 15 – we were in the woods near our house, and I was in a werewolf make-up. A bunch of much smaller kids came hiking in our direction and I heard one of them warn the others to stay in line behind him or the Creek Monster would get them. It was such perfect timing, I couldn't resist jumping out from behind a tree to give them a fright.

They screamed and took off running, far more terrified than I'd expected. I felt bad, and wanted to apologize, so I took off after them, which from their point-of-view I'm sure looked like a werewolf was chasing them. Scared out of their minds, they ran into a house, and as I'm approaching it this huge guy in his twenties comes out shouting and running straight for me.

Now I'm the one running away. I managed to get all the way back to my house, and I'm in the shower, ripping off the latex and scrubbing off the glue, when there's a knock at the door and Kevin shouts, "A police officer's here!"

I go down the stairs, nervous as hell, and as I'm walking past the hallway mirror I saw I still had big, black make-up circles around my eyes. I thought, "I'm dead."

The policeman looks at me, and says, "We, uh, had some kinda disturbing the peace call about an animal."

I explained to him what happened and apologized. A lot! He just laughed and wanted to know all about the make-up. He was fascinated. I guess he was a Monster Kid himself. Lucky break for me.

Jeff Yagher

"I COULDN'T RESIST JUMPING OUT FROM BEHIND A TREE TO GIVE THEM A FRIGHT."

I was ten years old and I guess I had a rotten babysitter because she rented *The Howling* (1981) and let me watch it with her. When Eddie [Robert Picardo] takes that bullet out of his head, that scene haunted me for years. Every time I got scared at night, I'd immediately think of his head bubbling and him saying, "I'm gonna give you a piece of my mind."

So I was frightened, yeah, but I was fascinated too. The transformation was just so pleasurable to my eyes. It looked real to me, like it was actually happening, so I couldn't look away, but at the same time I'm like, "I don't wanna die!"

It was a balance, then, of sheer terror and fascination, of intense viewing pleasure on one side, and "Please don't kill me" on the other.

It was the beginning of my lifelong love affair with werewolves.

Leanne Podavin

Above: Lycanthrope enthusiast and make-up artist Leanne Podavin hound sits a pair of KNB EFX-created werewolves for *Ginger Snaps 3* (2004).

Opposite: Made up as an alien for *Laserblast* (1978), make-up artist Steve Neill is touched up on set by the legendary Ve Neill.

My mom went to night school while raising me, my brother and sister. Brookdale Community College in New Jersey. *An American Werewolf in London* (1981) had only been out a few months, but somehow the college managed to get a print to show in a Halloween double bill with *Love at First Bite* (1979) in their gymnasium.

So we're all dressed as mummies and Mom takes us to see the movies. I was ten. *First Bite* was fun. I didn't get all the jokes, but there was nothing you couldn't get away with showing a kid. Then *American Werewolf* starts, and the sexual innuendo I didn't get, but there's f-bombs thrown left and right, and Mom's like, "If it keeps on like this, we're leaving."

Then Griffin Dunne's attacked. Torn apart on the moors. My brother's crying. My sister's freaked out. I'm stunned myself. So Mom grabs us. "We're out of here."

Worst part was, to get to the car park we had to walk across a huge, dark field with forest in all directions. There's no one else about, of course, as everyone's still watching the movie. And the moon's out! All I could think about was the scene on the moors... I don't think I've ever been more frightened in my life.

A year later I finally got to watch the whole movie, on HBO, at a friend's house. I was scared out of my mind and couldn't sleep at night because of the dream demons. Regardless of the trauma, that was my gateway movie to becoming a monster kid. That, and a short making-of documentary, also on HBO. Watching it, I realized that people made this sort of stuff for a job, and from that moment on, that's what I wanted to do.

Scott Stoddard

"[MY MOM WOULD] TELL PEOPLE, 'MY POOR BABY THINKS EVERY DAY IS HALLOWEEN.'"

Back when I was growing up, they had this thing on TV called *The Million Dollar Movie* (1955–88). It was the same film all week long at 5pm. I watched *The Beast with Five Fingers* (1946) three days in a row and it scared me so bad.

The monster was a hand. Just a single, crawling hand. So one day my mom catches me hiding, and she goes, "What are you doing?"

I'm like, "He could be round the corner."

She asks, "Who could be round the corner?"

I say, "The Beast with Five Fingers."

And she's like, "That's it. You're cut off. No more watching that movie."

She just couldn't figure out why I liked horror movies so much. She'd tell people, "My poor baby thinks every day is Halloween."

Ve Neill

I never thought Godzilla was real, but I loved the idea of someone in a suit masquerading and stomping around miniatures. There was something about the playful chaos of it that really rung my bell. When I was six I asked my mom to make me a Godzilla costume. I still remember the feel of the textured green fabric she used. I was already into model building, so my Godzilla had lots to destroy.

By the spark of puberty I got my first camera and decided to burn everything – all my soldiers and model buildings – and film the destruction. Then, of course, a creature would come along and crush everything, which was all super satisfying.

I've often wondered why I gravitated towards the 'Dark Arts'. I grew up in a loving, stable, suburban home, so it wasn't an escape fantasy. Years later my dad admitted that he and my mom worried why their middle kid was so laser focused on destroying lives and pouring blood on everything, but I was just having a blast!

Ultimately, he said they were glad I landed on my feet and was able to make a profession of it.

Gabe Bartalos

I was extremely young when I started watching monster movies. My mom would set an alarm and wake me up to go watch them. I don't remember where we lived, or what pet we had, but I do remember Godzilla.

Wayne Toth

I was a kid of four, maybe five, and my parents were out for the evening. *Godzilla: King of the Monsters!* (1956) was on TV but I was too terrified to watch it, so I hid underneath this huge chair. Suddenly my older brother drags me out, sits on top of me, grabs my hair and makes me watch it. Then at the end, he tells me, "He's coming for you tonight."

Oh my God! Best as I can recall, that was my introduction to monster movies and, obviously, it made an impression.

Chris Walas

When I was five we moved from Santa Barbara to Simi Valley. That first night, my father's like, "There's a movie on TV tonight we have to watch. It's called *The War of the Gargantuas* (1966)."

My father's the one who turned me on to monsters, Godzilla and so much else.

We had a black-and-white TV with the rabbit ears antenna, and the only place in the house we could get reception was my bedroom closet. So that night, I sat on my father's lap in the closet, watching the movie. Of course every time the green gargantua came out, my father grabbed me and scared me out of my skin. But it's one of the most endearing memories I have.

Many years later, the first time I saw *Godzilla Minus One* (2023), I thought it was a near-perfect film. But I did feel that some of the dialogue scenes dragged a little. Then I saw it again, about a month after my father died. Suddenly I hung on every word. Every reaction.

There's that moment towards the end when everyone goes out in boats to fight Godzilla. I looked to my left, and imagined my father sitting there, smiling and saying, "This is so great!"

The waterworks started and it was a struggle not getting butter and salt in my eyes as I rubbed them. No other Godzilla film has ever affected me so deeply. It's actually perfect.

Dirk Rogers

Opposite (top left): Gabe Bartalos behind bars with his Monster Copier.
Opposite (top right): Gabe Bartalos fine-tunes Alex Winter's sculpture for his part as Vlad for *Destroy All Neighbors* (2024).
Opposite (bottom): Wayne Toth and his brother, zombified for a fun day of shuffling around the neighbourhood, looking for BRAINSSSSSSSS...
Below: The most important thing a monster kid can hope for is parental support, and Dirk Rogers received nothing but encouragement from his dad, pictured here in a gloriously gory make-up by his future creature creator/performer son.

Two movies in particular made a big impression on me as a kid. I was four, maybe five, when I saw *War of the Colossal Beast* (1958), the sequel to *The Amazing Colossal Man* (1957). At the beginning of the movie, some guy's driving a dairy truck across the desert. He looks up and screams, then jumps out of his truck and runs away.

I could tell they were just about to show the thing, whatever it was, and I made a kind of worried gasp. My mother said, "If you're going to be afraid of it, I'm not going to let you watch it."

Click! She turned off the TV before they showed the monster. From a psychological standpoint, try to imagine what that does to a kid. I'm already afraid of what I might see. So now my imagination's working overtime. What was it? What did it look like? It's probably good she did that as the make-up's quite gory and disturbing, actually really well done and way ahead of its time.

I think it would have messed me up, but not as much as the other film did, a piece of sleazy trash called *The Brain That Wouldn't Die* (1962).

This movie is notoriously, horrendously gory. It features a woman's head in a saucepan of juice that somehow keeps her head alive. It's ridiculous, but it was very frightening.

There's a monster in the closet of this lab she's in, some mutation that she has a psychic connection with, and at one point it rips somebody's arm off. It's grotesque and the scene just goes on and on. The guy drags his bleeding stump across the walls and I was absolutely traumatized by that.

I also really wanted to re-create it, so like all good effects people, I farmed out the work. I asked my dad if he could make me a fake arm. He made one out of cardboard, and even at five years old, I remember thinking that it wasn't quite realistic enough for me, but that it would do.

I re-enacted that scene, and so many others, throughout my childhood. My mother was always yelling up the stairs, "What's all that screaming about up there?"

And I'd be like, "It's monsters, Mom. It's monsters."

Jordu Schell

"IF YOU'RE GOING TO BE AFRAID OF IT, I'M NOT GOING TO LET YOU WATCH IT."

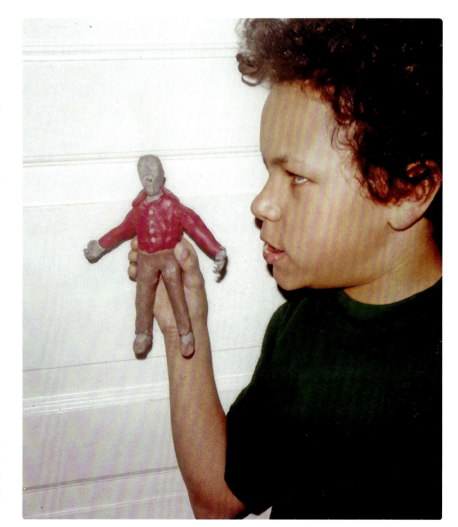

Right: Jordu Schell examines his latest clay monster creation.

Opposite (top): King of the Monster Movie Makers, director Takashi Yamazaki calls the shots on the set of *Godzilla Minus One* (2023).

Opposite (bottom): Little did Takashi Yamazaki's parents know that their son would grow up to make the best Godzilla movie ever.

Ishiro Honda's *Matango* (1963) terrified me as a kid. It's about a group of castaways on a desert island covered in giant, delicious, poisonous mushrooms. Anyone who eats them mutates into a mushroom monster.

We lived in the countryside and my father would go up into the mountains and harvest mushrooms. Back home, he'd sit and sort them. "These you can eat. These you can't eat…"

After watching the film, though, I wouldn't eat any of the mushrooms my father foraged. I'd tell him, "Any one of those could be a Matango."

Takashi Yamazaki

My first monsters were in a little book. From the age of four, every time I'd go to my grandmother's house, I'd leaf through *Where the Wild Things Are* (1963). I wanted to hang out with those things like you wouldn't believe.

Josh Turi

My father was a master dental technician with a huge lab in East London's Hackney Road. There was always someone there mixing a bowl of dental plaster and when I'd go to work with my dad, usually during the summer holidays, he'd sit me down with bowls of plaster, wax and teeth, and I'd make monsters.

I'd bring them home to my mother and they'd stand on the mantelpiece for two days before mysteriously vanishing. I'd always ask what happened, and Mum would tell me Dad had to take those supplies back to work. But actually they just made a horrible mess and would go straight in the dustbin.

Sometimes I'd make weird dentures with teeth sticking out in all directions. I'd put them in and surprise my mum. She'd tell me off: "They're dirty. Take them out!"

Little did we know then that a million years later I'd be making even crazier dentures for Austin Powers, with teeth going every which way, not to mention vampire fangs and mouthfuls of teeth for every monster under the sun – and the moon."

Gary Archer

I don't think a movie ever meant more to me than *The Exorcist* (1973).

I was 12 and my parents weren't loosey-goosey types at all. But I had such an obsession with movies that they let me see pretty much whatever I wanted. My dad would just take me to the drive-in and fall asleep. But my mother would not let me see *The Exorcist*. That's where she drew the line, so I became obsessed with seeing it. I begged and begged, but she wouldn't budge.

I got my sister to go to the drive-in with a little audio cassette recorder and tape the movie for me. Every night, before I went to bed, I'd listen to one of the tapes, and pretty soon I knew every single sound effect, music cue and line of dialogue from *The Exorcist*. So long before I knew it visually, I knew it aurally, and to this day, whenever I see it, I always know exactly what sound effect is coming next.

But back when I was still forbidden from seeing it, I tried to be clever and started bargaining. Like, what if I mowed the yard? Or did all the dishes for six months? Every deal I tried to strike, though, Mom said, "No, no, no."

I was a fat little kid, and out of desperation, I randomly threw out, "What if I go on a diet, and lose 35 pounds in a month?"

That seemed like something my mother wouldn't believe I could possibly do, and since I'd been so annoying, just to shut me up she said, "Sure. If you can lose 35 pounds in one month, you can go see *The Exorcist*."

So I lost 35 pounds in one month. I just starved myself to death, and finally I got to see *The Exorcist*, which did not disappoint in any way whatsoever. It was a masterpiece, and it still is.

Larry Karaszewski

I couldn't have had better parents when it came to encouragement and support. My mom and dad actually wanted me to be an artist, which is so weird. I have friends whose parents insisted they be doctors or lawyers and had a hard time accepting they wanted to make monsters instead.

I'll tell you my favourite story.

I was out in town with my mom and we went into a bookstore. My eyes zeroed in on a new magazine called *Fangoria*. Not only was it in colour, but it was full of gory pictures. It was the second issue with an article about *Alien* (1979), an interview with Tom Savini – whom I'd never heard of – on *Dawn of the Dead* (1978), and there was this amazing picture of an exploding head.

I ran up to my mom and asked if she'd get me the magazine. Of course, she opened it up at the shot of the exploding head, and was like, "No, no, no, no, no."

She was a strict pacifist, and didn't like the idea of me being exposed to such things. But this is how strong my passion was for this shit: secretly I rode my bike back downtown, seven miles to buy the magazine with some money I'd saved. I hid it from my mom. I'd just stare at it in my room, like seeing porn for the first time.

One day, I'm sitting with Mom in our kitchen, and I'm pleading with her to let me have *Fangoria* because I didn't want to hide it, or my interest, from her. I told her, "I really want to see this stuff. I think it's cool."

Again she says, "I don't want you to have that kind of violent stuff in the house."

Then I remember this like it was yesterday. I told her, "But this is what I want to do for a living."

And she went, "OK."

On a dime, she flipped, and that Christmas my mom and dad got me a subscription. They'd buy me supplies, too. And when I started my own studio in 1999, my dad gave me the money I needed to get set up. So they've been hugely supportive. I have no complaints.

Jordu Schell

Zombies were a big part of my life, growing up in Pittsburgh, and I was a huge *Night of the Living Dead* (1968) fan. Even though my grandfather looked exactly like the cemetery zombie at the beginning of the movie, and my middle-of-nowhere, farmland house was pretty much identical to the house in the movie, I'd still watch it, over and over.

I'd watch the movie, even though I was terrified there were zombies outside, coming for me. I'd watch it, and loved it, and tortured myself with it, because that's what monster kids do, right?

Christopher Nelson

I learned from *Jaws* (1975) that most shark attacks occur in three feet of water, ten feet from the beach. What a horrifying thing for a kid to carry around! Every summer after that, every time we went swimming, I'd measure exactly where the water reached three feet and keep well clear.

Jaws also introduced me to the concept of practical effects. I was traumatized by that moment the fisherman gets his leg chomped off, blood's everywhere, then it bounces on the estuary floor. It was so real to me, but my dad told me, "No, it's a rubber leg and the blood's just corn syrup and food colouring."

It took me a while to come around to it not being real, but once I figured out it was art, suddenly Mom's wondering where all the red food dye's going. Then she's like, "Oh, it's just John fucking around, making blood for his monster toys again!"

John Wrightson

My dad took me to see *Jaws* (1975) when I was six. I remember it like it was yesterday. As the film was an A – PG today – when it first came out in the UK, parents were free to take their kids, and mine were always willing to show me mad, monstery stuff.

It was the opening titles that got me. The camera's gliding across the bottom of the sea, the seaweed's swaying from left to right, and I was thinking, "The shark's coming out. Any second now, the shark's coming out and that'll be it..."

I was absolutely petrified. Those first few minutes, where nothing even ends up happening, were my first experience of sheer terror at the cinema. The rest of the film I got through OK! But ever since, I can't swim in the sea without thinking of *Jaws*. Even just paddling on the beach down in Brighton, it's in the back of my mind. And to be honest, I've even freaked myself out on the toilet, thinking about the film. That's what I call a legacy!

Duncan Jarman

Opposite: Christopher Nelson is one of the most talented and versatile make-up artists in the industry. He's also fearless, and can stand right beside a zombie and smile.

Above: Duncan Jarman and his siblings take an awful chance posing with a trio of apes who are clearly considering enslaving them and stealing their jumpers.

Top (right): The son of superstar artists Bernie and Michelle Wrightson, John Wrightson's a talented apple who fell right beside the tree.

M y parents are über-religious. Like, my mom could give Carrie's mom a run for her money. But, for reasons I've never understood, as much as Sunday was about church and Jesus, they never gave me shit about the horror stuff. There I was, fixated with monsters and demons and skulls and blood, and they were like, "He's just a little different. Kinda weird. Best not question it."

Mike Mendez

M onster movies never scared me. I was more excited by the idea that sometimes strange and inexplicable things happen. My mom likes to tell people that when I was a little kid I talked to dead people. Honestly I only saw, like, two ghosts, and I didn't know they were dead at the time. I guess I was just always open to vampires, creatures and spooks. Like Richard Dreyfuss in *Close Encounters of the Third Kind* (1977), I'm drawn to them the way he was to Devils Tower.

Silvi Knight

A local friend came over to watch *Halloween* (1978) at my house. We were thirteen, so old enough to handle it, but still young enough to be scared. Afterwards, he didn't want to walk home alone, so he asked me to come with him.

I said no, because then I'd have to walk home alone myself. Eventually I agreed to walk halfway, but felt I had to get him back for making me go outside, too, so just before I turned to go home, I told him, "I just saw someone by your bushes."

He said, "Shut up! You did not."

I'm like, "I swear to God. He was just there!"

It was tough getting him to come round to watch scary movies after that.

Terry Wolfinger

"I GUESS I WAS JUST ALWAYS OPEN TO VAMPIRES, CREATURES AND SPOOKS."

Opposite (top): Long before Mike Mendez found success directing horror movies, as a youth he dreamed of becoming a mariachi.
Opposite (bottom): Christopher Nelson, Silvi Knight, Mike Mekash, Eryn Krueger-Mekash and Kim Ayres go trick or treating on the set of *Halloween* (2018).
Above: Young vampire Terry Wolfinger fends off a gruesome twosome.

My dad and I were big campers and, no shocker, he was an amazing storyteller. So every night around the campfire he'd make up something new. One night he starts telling me a story, and I swear to God, it went like this:

"There's a bunch of people on a spaceship. They wake up to an alert and they're told to go investigate something. But as they're just waking up and having coffee, one guy's chest splits open and a creature bursts out of it. Then it starts moving around their spaceship, killing them one by one. And it has a mouth that opens up with another mouth inside, and it has acid for blood."

Basically he was just telling me *Alien* (1979) as a campfire story. Clearly, that night he'd come up empty and was like, "Fuck it. I'm just going to tell *Alien* from start to finish."

Shortly thereafter, I'm watching *Alien* for the first time, and I'm realizing I know every single beat of the movie. I know everything that's going to happen. And the first thought that goes through my mind is, "Oh my God, these assholes ripped off my dad!"

Eventually, I put two and two together, but ultimately it didn't matter. The film was so perfectly made, so honestly told and so dramatically authentic that it amazed me. It was unlike any film I'd experienced before. The work of a master. And that creature just buried itself deep inside my head. Every element of its design was so thoughtfully contrived, it scared the living shit out of me.

Jason Reitman

I wouldn't sleep in my bedroom for two weeks after seeing *Poltergeist* (1982). I was afraid a portal to the other side would open up in my closet. Even after I plucked up the courage to sleep in there again, I insisted the closet door be left open, so I could sneak peeks inside, to check it wasn't glowing.

I also had the same exact chair as the kids in the movie, but instead of that evil clown doll sitting on it, I had a Ronald McDonald. That was close enough for me, though, so Ronald had to go.

Tami Lane

"I WAS AFRAID A PORTAL TO THE OTHER SIDE WOULD OPEN UP IN MY CLOSET."

Opposite: Father and son filmmakers Ivan and Jason Reitman consider taking the Ecto-1 for a spin at a screening of *Ghostbusters: Afterlife* (2021).

Below: Make-up legend Tami Lane snuggles up with Revenant vampire Dirk Rogers during a cold night shoot for *Interview with the Vampire* (2022–present).

Karl: I'm haunted by the nightmares I had as a child, chased by rats as big as piglets through the dark. Those images are still so clear in my mind, and watching horror movies brings those feelings back. The anxieties of feeling trapped, or being pursued.

When you're making a horror movie, the challenges are technical, and the process is fun. But sitting through a horror movie is not enjoyable to me. I saw *A Nightmare on Elm Street* (1984) at a film festival, and that bathtub scene was horrible. Maybe I'm too empathetic, but how do you sleep after that?

Howard: So you and I are not going to go see a horror movie together anytime soon?

Karl: No, but we can make one!

Karl Walter Lindenlaub and Howard Berger

I was seven when *Gremlins* (1984) came out and it was amazing to me. My friend's father used to import toys and because I loved that film so much, he gave us loads of Gizmos. Also a really evil-looking, life-sized Stripe that lived in a dark corner of our toy cupboard.

My two sisters and I managed to convince ourselves that Stripe was coming alive and moving around at night. Every morning when we opened the doors to the cupboard, we were sure he'd changed position. We found it so terrifying, after a few weeks we ended up binning him. It was just so scary!

Sarah Gower

Above: Cinematographer Karl Walter Lindenlaub lines up a shot with the KNB EFX-created Aslan stand-in head for *The Chronicles of Narnia: Prince Caspian* (2008).

Opposite: Though there wasn't mushroom for him, a Clicker from *The Last of Us* (2023-present) managed to photobomb this shot with make-up designer Barrie Gower, Duncan Jarman, Victoria Bancroft and Sarah Gower.

School friends were fascinated and maybe a little horrified when they came to our house, but I didn't know any different. It was only when I started going to their houses that I realized not everyone lived the way we did.

I'd be like, "What, you don't have portraits of people being disembowelled by werewolves, or a naked *Bride of Re-Animator* statue clutching her heart in front of her boobs?"

John Wrightson

My mom took me to the Chiller Theatre convention in New Jersey. She bought me a Ben Nye make-up kit that had everything you needed to get started, and as soon as we got home, I dived right in.

I invited my friends over and started messing around. First thing I did was stipple a little liquid latex on their faces, folding their skin to make a wonderful gash and adding a trickle of blood to complete the effect. After that we went to each of their houses, rang the bell in a frenzy, and pretended they'd been in some terrible accident.

Every parent flipped the fuck out! Just freaked at the sight of their injured kids, and boy, fooling the adults was such a rush. That's when I knew I wanted to do this for the rest of my life.

Damien Leone

"IT WAS ONLY WHEN I STARTED GOING TO THEIR HOUSES THAT I REALIZED NOT EVERYONE LIVED THE WAY WE DID."

The first monster movie I saw in a theatre was *Jaws* (1975). After that, I wouldn't even go in the bathtub. To this day, if anyone asks if I want to go on a cruise, I go, "Have you not seen *Jaws*?"

Tyler Mane

My dad could draw and paint, and always encouraged me to do creative things, even if I messed up the house in the process. I was lucky because both he and my mom loved monster movies and got me excited about them too. I was born to be a Monster Maker!

Rick Baker

Opposite: The Gore the Merrier! Here's director, writer, producer, editor and make-up effects genius Damien Leone having a bloody good time on the set of *Terrifier 3* (2024).

3

WEIRD SCIENCE

Emerging from the primordial ooze of their beast-infused childhoods, driven by unbound monster-making dreams, our heroes set forth into the real world. Determined not to betray their younger selves by ever fully growing up, our dark Peter Pans sought gainful, gleeful, ghoul-making employment in the Business of Show.

Running the gamut of creature-themed creativity from stop motion animation to frightening tourists in theme parks, eventually our contributors met their destinies, and got to work.

I was always interested in the unusual. People thought I was a little peculiar myself. The film that set me on my path was *King Kong* (1933).

I wandered innocently into Grauman's Chinese Theatre one afternoon with my mother, and I haven't been the same since. I fell in love with the movie, with the fantasy, with the fact that someone dared put a 50-foot gorilla with a girl in his hand on the screen. Nobody had ever done that sort of thing before. It was so outrageous and so convincing that it titillated my imagination.

Kong haunted me. I kept going back to see it again and again. I desperately wanted to know how they'd brought the creatures to life, but unlike today there were no books on the subject, no DVD extras or magazines full of movie secrets. And that's the way it should be.

If you know too much about a film, it destroys the fantasy. Today's audiences are jaded by inside information. Back in 1933, I had no idea how Kong was made and I had no way to find out, so I had to be imaginative and devise my own methods. I started experimenting with a camera and animation models, then I started making my own dinosaurs, and gradually it turned from a hobby into a profession.

Ray Harryhausen

I used to complain to my teacher, Roy Harris, that I wished I had more technique. He'd always tell me, "Better to have ideas than technique. You can build techniques to meet your ideas, but if you don't have ideas, all the technique in the world isn't going to be enough."

That gave me the confidence to understand I didn't have to be John Williams. I didn't have to reach the peaks of these untouchable composing talents. So now I tell my students, if there's something you want to say, have faith you'll find the technique you'll need to express it.

Charles Bernstein

Preceding Spread: Kirk Thatcher finesses the final details of the Klingon monster dog puppet from *Star Trek III: The Search for Spock* (1984).

Above: Kong proves to tiny Ann Darrow (Fay Wray) and a hungry T-Rex that he's King of the Jungle in this dynamic battle from *King Kong* (1933), the film that inspired Ray Harryhausen to become one of cinema's greatest magicians.

Opposite: A lifesize Kong head on stage at RKO, ready to gobble up some extras as bananas barely register when you're the mighty *King Kong* (1933).

I wanted to work with Vincent Price, but was under contract with Hammer, and The Abominable Dr Phibes (1971) was an AIP production. Eventually, Hammer agreed to me taking a small role in the film provided it was uncredited. I don't think I got paid either, but I didn't really care.

I didn't have to do much! As the deceased Mrs Victoria Regina Phibes, I just had to lie there, dead in the coffin. That was more of a challenge than expected, though, as I'm a bit allergic to fluffy things and was wearing this beautiful gown with marabou feathers that kept going up my nose. I just tried to switch off and not breathe. Vincent, of course, was lying next to me in the coffin, and so thoughtful and caring. So gentle with the most beautiful, soothing voice. He'd say, "Don't worry love. You'll get out soon. We'll get the shot and you'll be home soon."

Off-camera, I loved watching magical Vincent work. I'd sit and watch and learn, like a little sponge. He was so charming and kind and funny and sweet. Not at all like the characters he played. On set he'd change into the most awful creature, and you'd appreciate then, what an extraordinary actor he was. He was so good at what he did, but so modest about it, and down-to-earth.

"I'LL TAKE THOSE MEMORIES OVER CREDITS AND SALARY ANY DAY."

He just always wanted to make sure everybody was all right. Every morning he'd bring in lovely food for myself, the make-up girls and hairdressers. Things he'd made the night before. So we'd be in make-up and everyone would be eating pâté at 6am! I'll take those memories over credits and salary any day.

Caroline Munro

Wes [Craven] was a good guy. A gentle soul. I wondered, sometimes, where did all the horror, all those movies come from?

Howard Berger

It wasn't until I was about 28 that I decided I wanted to make films. Before that I had wanted to write short stories and novels, but filmmaking jumped out of the bushes at me and, while I was at teaching college, I bought a camera without thinking much about it and started making movies. Then, at the end of that year, I quit, went to New York, and got my first job in film as a messenger and started learning.

Within a year or two, I had the opportunity to make my first feature. Sean Cunningham had just finished his first short, although he had never made a feature, and I had never written, directed or cut a film before. I ended up doing all three on The Last House on the Left (1972).

We just went off and made what we thought would be a very scary film, as that is what we had been asked to make by Hallmark Releasing, who were looking for a horror movie to show in their theatres, and thus we became horror film makers. But, before that time, I swear to God that neither one of us was an aficionado of horror, or knew much about it, or ever thought that we would be making them.

There were some very strong reactions against The Last House on the Left, against the explicit and protracted violence, and the ugliness of it. Since then I have moved towards being a little bit more abstract in the use of violence. Having an overall tone of violence rather than showing specific acts. To be honest, I've never been sure if that's right or wrong.

Certainly I don't think the violence in my films was ever gratuitous. I'm talking about violence, so it's not like the violence is irrelevant. If it were there simply to amuse I could understand, but I'm dealing with violence and violent people – how they operate and act and talk – so I don't see how it could be gratuitous.

The strange thing about horror films is that they can be made on a very low budget, and they afford a great amount of freedom. So there are two courses you can take once you become successful. The first is to pass over into mainstream culture and begin making films for other people, although there is some difficulty with that, as horror films have a very real taint and a lot of people will not entertain the idea of working with you. They think you're some sort of a Charles Manson.

The second course is to continue making horror films because you'll have the freedom to do what you want and you can become a sort of auteur within this forbidden, outlaw region of film, which some people think is terrific, and others believe is the work of the devil! Well, that's what happened to me.

Wes Craven

Opposite: Like every other man in the 1970s, Christopher Lee eyes Caroline Munro hungrily in this juicy scene from Dracula A.D. 1972 (1972).

Above: One, two, Wes is coming for you... Director Wes Craven sneaked into Scream (1996) as a familiarly dressed janitor named Fred.

Frankenstein's one of my favourite monsters, but not because of a movie.

When I was a kid, I went to Universal Studios, in Hollywood. I saw him performing, entertaining the crowd, and I was just completely enthralled. I loved the look of his mask and how he wasn't only scaring people, but making them laugh too.

I promised myself, "When I turn 16, I'm getting a job here playing Frankenstein."

And I did! I was 6'4", so tall enough for the task, and I doubt anyone ever pursued the job with more enthusiasm. The first time I stepped into the costume and put on Michael Burnett's slip latex Karloff mask, I immediately felt at home. Like, confident, comfortable and really just, "This is me."

You're only supposed to be out for maybe 30 minutes at a time, but as Frankenstein I'd stay out for an hour, easy. Eventually, though, I learned to pace myself and not skip breaks.

I performed to tourists from all over the world. First as Frankenstein, then as the Wolf Man, the Phantom and even Harry, from *Harry and the Hendersons* (1987). It was the beginning of my acting journey.

Walking around the park in those big boots, creeping up behind folks all slow and janky, I'd kick a trash can and they'd jump out of their skins. One time, I scared some guy's girl. He spun around and

Near where I grew up in Denver, there was a magic shop that had all these great masks. The best of them were made by a local guy called Ed Edmunds, who to this day, runs Distortions Unlimited, one of the biggest manufacturers of Halloween props and masks in the US.

We tracked Ed down and he was very kind. I spent a week with him, learning the in-and-outs of mask making, everything from sculpting and moulding to casting and painting. Ed helped me make my first full head mask and two-piece mould, and he liked it enough to put it in his 1982 catalogue. We called it the Saurian Trog and though it wasn't a big seller, for a 14-year-old kid to have a professionally produced mask on the market was pretty exciting.

Wayne Toth

kicked me so painfully, I almost fell over. In that moment, I became the monster, grabbing the guy and throwing him so hard, he went flying. Someone screamed, "Frankenstein just tossed that dude!"

It was awesome! I was sure I'd get fired, but got out of it as I had a good reputation.

In the end, I was at Universal for the best part of a decade and I still have the Frankenstein mask I wore in the park.

Five years later I was back in a suit at Universal, only this time, I wasn't down in the park. I was the Head Sleestak in *Land of the Lost* (2009) and happy to be doing what I'd always felt I was meant to do.

Douglas Tait

Troma is where I went to college. I was about to graduate high school. My mother was one of the first location caterers in New York, and through her I met Tim Considine. He was the prosthetic make-up artist on the job she was working on. He was always very nice to me and let me hang out and help at his shop.

I remember one day – I felt so privileged – he asked me to make some blood. I was like, "Where's the formula?"

He goes, "There's no formula! You prick your finger and match the colour."

Even though that sounded like bullshit to me, I didn't know any better, so by lunchtime I'm cut to ribbons, my fingers are like bloody claws, and I'm mixing all sorts of shit trying to match it with the stuff leaking out of me. Then Tim comes by with a piece of paper, throws it on the table, and says, "Why don't you use the formula?"

I pull that trick on all my interns now!

Honestly though, scrubbing plaster buckets and sweeping the floor around mould makers and sculptors was the best education I ever got. Because while I was sweeping and cleaning and taking lunch orders, I saw how they did a wrinkle. I saw how a clay build-up happened. And then literally on the day I graduated, Tim asked if I'd like to come help on his next movie.

The following Monday I was in the shop for *Sgt Kabukiman N.Y.P.D.* (1990). I was a 17-year-old kid and they told me to go make monsters! Everything I'd dreamed of up till then I just poured into the movie. The older guys in the shop, I picked all their brains. I even got to wear creature suits. That's me, at the end, playing The Evil One.

For all that, working 22 hour days, I made just $81 a week, but the experience, man, that was gold. I can never thank Lloyd Kaufman enough for that.

Josh Turi

Opposite (top): Accompanied by his father, 14-year-old Wayne Toth presents his Saurian Trog sculpture at Ed Edmund's Distortions Unlimited mask studio in Colorado.

Opposite (bottom): Douglas Tait models a Sleestak costume created by Mike Elizalde's Spectral Motion for *Land of the Lost* (2009).

Top: Tami Lane, Peter Montagna and Josh Turi apply the Electro make-up to Jamie Foxx's stunt double, Clay Fontenot, for *The Amazing Spider-Man 2* (2014). Sculpted by Norman Cabrera, it was a multi-piece silicone creation from KNB EFX.

Above: Josh Turi ensures Ben Barnes is bloody enough for a scene from *The Punisher* (2017-2019), while Jon Bernthal waits his turn to get equally messed up.

I graduated from film school with a zombie short called *Brain Death* (1992). I was surrounded by pretentious tutors and filmmakers who wanted to make artsy, worthy, black-and-white message movies, but I said, "No. I'm going to do a zombie film. It's going to have blood, guts and explosions."

Because it was an action film too! I made miniatures and blew them up. We had axes and machine guns. It was such a good laugh. But we almost didn't get to make it, as the tutors wouldn't approve my script. So I wrote a fake script they'd like, and once that was approved, we grabbed the gear and made our zombie action film.

Tempting fate, we even shot it in the film department. We needed an interior and it was conveniently right there. We bribed the security guy to let us in. We'd film all night, then clean up the blood, and nobody knew until we showed them the film.

Most of my tutors dismissed it as nonsense that no one would ever take seriously, but every year the graduation films got a public screening and it was clear from the applause which film the audience enjoyed the most!

In the end, I passed the course, and there were industry guys at the screening who offered me some editing work when I graduated. Really everything went from there.

Neil Marshall

"THE TUTORS WOULDN'T APPROVE MY SCRIPT, SO I WROTE A FAKE [ONE] THEY'D LIKE."

The stunt co-ordinator for *X-Men* (2000) reached out to me. I was wrestling professionally at the time and had long blond hair, so I kind of resembled Sabretooth. He wanted me to come aboard as a stuntman, but I was humming and hawing about it because, well, I wasn't a stuntman.

He showed Bryan Singer my picture, but actually Singer wanted to see me for the part. So I got the fake teeth, though I felt a damn fool about it, and walked into the office. There's this kid sitting on the edge of the couch, typing on his computer. I go, "I'm here to see Bryan Singer."

He doesn't look up. Just raises a finger to hush me, and I'm thinking, "You little shit."

Finally, he looks up and goes, "I'm Bryan Singer, and you're Sabretooth!"

Then he jumps up on the coffee table, shouting, "Choke me! Choke me!"

So I grabbed his throat and roared. That's how I got cast!

Tyler Mane

Hollywood, to me, always felt so out of bounds. But the independent film boom of the Eighties and Nineties taught me regular people could make movies too.

Peter Jackson and Sam Raimi's vision and enthusiasm transcended their budgets. Like them, I had no Hollywood connections, but I did have woods behind my parents' house. I could go out there with a camera and figure things out. I didn't think it would be easy. I didn't know if I would be any good at it. But the barrier to entry was no longer there.

Ti West

Opposite (top): The poster art for Neil Marshall's first short film, *Brain Death* (1992).
Opposite (bottom): Neil Marshall with the cast and crew from his gory student short, *Brain Death* (1992).
Top: Tyler Mane had a roaring good time returning as Sabretooth for *Deadpool & Wolverine* (2024). The make-up was originally designed by Gordon Smith for *X-Men* (2000), then re-visited by Bill Corso for the hit MCU action comedy.

4

STOMP AND CIRCUMSTANCE

From lost worlds and the ocean depths to mad labs and the pits of hell, the monsters are coming. Grotesque, gargantuan, grumpy and gluttonous, they're of a size and a mind to do as they please. To terrorize and chase us. To claw and chew and squish us. To feed our nightmares and forewarn us that we may not always be top of the food chain. For all those who identify as Kaijuish, this collection of colossal terrors is for you.

Max Steiner set the template for how we score movies. He took the same approach to composing the music for *King Kong* (1933) as someone would an opera: taking a theme or even an instrument, and applying it to a character. So every time that character comes on, you'd hear their theme and it was a great way of helping audiences track a story without realizing they were being led in any particular way.

Kong was the first example of leitmotif in movies, a classical way of scoring that's been the norm ever since. Every score since *Kong* has been influenced by Max Steiner making that choice more than 90 years ago.

Michael Giacchino

"IT WAS A GREAT WAY OF HELPING AUDIENCES TRACK A STORY WITHOUT REALIZING THEY WERE BEING LED."

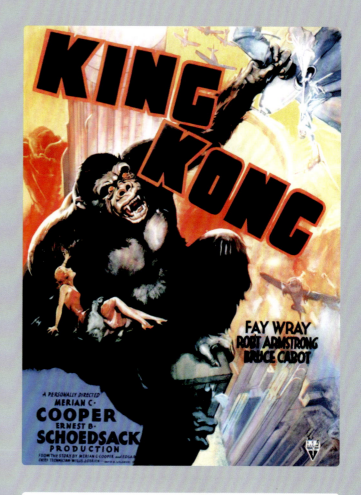

Preceding Spread: You'd never know that behind all that fur, foam rubber and contact lenses hid movie make-up royalty, the true King of *King Kong* (1976), Rick Baker.

Below: Three-time Oscar-winner Max Steiner conducts his game-changing score for *King Kong* (1933).

Right: A striking septet of vibrant, dynamic movie posters for the adventure classic that made a monster kid of Ray Harryhausen – and millions more – *King Kong* (1933).

John Landis said, "Some Italian guy's gonna remake *King Kong* (1933)."

I told him, "Well, that's a mistake. They're probably going to get some idiot and put him in a gorilla suit."

I was right!

Even though the stop motion's kind of jerky, the original *King Kong* is still the best. They came up with so many brilliant ways to do things, and the scale and visuals still amaze me.

I was against remaking it, especially since my friends at the time were all stop motion animators. But somehow the producers got my number. As I'd thought, they wanted a suit, then they ragged on the original movie, telling me how much better their version was going to be. That pissed me off. I told them, "You'll be lucky if you make something half as good."

They said they wanted Kong to be less like an ape this time, and more like a neanderthal man. They had all these drawings by Mentor Huebner, a great storyboard artist, of a primitive but human Kong, and I'm 25-year-old Rick Baker, with no filter, and I go, "What the fuck's wrong with you guys? If anything, King Kong should be a Super Gorilla. Not less of a gorilla. More of a gorilla. A gorilla on steroids!"

Anyway, I was just about to start *Squirm* (1976) and I said, "If you really want me to build you a suit, if you can let me know soon, I can probably get out of this other film before I start. But if I don't hear from you, I'm going to get on with *Squirm*."

I didn't hear from them, so I started *Squirm*, and then of course they called to ask me to build their King Kong suit. I said, "I told you I was going to do this other movie and you didn't call, so I'm going to be busy for a few weeks."

While I was away, Dino De Laurentiis brought in Carlo Rambaldi – his friend from Italy. I wasn't familiar with his work, so they showed me his portfolio and there was some cool stuff in there. Still, I told them, "I don't know how we're going to work together. I don't speak Italian, he doesn't speak English, and we have different techniques."

They said, "We think you both have good ideas and we want you to do a test costume."

My friend John Berg made these cool mechanical arm extensions. I took them to the producers and told them we could use them to build a proportionally accurate ape suit. But they didn't care. They wanted the caveman guy. With only six weeks and very little money, I got started in my little garage workshop, but decided to ignore their drawings and do what I thought was right. I thought, "I'm going to show them they're wrong and build a gorilla suit."

It was a scramble to get my suit done in time, but I managed, and showed up to meet with everyone. I was dying to see what Carlo

"I GOT THE BEST GUY FROM ITALY. I GOT THE BEST GUY FROM AMERICA. TOGETHER, YOU'RE GOING TO MAKE THE BEST FUCKING APE ANYBODY'S EVER SEEN."

would turn up with, but he wasn't there. They told me, "Carlo didn't have the time to get finished."

Neither did I, but there I was with it. Of course, they were furious with me. "This doesn't look anything like what we wanted you to make."

"I know – it's better!"

They said, "Yeah, well, Carlo's going to build a robot King Kong that'll do the whole movie, so we may not even need your suit." I told them, "Well, that's bullshit. NASA can't even make a walking robot, let alone a 40-foot one."

Many weeks later, if not months, Carlo finished his suit and it was a disaster. Though he built it closer to what they wanted, more of an Australopithecus kind of guy, [director] John Guillermin wasn't happy with it at all. They wanted to do some test shots, so they sent for my suit. Even though they hated it, they'd kind of gotten used to it.

So I'm in my Kong suit, and Guillermin's pointing at me, then he's pointing at Carlo's suit, and telling everyone what's wrong with both of them. At which point, I said, "You know what? I fucking quit. All I've been hearing is what I did was crap, and Carlo's a genius, and he's making a robot that'll do the whole movie. So go make the movie with your genius."

I got called into Dino's office, and he was like, "I got the best guy from Italy. I got the best guy from America. Together, you're going to make the best fucking ape anybody's ever seen."

I didn't know how we could possibly work together, as most of the time, it was less a collaboration than a fight. But I was threatened

Opposite (top): Rick Baker's hand-drawn designs for the Kong expression heads he was tasked with creating for *King Kong* (1976).

Opposite (bottom): Rick Baker's roaring head sculpture for *King Kong* (1976).

into figuring something out with him, and in the end, it became a contest. I sculpted three heads, he sculpted one, and they picked mine. I sculpted the body with a studio sculptor named Steve Varner, and supervised the sculpture of the hands and the feet. Meanwhile, Carlo's drawing pictures of everything after I made it, then going, "Look at my design."

Even though Dino chose my head and liked what I did better with my initial suit, Carlo still had his ear. Like, I wanted to do a hand-tied suit, with the hair going in the right direction. But Carlo went to Bischoff's Taxidermy and bought a black bear hide, took it in to Dino's office and went, "Look at this, it's beautiful."

Carlo got his way, but once they'd made the suit and put it on the padding, it became this great, big fuzzball. The hair just stuck up everywhere, so they ended up cutting it all off.

In the end, the suit wasn't what I would have built on my own. In a lot of ways, mine would have been better, except for the mechanical aspect. Carlo and Isidoro Raponi were responsible for the mechanics of the face, and they were way beyond what I could have made at the time, even though I had to drag a giant bundle of cables that came out the back of my head, went through my suit and down my leg, for the entire movie.

Though I was upset pretty much the whole time, *King Kong* (1976) is better because I fought for what I thought was right. I didn't win every battle, but I did what I could. And yeah, the irony that I ended up being the guy in the gorilla suit was not lost on me.

Playing Kong could be scary, like when there were big-ass explosions behind me, and I'd get so hot I'd think I was on fire. But it was also fun, sometimes. I got to stomp around on miniature sets, break buildings and throw trains. Who wouldn't want to do crazy shit like that?

Rick Baker

"I GOT TO STOMP AROUND ON MINIATURE SETS, BREAK BUILDINGS AND THROW TRAINS."

Above: Rick Baker's Kong shoots a furious glare at producer Dino De Laurentiis for only giving him a "Special Thanks" credit for all his hard work on *King Kong* (1976).

Right: Rick Baker tests one of the hard contact lenses he endured throughout the making of *King Kong* (1976).

Opposite (top): An exhausted Rick Baker rests between takes while playing the 8th Wonder of the World for *King Kong* (1976).

Opposite (bottom): A glance at Rick Baker's workspace at MGM Studios where he built his remarkable suit for *King Kong* (1976).

Phil Tippett's take on *Dragonslayer* (1981) was, like, "I'm never going to get a chance to design the ultimate dragon again. So this is going to be mine."

And it was good!

Dennis [Muren] came back from first unit to tell me they had a visual problem with the full-scale head. It was very long, and too perfectly aligned, so when it faced camera, it compressed and completely flattened out. It looked two-dimensional.

I built a puppet, throwing everything off kilter just enough to register as depth. It was only intended for one close-up, but suddenly everyone was like, "We have a puppet now! Let's shoot the hell out of it. It can breathe fire, and nudge baby dragons!"

And I'm like, "Fine. I can build all that in."

Chris Walas

I love the smoothness of the stop motion in *Dragonslayer* (1981). The Cain Robot from *RoboCop 2* (1990) is also incredible. There's nothing more exciting than a Phil Tippett creation.

Takashi Yamazaki

Vermithrax Pejorative from *Dragonslayer* (1981) and the dragons from *Reign of Fire* (2002) were our main references going into *Harry Potter and the Goblet of Fire* (2005). That was the benchmark we tasked ourselves with topping.

Nick Dudman built a full-size animatronic dragon that breathed real fire from big, hidden propane tanks. It was crazy! For me though, the fun is freeing them from a corner of the stage, and making them walk and fight and fly. Bringing those creatures to life is what we all live for.

We animated the Hungarian Horntail. I don't really buy quadruped dragons, so we made ours more bat-like, and had him move around on his wings. That just seems scarier to me. Most of my monsters I prefer a little bit vicious. Kids love that stuff! I know I did growing up.

Jim Mitchell

I'm good with organic things, but terrible with anything mechanical, so I hired Craig Hayes to design ED-209 for *RoboCop* (1987). Ed [Neumeier] had some artwork he liked, of robots whose arms terminated with guns, so we started there. Paul [Verhoeven] wanted legs like a 'Z', without any anthropomorphic qualities. So we just slowly built it up, avoiding any kind of organic flow. Everything was axial and quick and snapped.

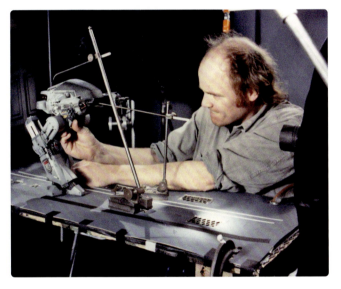

Whenever I'm making something, there's got to be some kind of sound component in my mind. It's generally not what the sound designer comes up with, but it helps me frame what the character is. For ED, I imagined lathes and mills and drill presses, and when he's off camera, I proposed that Paul keep him alive with a bass pedal note, just a deep subwoofer hum that keeps him present.

The scene where ED's at the top of the stairs, and wiggles its toes uncertainly over the first step, was really an afterthought. I was just getting ready to shoot that shot when Jon [Davison] called me and said, "Can you do something funny?"

I was like, "I guess so."

So I came up with something funny.

Phil Tippett

Opposite (top): Peter MacNicol rides Vermithrax Pejorative's full-size head and neck to make a point in *Dragonslayer* (1981).

Opposite (middle): Dragon wrangler Chris Walas readies his insert puppet head of Vermithrax Pejorative from *Dragonslayer* (1981). This puppet was used for close-up shots requiring more detail than Phil Tippett's go-motion puppet was capable of providing.

Top: Nick Dudman's magnificent full-scale Hungarian Horntail dragon has a serious case of fire breath on the set of *Harry Potter and the Goblet of Fire* (2005).

Middle: Phil Tippett brings ED-209 to life through the magic of go-motion, for *RoboCop* (1987).

Bottom: Phil Tippett and Craig Hayes admire their handiwork as the full-scale ED-209 they built for *RoboCop* (1987) prepares to pump the residents of Old Detroit full of lead and catchphrases.

I was brought on to Jurassic Park (1993) before the edict came down that everything was going to be computer graphics. I got the job, not only because I knew pre-production, production and post-production, but because I knew all the dinosaurs, I was up on the latest palaeontology, and I'd made some short films with dinosaurs. So I knew stuff, and they knew I knew stuff, so even after we went digital, they kept me on.

Technology changes everything. When the digital revolution came, and I saw that dinosaur test footage, I thought it was the end. Steven [Spielberg] asked me how I felt, and I told him, "Extinct."

He said, "I've got to put that in the movie!"

Steven's such a sweet, thoughtful guy, though. He realized it was a big deal for me to make the transition from analogue to digital filmmaking. And I did it begrudgingly at first, but it taught me a valuable lesson: besides adapting to survive, if you can embrace new tools, there's so much more you can do than you could before.

Micromanaging the animators on Jurassic Park was a pain in the ass, but their skill level just wasn't up to speed. At the time, in the US, no one was being taught computer animation. There was a team from Sheridan College in Canada who'd been trained in Disney's 2D style, but it's a totally different animal when you're animating things with specific weight in a real-world environment.

I made articulated stop motion puppets to show them the poses. I traced the dinosaurs' forward momentum on clear acetate cels with a black Sharpie. And I mapped out the movement and timing of every joint. It was slow, painstaking work, but we got there.

When the film was finished, Kathy [Kennedy] invited me to a screening at Amblin, and afterwards she turns around and asks me, "What do you think?"

I told her, "It doesn't suck!"

She said, "That's exactly what I thought!"

Holy shit! It actually worked. It was on a level that you always aspire to, but rarely achieve.

Phil Tippett

"STEVEN [SPIELBERG] ASKED ME HOW I FELT, AND I TOLD HIM, 'EXTINCT.'"

We're all masochists to some degree. The thrill of creating something is so great, by hook or by crook, no matter how huge the effort, or how many late nights, we're going to find a way to make it happen. There were a lot of people like that at ILM at the beginning of the transition. Back when the idea took hold that computers were going to be part of the equation.

Somehow I ended up down in the pit with Steve ['Spaz' Williams]. I remember watching Steve build the T-Rex skeleton from scratch, then animate the walk cycle all on his own. It was amazing and led us to creating the full CG T-Rex test for [Steven] Spielberg that Dennis [Muren] put together with a background plate he shot. After we saw that, we suddenly had the feeling ILM was going to be a much bigger part of *Jurassic Park* (1993) than we'd originally expected.

Something was definitely changing with the way movies were going to get made. We'd watch the dailies and even from the crudest initial tests and takes, we felt like we were seeing dinosaurs come back to life. That this was the next evolutionary step after Ray Harryhausen's stop-motion magic.

Ultimately, we only created about 85 computer-generated shots – these days movies have 2,000 or more. So much of the movie was still created in-camera. Really it was the perfect blend of digital and practical disciplines, thanks to Steven Spielberg bringing everything together so beautifully and seamlessly.

It was a very special time, and I think we knew it. What more could monster kids ask for than the opportunity to go make dinosaurs?

Jim Mitchell

I was on a panel at the Academy one night and I saw the look in Ray Harryhausen's eyes after he saw *Jurassic Park* (1993). All the things he'd tried to do, Phil Tippett did. His acolyte had bested him. It was almost sad to see.

Richard Edlund

Jim: We're watching dailies of John Rosengrant in the pteranodon suit for *Jurassic Park III* (2001), and Stan Winston's like, "There's bits. There's bits..."

Howard: Stan would always say, "Little pieces of film cut into one big piece of film."

Jim: A glimpse is sometimes all you need. Even if John fell over in the suit after half a second, we still had 12 frames in front of that where maybe the beak turned towards the camera in a striking way, or there was an amazing glint of light in its eye. Bits are what made *Jaws* (1975) work.

Jim Mitchell and Howard Berger

Opposite: Phil Tippett (on the right, pictured here with Adam Valdez) used his expertise in motion, physics and kinetics to help bring the digital dinosaurs to life in Steven Spielberg's *Jurassic Park* (1993).

Top: Computer graphics artist Jim Mitchell works patiently on a computer-generated shot for *Jurassic Park III* (2001).

Above: Senior animator Randal M. Dutra manipulates one of Phil Tippett's stop motion armatures for *Jurassic Park* (1993).

I went to New Zealand to apply a make-up for the pilot episode of *Xena: Warrior Princess* (1995–2001). Xena had to fight a cyclops, but they didn't have the money for a mechanical eye, so we made him blind, with his eye stitched closed.

Howard [Berger] put me in charge of the thing. It was such a great opportunity! So I sculpted and ran it, put my kit together and jumped on a plane. Early the next morning, I'm applying it to the actor and get about halfway through when I realize something's not quite meshing with the colours.

Then it hits me: I'm not on a set down the street. I'm 14 hours away from the closest help and it's a miracle I packed enough of the right stuff for my kit. So I had a panic attack, quietly to myself. Finally something happened, and it all worked out. One bad stroke can send you way off track, but another can reset everything.

In the end, it didn't even matter though, as the instant we got to the location, the actor went up to the damn catering truck and ordered a frikkin' bacon sandwich. Ridiculous! So he's eating his breakfast and next thing you know, his chin's falling off. I had to fix it again, this time on set, but everything worked out in the end. The cyclops even ended up in the title sequence for the entire run of the show!

Mark Tavares

For the longest time, CG was a four-letter word and something to avoid. The odd exception aside, practical creatures are so much more powerful than computer-generated ones. There's just something special and mesmerizing about seeing a real thing in action. Something puppety or mechanical, live, on set.

But I was making a movie about a giant spider and had to be realistic. Stop motion would have given it a cool, Harryhausen-ish look, but this was a $600,000 movie and there's no way I could have afforded effects like that. CG was the only way to go.

What an eye opener it was for me. We were lucky to get a start-up company out of Pakistan. They were eager to prove themselves and did an amazing job animating it. They also opened my mind to augmenting existing sets with vehicles and background things. There's no way I could have made *Big Ass Spider!* (2013) without them.

From then on, I realized digital isn't something to fear, but a valuable tool to enhance the practical side of your production. It makes everything seem just that little bit more realistic.

Mike Mendez

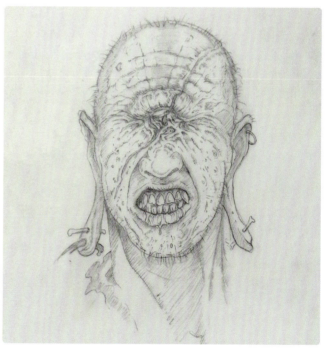

"THE PRIORITY ALWAYS WAS, WHAT'S THE MONSTER, AND HOW CAN WE HAVE FUN?"

When I was a kid, I wanted to be in horror movies. Even as I got older and discovered that my real talent was for being funny, I still thought, "Fine, I'll become a comedian. I'll get famous and powerful, then I'll write a horror movie and put myself in it."

It was the dumbest, most circuitous route, but that was always the goal, and it worked! I created the show, *Stan Against Evil* (2016–18), and put myself in it.

The premise of the show was, what if you took *The X-Files* (1993–2018), but instead of Dana Scully being with Fox Mulder, she was with my dad? Like, he believed in monsters, but he just didn't give a shit. We used to joke that if our father had been in one of the planes shooting King Kong, he'd fly over, check the score of the baseball game, shoot at Kong some more, then go back to the game.

That was how *Stan Against Evil* came about. It was a current sheriff and a retired sheriff in a haunted New England town fighting demons, and it allowed me to write everything I'd ever wanted to about monsters. The priority always was, what's the monster, and how can we have fun?

My favourite episode ['Larva My Life'; S03,E03] was about a guy who'd turned into a moth battling a local alcoholic who was trapped in a gorilla suit. And they fought on a miniature of the town, so we got to do a kaiju episode that remained within the bounds of the show's reality.

Most people have never heard of *Stan Against Evil*, but those who saw it, and got it, loved it. That's good enough for me.

Dana Gould

Opposite (top): Patrick Wilson bellows as the vengeful Cyclops in a make-up designed and applied by Mark Tavares for the pilot episode of *Xena: Warrior Princess* (1995–2001).

Opposite (bottom): John Bisson's Cyclops concept art for *Xena: Warrior Princess* (1995–2001).

Top: Wallace Shawn grimacing at the pleasure of wearing a hot ape suit, with Dana Gould sympathetic in the corner there, on location for *Stan Against Evil* (2016–18).

Middle: Dana Gould ain't 'fraid of no hideous horror hag (Morgana Ignis) – created by Jason Collins' make-up effects studio Autonomous FX – on the set of *Stan Against Evil* (2016–18).

Right: The big ass spider from *Big Ass Spider!* (2013).

Japan is a beautiful country with incredible architecture. It's where I proposed to my wife, Soni. For that, I chose the most perfect spot, my mecca: the Godzilla statue beside the guard gate at Toho Co. I was so nervous before I proposed, I was shaking, but Soni just thought I was excited to see Godzilla. Anyway, I got down on one knee and she said, "Yes!"

That night we stayed in Tokyo's Godzilla Hotel, the suite with the full-size hand coming through the wall. There's a button by the bed that activates subwoofers that shake the room like Godzilla's approaching. Then the lights go out, the TV comes on, and there's a newscast showing Godzilla destroying everything around the hotel. There are etchings on the windows so you can take photos of the city with, say, Mothra swooping down. And there's another button, right beside the toilet, that turns the bathroom into a spaceship, with Godzilla on a monitor in front of you.

So there I was, newly engaged, a grown-up man, but really I was just five years old the whole time!

Dirk Rogers

"I WAS SO NERVOUS BEFORE I PROPOSED, BUT SONI JUST THOUGHT I WAS EXCITED TO SEE GODZILLA."

Opposite: From artist Paul Mann comes Mondo's glorious tribute poster to Toho's classic *Destroy All Monsters* (1968), the ultimate monster mash.

Below: With Godzilla as his wingman, Dirk Rogers found the courage to propose to his wife Soni.

As a child, I was drawn to Godzilla. I read once, in a magazine, how Toho made their kaiju movies and I remember thinking it wasn't fair. I felt jealous that adults got to do fun stuff like dress up in costumes and trample miniature buildings. I thought, "I want to be part of that group one day."

Every time I saw Godzilla or Ultraman on TV, I'd draw what I remembered at school. I'd voice the characters and do atomic breath sound effects. My classmates would line up with their notebooks, asking me to draw their favourite characters.

I moved on to clay so I could make my own figures. Once I was so focused on sculpting that I didn't notice a small fire had started in the house and my room was filling up with smoke. My mum was out shopping and my little sister had to run to tell her the house was on fire! Fortunately it was only food burning on the stove, but I was oblivious to everything till my mum ran into my bedroom yelling, "What are you doing?!"

Years later, I made a film called *Always: Sunset on Third Street 2* (2007) that opens with a fantasy sequence featuring Godzilla. After that, Toho knocked at my door, and kept knocking. "Do you want to do a Godzilla?"

Back then I didn't feel the technology was quite up to creating the Godzilla I wanted, but by the time *Shin Godzilla* (2016) was released, and the tech was sufficiently advanced, that movie already achieved what I'd wanted to do. So then it became a matter of, "How can I make a better Godzilla movie than *Shin Godzilla*?"

I came up with a story, set right after the war, where the only weapons available to fight Godzilla are decommissioned underwater mines and the like. At that time, Japan didn't have any effective weapons. Just wooden ships, for the most part, that showed how impoverished they were. And I made the hero a kamikaze pilot survivor. Although Toho had previously considered setting a Godzilla story prior to the first film as taboo, after I presented them with my ideas, they said, "Let's do it."

A year before we went into production on *Godzilla Minus One* (2023), I was directing Seibuen Amusement Park's *Godzilla the Ride: Giant*

Opposite: Presented with a wealth of stomping options, Godzilla's like a kid in a candy store in this classic lobby card from *Godzilla Vs. The Thing* (1964), a.k.a. *Godzilla vs. Mothra*.

Left: A 'Stomp' of Godzilla figures from the collection of Marshall "More is More" Julius.

Monsters Ultimate Battle. Taking the coolest elements from my favourite Godzillas over the years, I created a Godzilla I really loved. It was a design I'd been working on, I suppose, since childhood, and many people said it was my best work!

As I'd already created my ideal Godzilla, I kept coming back to it during the design process for *Godzilla Minus One*, and so ultimately we just tweaked elements of that for the movie. I wanted to bring back the destroyer Godzilla, not a protector of Earth or kaiju wrestler, but a merciless, destructive force. My Godzilla is Nuclear War Godzilla and it was time to bring him back.

It is very gratifying to me that the film was so well received, both at home and around the world. Seventy years ago, when the first *Godzilla* (1954) was in cinemas, Toho stated in their advertising that the special effects surpassed anything ever seen in the West. So all these years later, winning the Oscar for Best Visual Effects, I felt we'd earned our place in the franchise's long and celebrated history.

At the Academy Awards I carried a Golden Godzilla. Prior to that, a regular Godzilla figure accompanied me to every event, screening and interview. Though it wasn't my idea – more a command from Toho – I couldn't argue with the results. Everywhere we went, everyone knew who we were, thanks to the figure, and even Steven Spielberg wanted a picture with Godzilla!

In fact, Steven loved the figure so much, he asked me where he could buy one. When I told him they were rare and hard to get, he looked so sad, so I offered him one of the two I had. He looked at them for a long time, struggling to decide, like a kid in a candy store torn between two favourite chocolate bars. It was wonderful to see just how much genuine love he has for Godzilla. No wonder his films have so much magic and warmth. In the end, he chose one and we took a lot of photos together.

From beginning to end, *Godzilla Minus One* was an unforgettable experience. I fulfilled my childhood dream and shared it with like-minded people from all around the world.

Takashi Yamazaki

Godzilla means so much to the Japanese, in terms of reflecting the country's psyche. Not only how they feel about the bombing of Hiroshima and Nagasaki, but also their guilt at maybe bringing it upon themselves. *Godzilla Minus One* (2023) did a perceptive and sensitive job of addressing those post-war issues. It's a beautiful film, and also I love that Godzilla looks like a man in a suit, even though he's a brilliant CG creation.

For the Japanese, Godzilla is a complex and potent metaphor for war, but for America, the country that dropped the bombs, he's just a monster. That's why I'm uncomfortable when Hollywood does Godzilla, because it feels like cultural appropriation.

Simon Pegg

FANGS FOR SHARING

Immortal, mesmerizing, shape-shifting predators who hold dominion over the creatures of the night, vampires boast more superpowers than an entire legion of comicbook heroes. And they have so much more fun!

Free of the ravages of conscience, emotion or consequence, they're our darkest desires, with wings on. Compelled to sleep all day, then driven by a relentless hunger, they are the teens of the monster world and no less terrifying.

Stakes at the ready, all...

Fright Night (1985) was my love letter to the genre I grew up with, as I mainly watched AIP and Hammer horror films. I had the idea while I was writing *Cloak & Dagger* (1984), a juvenile version of *Rear Window* (1954). I said to Universal, "If you really want a fun story about a kid who sees something out the window, you should make him a mad horror fan, and let him see a vampire next door, chomping down on a beautiful woman."

They hated the concept. The only successful vampire movie in recent memory was *Love at First Bite* (1979), and at the time, the thinking was that once a genre got the spoof treatment, it was exhausted. Still, I couldn't get the idea out of my mind.

I just didn't have a story, but eventually remembered all the Friday Night Frights I'd grown up with. Local horror hosts like Zacherley and Vampira. Then everything clicked. I'd have the boy run for help to a local horror host, a vampire killer in the style of Peter Cushing or Vincent Price. And Peter Vincent was born!

The story came together very quickly after that. Charley Brewster, the kid, is the engine. His quest to stop the vampire, Jerry Dandrige, is what drives the movie. But it's Peter who takes the hero's journey. He's the one who starts out as a coward and eventually finds the heart to go fight the vampire.

Originally I considered casting Vincent Price, but his health at the time made that impossible. Then I spoke to Roddy McDowall, who told me Peter Vincent reminded him of the Cowardly Lion. He just got it, and was brilliant in the role. Really nailed the humour and the pathos. The absolute heart of the movie.

Tom Holland

Preceding Spread: Wesley Snipes flashes his pearly whites – artfully supplemented with Gary Archer's dental prosthetics – as a day-walking, human-vampire hybrid in Marvel's first successful movie, *Blade* (1998).

Above: Roddy McDowall as late-night horror host turned fearful vampire hunter Peter Vincent, in Tom Holland's classic vampire tale, *Fright Night* (1985). "You have to have faith, Mr. Vincent!"

Below: Director Tom Holland lines up a shot with Roddy McDowall and Stephen Geoffreys as Evil Ed for *Fright Night* (1985).

Opposite (Top): Master monster maker Randy Cook knocked out Amanda Bearse's shark mouth make-up in record time, delivering one of the most iconic scares in *Fright Night* (1985).

Opposite (bottom): Randy Cook's startling shark mouth looms large in "the fucking poster" for *Fright Night* (1985).

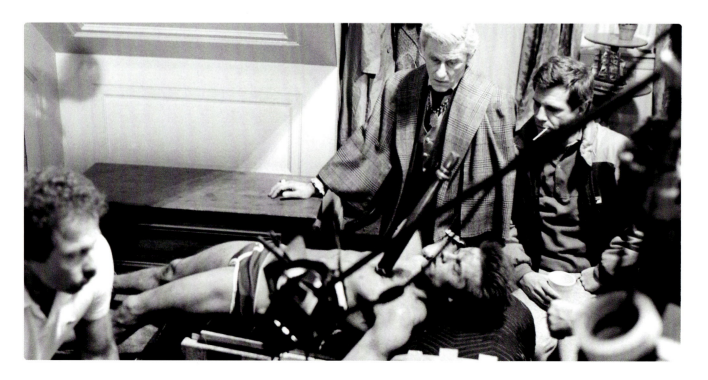

T om [Holland] called upon our friendship to persuade me to work over the weekend on a freebie. The shark mouth from the scene in *Fright Night* (1985) where Amy [Amanda Bearse] attacks Charley [William Ragsdale]. He said, "It'll only be on screen a few frames. Just a second or two."

Of course, I did it. But I told him I didn't have the time to make something that would stand up to close inspection. "For God's sake," I warned him, "don't overdo it!"

Of course, he did. It was in shot after shot, then it wound up on the fucking poster!

Randy Cook

"IT WAS IN SHOT AFTER SHOT, THEN IT WOUND UP ON THE FUCKING POSTER!"

I've lived with the idea of Count Crowley since I was twelve years old. Inspired by Roddy McDowall's character in *Fright Night* (1985), I thought how awesome it would be to tell stories about someone whose cover is a horror host, but in reality he's secretly out there protecting the world from monsters.

As an adult I had to confront the sobering – to coin a phrase – reality, that I not only wrestle with mental illness, but that I am an addict and an alcoholic. So, 21 years ago, I got clean and sober. But that was just the beginning of my journey, fighting the monsters and demons that exist within myself, including an oftentimes crippling struggle with suicidal ideation, abandonment anxiety and anxious attachment disorders, racing thoughts and abject depression.

I've had conversations with different women in my life who've had horrible, gut-wrenching experiences, at home, in school and at work. But no one's believed them. So I thought it would be more interesting to make my hero a woman who struggles to be heard. Jerry became Jerri, but not a sexy cover star like Vampirella and Buffy. As much as I love those guys, I wanted to see a badass woman in combat boots and ripped-up jeans who's just trying to stay sober long enough to figure out how to stop a vampire from eating her brother.

My journey taught me much about my influences over the years, and I began to think about how grotesquely manipulated the media is by politicians and money men. Just the worst people feeding us lies, so I thought, why not monsters too? What if monsters have fed us disinformation for centuries? So we think we know how to take them on, but really we don't. Say Dracula walks into your house. We'd look for a crucifix, a sharp piece of wood or maybe holy water. But Dracula would laugh and say, "Ha! You fell for it. You believed what we've been putting out there, but none of that stuff works. It's all bullshit."

That's how *Count Crowley: Reluctant Midnight Monster Hunter* (2019–present) came together.

Dark Horse accepted the idea and paired me with this incredible editor, Megan Walker. She asked me what I wanted the book to look like, and I told her it had to feel like *Mad Magazine*'s Al Jaffee meets EC Comics and Bernie Wrightson. She sent my first script to artist Lukas Ketner, who immediately knew what I was looking for and sent me a spread of potential Jerri looks. We hired him immediately!

Count Crowley's changed my life as I get to tell stories about incredible people, share my love of all things fantastical and wild, and at the same time, explore all of the complicated and complex ideas that make it so difficult for us to be human beings today.

David Dastmalchian

Right: *Count Crowley: Reluctant Midnight Monster Hunter* (2019-present) is creator/writer David Dastmalchian and artist Lukas Ketner's modern, comicbook take on classic creatures.

Opposite: Ve Neill flanked by *The Lost Boys* (1987) – from left to right – Brooke McCarter, Billy Wirth, Kiefer Sutherland and Alex Winter. Below, Neill transforms Sutherland with a groundbreaking vampire look from Greg Cannom.

God, I loved Christopher Lee. Those Dracula movies of his scared the bejesus out of me. Oh, but he was sexy as well. Creepy, but handsome and tall. And British! He had it all going on.

Vampires are supposed to be sexy. That's what I told Joel Schumacher, a director I absolutely adored. When he told me he was hiring Steve Johnson to make the vampires for *The Lost Boys* (1987), I asked him to reconsider. I said, "Steve's great, but if you hire him, they'll be horrible-looking monsters. We need our vampires to be sexy, cool and beautiful. Like dark angels."

Greg Cannom and I collaborated on a design that came out freaky, scary and beautiful. Joel loved it and passed on Steve's more monstery look. We aimed for that sweet spot between human and inhuman, and sculpted a slightly different look for each of the vampires. They came out bitchin'!

None of the guys had long hair, so I suggested they get extensions, which weren't so widely used back then. The guys all moaned that braiding hurt, so [hair stylist K. G.] Ramsey and I got extensions too, in solidarity with the guys. We had mullets for a while, and that was fun, but better still, we had our Lost Boys.

They were spooky, cool and so Eighties! I loved seeing them all together. My beautiful, sexy vampires.

Ve Neill

When I first got my fangs for *Buffy the Vampire Slayer* (1992), I was thrilled. My character had a gold tooth that turned into a golden fang! I thought that was hilariously funny. Unfortunately, most people missed that detail, as it didn't read too well on screen. Still I became obsessed with my fangs and asked to take them home. I'd wear them out to clubs! And my daughter's the same. She wore fangs for her senior picture!

David Arquette

I got a call from Michèle Burke saying, "Can you make vampire teeth?"

The film was *Interview with the Vampire* (1994). Tom Cruise has a midline that goes up his right nostril, so the challenge was to make a set of teeth that would give him symmetrical fangs. John Rosengrant was in charge of the sculpt, and after we'd made a test set of teeth, my dad and I went to Stan Winston's place to do the first fitting.

I'll never forget what happened as it was one of the most frightening moments of my life. I put the teeth on the table, ready for the fitting, and without looking, my dad put his hand down and broke them. We'd only made one set and they were snapped in two, right down the centre. Then in walks Stan and Tom.

Fortunately they were veneers, which are like shells that fit over your teeth, with no gums. So I took a breath, picked them up and said, "Let's see how these fit, then."

Actually, they fitted really well! Tom liked them, but Stan was curious why we'd made them in two halves. I told him, "Just in case there was any discrepancy in the mould, I thought maybe we could make them fit a bit better this way."

I'm sure he realized we'd had a little accident with them, and that I made that up on the spot, but Stan was very nice about it and we ended up making teeth for Tom, Brad Pitt, Antonio Banderas, Kirsten Dunst and a few others.

Gary Archer

I had an idea for a movie where the characters are trapped in an isolated setting. Kind of like *Night of the Living Dead* (1968) or *Assault on Precinct 13* (1976), but with vampires. I was looking for a writer to do a first draft of the script and I believe it was Dave Goodman who said, "Hey, there's this guy who works at a video store and has a real cool thing going on with his writing."

So I called the guy and he sent me three sample scripts: *Reservoir Dogs* (1992), *True Romance* (1993) and *Natural Born Killers* (1994). This was back before any of them had been made, and the dumbest thing I ever did was not option all three of them immediately.

I read them and loved them, then I asked Quentin Tarantino what he wanted in return for writing *From Dusk Till Dawn* (1996), his first commissioned screenplay. He said, "Look, if I can get out of working at the video store, that's what I want."

He wanted $1500, so that's what we, my co-producing partner John Esposito and myself, paid for his first draft, and the rest is history.

Robert Kurtzman

From Dusk Till Dawn (1996) was the most fun to make. Hard work and long hours, but we were young, so we just got on with it. I got to do Quentin Tarantino's make-up, based on a rough design by Evan Campbell.

It was cool that Quentin went for it as it was a huge exaggeration of his face. Like one of those caricatures you'd get at Disneyland. But he was game, so we just added lots of realistic detail, toning it down just enough to make it believable and scary on screen.

Wayne Toth

"IT WAS SO COOL THAT QUENTIN WENT FOR IT AS IT WAS A HUGE EXAGGERATION OF HIS FACE."

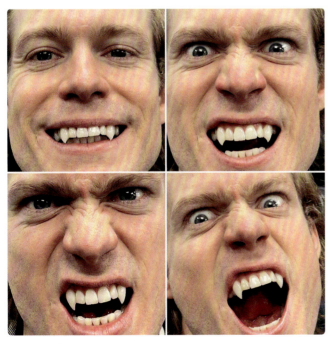

Opposite: Director Robert Rodriguez hangs out at the Titty Twister with Quentin Tarantino in his vampire look for *From Dusk Till Dawn* (1996).

Top: Emerging from decapitated blood-sucker Tom Savini, a giant rat creature aims to chow down on George Clooney in *From Dusk Till Dawn* (1996).

Above: Ahead of playing Lestat de Lioncourt in *Interview with the Vampire* (2022–present), Sam Reid takes Gary Archer and Jac Charlton's fangs out for a test bite.

In early drafts of the script for *From Dusk Till Dawn* (1996), there was a sequence where a subterranean rat creature comes out of a deep, dark hole in the floor and there's a fight. The scene got cut but we'd already built the rat, and it would have been such a shame to waste it, so Robert [Rodriguez] built it into a different scene. Which is why Tom Savini turns into a giant rat after George Clooney whips his head off!

Robert Kurtzman

Being invited to create the fangs for AMC's *Interview with the Vampire* (2022–present) series was a real full circle moment for me, as my father and I had made the fangs for Neil Jordan's film almost three decades earlier.

Particularly challenging was the fact that the show was shot during the pandemic, but I'd recently partnered up with Dominic Mombrun at Bitemakers, and he's a genius with digital. Working with Jac Charlton, we found we could scan an actor in one country, send the files to another, print and construct the teeth, FedEx them to the actors and test fit them on Zoom.

It was a very modern, very remote, but extremely effective way of doing things. By the time the actors and their fangs arrived in New Orleans, pretty much everything was already bang on.

Gary Archer

Dirk Rogers is great! There's an unspoken language when you make up someone who works in special effects. They know exactly what to do and when to do it. At the same time, Dirk brings a cheeky, childlike silliness to the process, so it's always fun working with him. He's a fantastic performer, too, with the perfect build and vigour to wear both full creature suits and make-ups. He's an incredibly rare talent.

Kerrin Jackson

Right: Accomplished monster performer Dirk Rogers as a haunting spectre in Justin Dec's *Countdown* (2019).

Below: Dirk Rogers as KNB EFX's Skinny Devil with the Yellow Eyes for Noah Hawley's *Legion* (2017-2019). Dirk is adept at enduring any sort of discomfort to help bring creatures to life.

Opposite (top, left and right): For Mick Garris's *Nightmare Cinema* (2018), Dirk Rogers played the sutured patient in a make-up created by KNB EFX that was masterfully applied by Kerrin Jackson.

Opposite (bottom): Longtime collaborators Dirk Rogers – in a full-body make-up as the crippled Minotaur – and Howard Berger discuss a scene on the set of *Legion* (2017-2019).

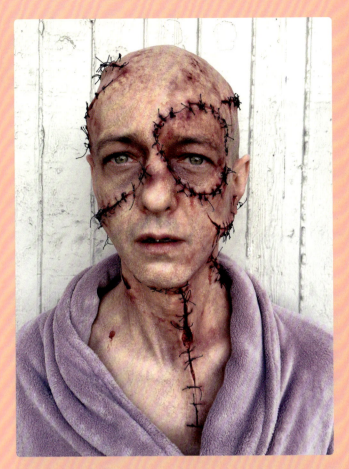
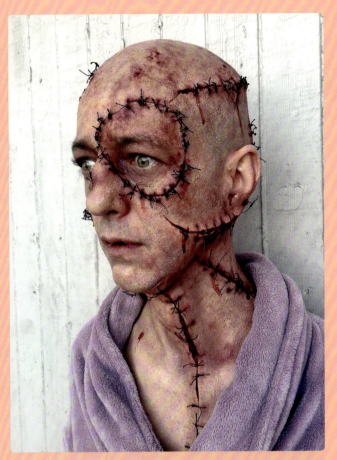

Haruo Nakajima was the original Godzilla suit actor and a huge inspiration for me. While shooting the kaiju movie *Varan* (1958), an explosive-filled prop truck exploded near his crotch and he was pretty badly burned.

He later gave an interview saying, "I looked out of the eyelets and could see the entire crew. I knew if I called stop that none of these people would get paid. So I felt an obligation and a duty to maintain my character."

I took his work ethic to heart.

One of the things I most enjoy about being an effects artist is not going to set, but being in the lab. Like most monster kids, I grew up a bit of a loner, but once I got into the labs, I found myself surrounded by like-minded people. You solve problems together, you make monsters together, and they begin to feel like family.

So any time I'm put into a monster suit, I know what's gone into it. Most of the time, it meant staying up all night, the night before, trying to get it done because the schedules are so short. So I feel an obligation to do justice to the hard work of my effects artist brothers and sisters.

To this day, whenever I play a monster, I put up a scroll in my trailer. It's a picture of Haruo Nakajima wearing the lower half of a Godzilla suit. I always touch it before I head out to set, and say, "Give me the strength, Haruo, to make you proud."

I played a nasty, feral vampire called the Revenant in season two of *Interview with the Vampire* (2022–present). We shot in Prague, all night in a fairy tale-looking forest. I had to dive on someone and tear them to shreds, but when I did, I landed straight on a root that was sticking out of the ground and split my kneecap.

It was my Haruo moment. I was like, "I'm not going to screw this up. I'm not going to say anything. I'm just going to take it. I'm going to channel the pain and make it work for my character."

My knee was seriously swelling up but no one could see it under the suit. At one point I had to fall to my knees and it wasn't hard to express pain in that moment. But the adrenaline of being on set, of knowing how many people were counting on me, helped me push it all away. I felt Haruo was there with me, in spirit, and despite everything, I had a blast!

Dirk Rogers

Dirk Rogers is a dream. We've done several make-ups on him, but because he's such a huge Anne Rice fan, it was pretty special transforming him into the Revenant for season two of *Interview with the Vampire* (2022–present).

The Revenant's a primal, mutant vampire who preys on everything, even other vampires. The make-up was great, but Dirk made it epic, and he was such a good sport.

There's a scene in the forest where Claudia (Delainey Hayles) jumps on the Revenant's back and rips out its eyes. To achieve that practically, I had to make up Dirk in the middle of the forest, in the middle of the night, plus it was freezing and he was blind. Couldn't see a thing as his face was rigged to spurt a lot of blood.

Dirk and Delainey rehearsed it, counted the steps, but even on the night, I was wondering how the hell they were going to pull it off. Of course, they did. It was like watching a beautiful, bloody dance.

Tami Lane

Opposite and below: Dirk Rogers suffered through long winter nights in a Czech forest to play the terrifying, eye-popping Revenant on *Interview with the Vampire* (2022–present).

Left: Make-up artist Tami Lane keeps an eye on Dirk Rogers in a KNB EFX-designed make-up sculpted by Mike Rotella.

Bram Stoker's *Dracula* (1897) is one of my favourite books of all time. In it, there's this captivating chapter about the journey of a doomed merchant ship, *Demeter*, as it unwittingly carries Dracula from Bulgaria to England. Basically, it's *Alien* (1979) in the 1800s, and for years I fantasized about putting a movie together about it.

Here we are in the pandemic, then, and I read in the trades that André Øvredal is making a movie called *The Last Voyage of the Demeter* (2023), an adaptation of the chapter, 'Captain's Log', from *Dracula*. I freaked out.

I tracked André down and wrote him a letter, asking to audition. He was kind and replied that he liked my work, but wasn't sure if there was anything right for me. The UK casting director, meanwhile, said there was one role, a Polish man, but that he was an alpha, and didn't seem my type. But I was more than welcome to put myself on tape and see what I could do with it.

With help from my amazing wife, we built little sets, I made a costume and props, we taped maybe 15 pages of material and André loved my take on Wojchek. He gave me the role!

We shot all of the below-deck sequences on a stage at the Babelsberg Studio, just outside Berlin. It's where Fritz Lang made *Metropolis* (1927)! Then we went to Malta to shoot the exterior work in an infinity pool that makes it look like you're out at sea. It was the classic filming experience I'd always wanted. Getting blasted by seawater, wind and lightning effects was so much fun!

I'd always assumed that if I was ever in a Dracula movie, I'd play the Count. But to be playing the guy who's fighting him? I never expected that. Actually Dracula was played by Javier Botet, who's one of the finest physical performers when it comes to creature acting. Going toe-to-toe with Javier, while he was in his full Dracula make-up, was incredibly powerful. It reminded me of the first time I was ever on a film set, standing next to Christian Bale on *The Dark Knight* (2008), thinking, "I can't believe I'm standing next to Batman."

David Dastmalchian

Below: David Dastmalchian, Chris Walley and Corey Hawkins go vampire hunting in *The Last Voyage of the Demeter* (2023).

Opposite (top left): Make-up masters Göran Lundström and Pamela Goldammer ready monster performer Javier Botet as Dracula for *The Last Voyage of the Demeter* (2023).

Opposite (top right and bottom): Javier Botet strikes a pair of monstrous poses in a Dracula make-up designed and created by Göran Lundström for *The Last Voyage of the Demeter* (2023).

Rather than completely cover an actor, I'm always happier with a canvas I can accentuate rather than conceal. Boris Karloff's make-up for *Frankenstein* (1931) is a perfect example of using as much of an actor's face as possible. So much of the monster was him, it's never looked quite right to me played by anyone else.

For *The Last Voyage of the Demeter* (2023) I was originally worried when they wanted to cast Javier Botet as Dracula, as his head is somewhat large against his strikingly thin body frame. Because of this it's very easy to recognize his silhouette in most types of prosthetics, so to counteract that I ended up extending his jaw and moving his eyes up a little bit to balance things out. And that made it work, but it was a stretch.

The last thing I wanted to do was create a homage make-up. We weren't looking to reinvent the wheel, but I didn't want anything so familiar that people would immediately feel we lifted things directly from *Nosferatu* (1922) or *Bram Stoker's Dracula* (1992). We even watched Coppola's movie to make sure nothing we'd designed came too close to anything of Greg Cannom's.

The more general directive I got was to make the monster look rough and rotting. Their only specific request was for him to have no eyelids, like Dick Smith's undead Eva make-up from *Ghost Story* (1981). For my part, I just wanted to make something that looked cool and scary on Javier.

In the end, unfortunately they barely showed the make-ups at all. So much was replaced by CGI, and even Javier's unique silhouette was erased in favour of something more generic. It looked a little too much like a videogame design to me. I'm still not sure why they made that choice.

Göran Lundström

INFERNAL AFFAIRS

What the hell possessed us to include a chapter about demons? Why not read aloud from the *Necronomicon* while we're at it? Paint a pentagram with goat's blood? Get a 666 tattoo on our scalps?

Maybe we're playing with fire, even risking our immortal souls, ushering you through the infernal regions, but damn it all, from Damien and the Deadites to the Devil himself, we love a good fright, and the hellspawn ahead will surely keep you up all night.

I grew up very Catholic. Very religious. I almost went to seminary. I was that close to becoming a priest. Instead, I became a make-up artist.

So I'm building all sorts of crazy stuff for a demonic horror movie called *Evilspeak* (1981), and next on my to-do list is a life-size, melting statue of Christ on the Cross. We built it up with layers of wax so that as it melted, it would bleed, and once all the wax was gone, underneath was a demon skeleton.

The whole time we're doing it, I'm thinking, "I'm not sure this is a good idea."

We made a mould on the statue, built a cellophane tent in the back part of our shop and left it with an electric heater to cook overnight. In the morning, we'd de-mould it.

So it's late, eleven at night, and everyone's leaving. I'm last in the shop, cleaning things up and turning off the lights. I'm out the door and heading to my car when I realize I forgot my keys. Shit!

I go back, open the door, and remember I left them near the statue, which, surrounded by heater lights, is literally glowing red. I figure I don't have to turn the lights back on. I'll just feel my way through and get in and out quick. Talk about a classic horror movie set-up.

As I crept through the shop, I remember thinking, if the statue moves, I'm gonna freaking die. The keys are just three paces past the statue, and as I hurry to grab them, of course the plastic whooshes up in the air and I scream so loud, my ears ring. Then I turn and run, but it's dark and I slip and hit the ground. My head's spinning and my heart's beating out my chest as I drag myself up and run the last few feet to the door.

Finally I'm out. Slam! I took a breath and regained my senses. "Oh my God," I thought. "I just scared the shit out of myself."

Allan Apone

My poster for *The Evil Dead* (1981) was my first notable commission, two years after I left art college. That movie was all the things I loved – B movies, horror and punk rock – and I wanted the poster to reflect that.

Graham Humphreys

Howard: Yeah, Sam was like, "Oh my God! It's the most horrifying thing I've ever seen. It's a horrible, hideous horror hag!"

Robert: And Sam pretty much recreated that reveal in the movie, when – BOOM! – Pit Bitch bursts out of the moss and lunges at Ash.

Robert Kurtzman and Howard Berger

"IT'S A HORRIBLE, HIDEOUS HORROR HAG!"

Sam Raimi has so much energy. And he's so kooky! When we were on the set of *Evil Dead II* (1987), we'd watch him do things like lie on his back with a camera between his legs, then get dragged through the cabin on a blanket. Then he'd attach a camera to something, like the end of a two-by-four, and go charging through doorways.

We'd stand there, wondering, "What the hell is this all about?"

Then we'd see the footage, and be like, "Oh, right. Sam knows what he's doing."

Howard Berger

Robert: Every day on *Army of Darkness* (1992), Rob [Tapert] and Sam [Raimi] wanted more exploding skeletons. More bones flying. But we could only afford so many, so after blowing them up, we'd pick up the pieces and a team of people would put them back together. From the remains of two or three skeletons, they could piece a new one together, polyfoaming skeletons all night long for the next day.

Howard: Sam wanted everything, every single day. We'd meet in the morning with the storyboards, and he'd be like, "How many suits do we have?"

We'd tell him, "We have 16."

He'd say, "I need 16. How many puppets?"

"We have 20."

"OK, I need 20."

And so it went on. He used everything we had and there was nothing left at the end of the show.

Robert Kurtzman and Howard Berger

Robert: The Pit Bitch in *Army of Darkness* (1992) was played by Billy Bryan. He played the Stay Puft Marshmallow Man in *Ghostbusters* (1984) and is an effects guy, so he was working on the show with us. We spent several months designing and building everything for the movie, and every week or two Sam [Raimi], Bruce [Campbell] and Rob [Tapert] would come into KNB to check on our progress.

One day they're walking around the shop, and as we'd just finished the Pit Bitch, we put Billy in the suit but had him stand really still, like he was a mannequin. So Sam's looking at it, but he's not convinced. He says, "Let me think about it."

Suddenly Billy comes to life and lunges at him, Sam screams, then everybody laughs. Immediately Sam says, "That's going to be in my movie!"

Just the fact that we scared him, sold him on it.

Preceding spread: Artist and satirist Mark Tavares traded in his poison pen to burn time as a demon in the horror comedy *Little Nicky* (2000).

Opposite: Graham Humphreys' first big commission was the gloriously blood-spattered UK poster art for Sam Raimi's *The Evil Dead* (1981).

Above: The Pit Bitch from *Army of Darkness* (1991) only made it into the movie after actor Bill Bryan wore it to give director Sam Raimi the scare of his life!

Left: Gorgeously gruesome concept art of the Marauder from *Evil Dead Rise* (2023), courtesy of Odd Studios' Adam Johansen.

Below: Warwick Davis prepares to chug a pint of Guinness after emerging from Gabe Bartalos's make-up chair as the fiendish *Leprechaun* (1992).

Opposite: Terry Wolfinger conquered the considerable challenges of painting (left) Doug Bradley's Pinhead from *Hellraiser* (1987), and (right) Tony Todd's *Candyman* (1992).

The most difficult creature suit we've ever built was the Marauder for *Evil Dead Rise* (2023). The mother's children push themselves into her body to create this menacing, twisted-limbed, spider-like deadite. In silhouette it sort of resembled the Australian funnel-web spider, specifically when it rears up in attack mode. It looked pretty damn scary, we thought.

We built the suit in Sydney [Australia], but Covid restrictions kept us from taking it to set in New Zealand, where ideally we'd have put it together, then operated and maintained it. It felt so wrong, just sending it away, not seeing it through to the end, but we sent it with a bunch of detailed, instructional videos and it turned out fine. Obviously it would have been a joy seeing it come to life on set, but I still really love it. It's freaky!

Adam Johansen

Going into *Leprechaun* (1992), my only reference for leprechauns was Lucky Charms cereal. What appealed to me about the job was the studio had no idea what he should look like either, so it was fun to be able to design a character with a blank slate.

For the first film I designed three stages of prosthetics, steadily ramping up the evil till he's at his angriest and most aggressive for the final act. For the sequels, though, the executives just wanted me to go straight to the third make-up. I explained there was a subliminal architectural character arc in my designs, but they wanted me to cut straight to the aggression.

Certainly I had no reservations about going really bold with my work, but no matter how outrageous the stories got, even with the giant spider monster in part three, I always took the work seriously. Warwick [Davis] approached his performance exactly the same way, always keeping a straight face. All the winking, tongue-in-cheek and camp we left to the production.

Gabe Bartalos

The toughest monster I've ever painted was Tony Todd's Candyman. I was commissioned to paint him in oils on canvas. It wasn't easy finding good reference material, but the real challenge was painting all those damn bees. There were just so many! I don't think I ever need to paint him again.

Doug Bradley's Pinhead also presents a unique set of challenges. Each nail has to be in its own perfect space, and then the shadows from each nail have to be painted just right. Usually there are multiple light sources too, which means every nail casts multiple shadows. It just gets crazy!

Terry Wolfinger

"THE REAL CHALLENGE WAS PAINTING ALL THOSE DAMN BEES."

Tim Burton didn't want *Beetlejuice* (1988) to be scary. Unsettling and whimsical was more the tone he wanted to set.

Michael Keaton comes in to test, and I'm thinking, Beetlejuice lives underground, so we'll make him really pale. Tim wanted dark circles around his eyes. Like, really dark. So I did this make-up on him, but he ended up looking like a creepy, old derelict. "Too scary," said Tim. "Nobody will be able to look at him like that."

I asked Tim if I could take him back to the trailer and let me do what I thought was right for the character. He agreed and left me to it.

Michael told me he wanted a broken nose. We didn't have any money to make anything so I asked Steve LaPorte, who was my second on the film, if he had any broken noses from stuff he'd done in the past. He goes, "No, but I have some swollen lips. We can put one on each side of his nose, and it'll look broken."

So we did that. We also mucked up his teeth, but just for the test. For the movie, Steve wound up making a set. Then we added broken, nasty acrylic nails and a bald cap. I said, "He needs to look like he crawled out from beneath a rock."

I sent a runner to a hobby store to get some crushed foam, the sort they use when building landscapes for model trains. I wanted different colours, textures and fake moss. We painted it up and stuck it on, like it was rot and mange crawling out from under his hair and collar.

When we were done, Tim came to see and he was like, "Yes! That's it. He's funny, he's creepy, he's everything at once."

It was a weird and messy monster make-up. Pretty basic, really, because at the time, we didn't have any other way to do it. So we just pulled it out of our you-know-what!

Ve Neill

John Bisson was my key designer on *Wishmaster* (1997). We did maybe 60 different sketches of the Djinn before we honed in on his look. He's not a physical sort of monster who claws at people and throws them around. He's more like the god of another realm, so we wanted something majestic and kind of sexy.

Robert Kurtzman

Silvi: I did a full body burn make-up for a girl on *Necronomicon* (1993). A producer comes along, looks and her, and tells me, "I need it to be more sexy."

I'm like, "Sexier burns?"

Howard: We built a robot once for a show, and the director asked us, "Can it be a little more sexy?"

Tami Lane went into the trailer, came out with a big pair of eyelashes, and glued them on the robot. And she asks, "Is that sexy enough for you?"

He's like, "Yeah. OK. Never mind."

Silvi Knight and Howard Berger

Left: Michael Keaton, as demonic bio-exorcist *Beetlejuice* (1988), and make-up artist Ve Neill get their hug on.

Above: Andrew Divoff's Djinn invites director Robert Kurtzman to make a wish on the set of *Wishmaster* (1997).

Opposite: Andrew Divoff as the fearsome *Wishmaster* (1997), sporting a startling make-up that was sculpted and applied by Garrett Immel.

H oward [Berger] made a deal for a number of us at KNB to earn our SAG [Screen Actors Guild] cards playing background demons on *Little Nicky* (2000). Also, we got to sculpt our own characters, which was great. Everyone followed the same design ethic: standard horns and skeletal structure, pointy chin and nose. So I thought, "I'm going to do something different. I want my guy to stand out."

Once we started shooting, I realized the mistake I'd made, as basically I got a couch glued to my face every day for eight weeks. And while my make-up was big and bulky, everyone else's was lightweight. So I'm like, "Now I see why you were doing it that way."

Every make-up artist should have that sort of experience. To know what it feels like to wear prosthetics for weeks on end. To wear them till the smell of the glue in the morning freaks you out a little bit. It definitely makes you more sympathetic to what actors go through.

The second mistake I made was making my demon much scarier than the director was looking for, so while the more handsome demons were prominently placed, mine was hidden further and further back each scene.

I drew a little cartoon in my Poison Pen Sketchbook to memorialize the experience. The 2nd AD's placing me outside the studio door, by the exit, right on the street. And he's like, "OK Mark. You're going to hang out here. We'll get to you for sure. You're definitely in the shot this time..."

Mark Tavares

Top: Make-up artist Howard Berger is surrounded by a squad of his demons on the set of *Little Nicky* (2000). Most of the demons were played by KNB EFX artists who wanted to be in the film.

Above: Artist Mark Tavares is hungry for souls in a demon make-up of his design that was later applied by Craig Reardon for *Little Nicky* (2000).

Opposite: Joseph Bishara sneers through Justin Raleigh's iconic Lipstick Demon make-up, created for James Wan's *Insidious* (2010).

James Wan invited me to work on a super-low-budget project for this new company, Blumhouse. Aaron Sims sent me rough designs of a character they were calling the Red Face Fiend. Kelly Golden and I built everything out of my garage: sculpting, moulding and casting everything together. On set, it was mostly a paint make-up with hand-laid hair.

I never anticipated the Lipstick Demon would become my Freddy Krueger. The monster I'm most closely associated with. But I'm so thankful to have been brought in on *Insidious* (2010) and the many movies we made in that and the *Conjuring* universes.

The idea of the Lipstick Demon is that in The Further, the dark dimension between Heaven, Earth and Hell, there's no colour. So to stand out, he took this old, blood-red lipstick and smeared it all over his face.

Joseph Bishara, who plays the Lipstick Demon, also composed the music for the movie. Those crazy strings and dissonant tones are all him. He also played Bathsheba in *The Conjuring* (2013). In the make-up trailer, he'd play us the darkest, most sinister music you've ever heard. Screaming, chanting, evil chords... That really set the tone for everyone, and got him into character.

In general, too, *The Conjuring* sets felt weird. The Warrens' occult museum set felt particularly ominous. People were scared to go on it, and a night guard quit after hearing something running around. Lorraine Warren visited the set and blessed us. That was pretty intense. She told me my Bathsheba looked exactly as she remembered. Everyone was really creeped out, to be honest.

Justin Raleigh

"I NEVER ANTICIPATED THE LIPSTICK DEMON WOULD BECOME MY FREDDY KRUEGER."

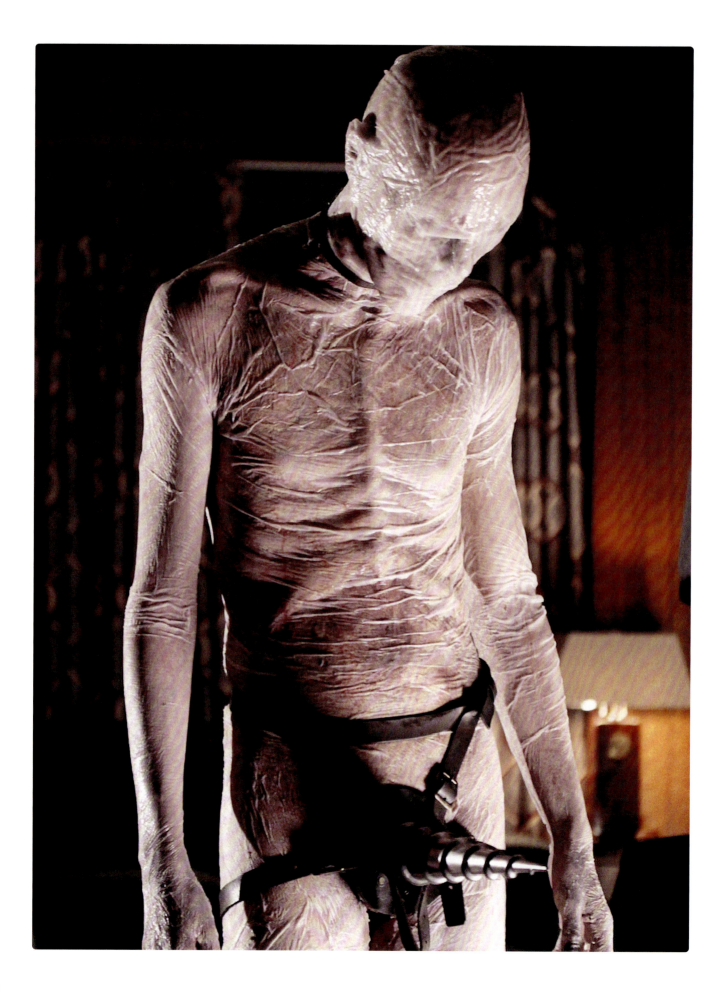

"HE COULDN'T SEE. HE COULDN'T HEAR. HE COULD BARELY BREATHE!"

Eryn: Mike and I were on the first ten seasons of *American Horror Story* (2011–present), and working with the same cast over all those years, they became familiar with prosthetics. Make-up effects were a big part of the show's appeal and it wasn't long before the cast started asking for more, always pushing to take the transformations further. We were happy to oblige!

Evan Peters was gung-ho for anything. Angela Basset too. Cheyenne Jackson you could cover in blood from head to toe. And it might sound like fun – Sarah Paulson playing a two-headed character in *Freak Show* (S04, 2014–15) – but carrying around an extra head for six hot months is a gruelling gig.

Of all the characters we created, the Addiction Demon from *Hotel* (S05, 2015–16) was possibly the most challenging to play. Like sealing someone in their own, personal sensory deprivation suit. I worried it was too much, but Alexander Ward, our creature performer, never complained.

Mike: He couldn't see. He couldn't hear. He could barely breathe! You'd tap him, he'd walk a few steps, make a turn, act scary, then we'd reset. His shots took a lot of takes. Sometimes we'd sit him down and people would go over to chat, but he didn't even know they were there!

Five hours it took to get Alex in that make-up, and we put him in it ten times. It was an enormous physical and mental challenge, but Alex aced it. His fortitude was inspiring. All that for a character you see for just 20 seconds, total, over the whole series!

Eryn Krueger Mekash and Mike Mekash

We had just a few weeks and limited funds to make the Meat Monster for Don Coscarelli's *John Dies at the End* (2012). It was such a wild, original film though – I had to be involved. We fabricated all these different cuts of meat and glued them together – Thanksgiving turkey head, beef rib cages and dangly sausage fingers. Definitely one of the strangest monsters I've ever been involved with making!

Robert Kurtzman

I played a demon in a short called *House Mother* (2017). Because why should I always be the damsel in distress, or the one who dies? Bruce Fuller did the make-up and under all those prosthetics, with the teeth, the paint, and these four incredible horns, I was unrecognizable. I looked at myself in the mirror, but it wasn't me looking back. It frightened me.

I've never been as scared watching a movie as I was seeing myself as a monster that day. It made me wonder what demons I might have inside, and took me a good half hour to calm down.

I played a monster again, a vampire this time, in a feature called *Jakob's Wife* (2021). It got very bloody, and I enjoyed it. It wasn't a shock, that time, seeing myself as a monster, and now I want to do it more!

Barbara Crampton

Opposite: Alexander Ward went through hell to play the Addiction Demon in *American Horror Story: Hotel* (2015-16), but with help from make-up duo Eryn and Mike Mekash, he aced the challenge.

Above: Robert Kurtzman hungrily accepted the challenge of cooking up a Meat Monster for director Don Coscarelli's *John Dies at the End* (2012).

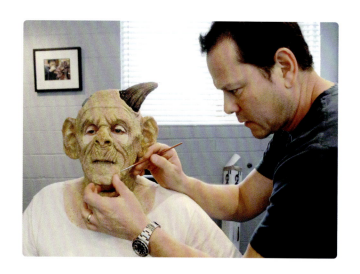

"GETTING CONTINUALLY TRAMPLED BY A MONSTER WOULD TEST ANYONE'S PATIENCE."

It was exciting to be invited to contribute to the Troll Market sequence in *Hellboy II: The Golden Army* (2008). What a wonderful opportunity to be involved in something so richly textured with such depth and so many stunning characters. We shot in an underground quarry and everywhere you looked there was something amazing.

Of all the creatures Guillermo [del Toro] asked us to create for the movie, from the moment we first saw Mario Torres Jr's maquette, it was clear that Mr. Wink was going to be something special. An interesting build, as there were so many components and points of articulation, and so much expression in the face. Certainly it had a high capacity for emotive performance.

The biggest suit we'd ever built, Wink was beautiful in his own way. Everything you see, except for the rubber skin, is real. Those are genuine leather pieces he's wearing. From an artisan's perspective, it was a golden opportunity to do a lot of different things. Every discipline of our community was required to make him happen.

Mike Elizalde

Hellboy (2019) was a tough one. Really tough. I played Gruagach and the suit looked amazing, with an incredible animatronic head, but it was difficult to wear and perform in. As I could only see through the mouth, if I stood straight, Gruagach looked oddly up in the air, so I had to squat in this heavy suit that really put a lot of stress on my neck.

So I'm in the suit, staring at the floor, bent over and struggling to breathe. I kept stepping on Milla Jovovich, who's awesome, but getting continually trampled by a monster would test anyone's patience. All I could do was apologize, over and over.

Then one day I smell smoke. It's getting stronger and stronger and I'm like, "What the hell is that?"

I was on fire. We were shooting in Bulgaria and there was an issue with voltage conversion. I was the only one who knew I was on fire, though, as everything was happening inside the head, which I couldn't take off myself.

Luckily, though none of the crew realized what was happening, Milla figured it out and yelled, "Get that fucking head off him right now."

She saved me! Even though I'd trodden on her all those times. I'm glad she didn't hold a grudge.

Douglas Tait

Top: Enlisted by Guillermo del Toro to populate the magical world of *Hellboy II: The Golden Army* (2008), Mike Elizalde of Spectral Motion applies a characterful troll make-up.

Above: Mike Elizalde gets closer than most would dare to the mighty Mr. Wink (Brian Steele), making a last-minute adjustment on the set of *Hellboy II: The Golden Army* (2008).

Opposite: Actor and creature performer Douglas Tait isn't afraid to suffer for his art, and suffer he certainly did, playing Gruagach, designed and created by Joel Harlow and Norman Cabrera for Neil Marshall's *Hellboy* (2019).

Opposite (inset): Douglas Tait always has a smile on his face, no matter what creature suit he's stuffed into!

*T*he Witcher (2019–present) was the first TV show I did after lockdown, and everyone was petrified that Covid would spread like wildfire through the crew. We had to wear so much PPE, though, it was almost impossible to work.

Vicky Bancroft and I applied Agnes Born's Vereena make-up for Season 2, and it was summer, so already bastard hot, but on top of that, we were wearing plastic aprons, masks and visors. I was sweating buckets and my glasses steamed up, then my visor too. I might just as well have done it with my eyes closed, as I couldn't see what the fuck I was doing.

Duncan Jarman

Below (left): Courtesy of Barrie Gower's BGFX studio, here's Duncan Jarman's beautiful sculpture for Agnes Born's Vereena make-up in *The Witcher* (2019 – present).

Below (right): Agnes Born in her final look make-up as Vereena in *The Witcher* (2019 – present).

Opposite (top): Alex Winter is no stranger to wearing heavy prosthetic make-ups, and for *Destroy All Neighbors* (2024), he had Gabe Bartalos (left) design and create his look as Vlad, with Bill Corso (right) applying and executing the make-up on set.

Opposite (bottom): Alex Winter ain't got no body, on the set of *Destroy All Neighbors* (2024).

*L*ike Benicio Del Toro and Gary Oldman, Alex Winter loves make-up. He's just one of those guys. Like, Mark Ruffalo's dream is to play Quasimodo in *The Hunchback of Notre Dame*.

We worked together on this crazy, low budget horror movie called *Destroy All Neighbors* (2024). It was a ten-day job and, originally, I was just going to do Alex's face. But on the first day, he told me, "I don't think any of these people have ever made a movie before, so anything you can do to help, I'd really appreciate it."

Though it was clear from the script that it was going to be a very bloody movie, on the first day, there wasn't any blood. The make-up department didn't realize they were supposed to supply it. They asked me, "Do you have any blood?"

I ended up helping in lots of different ways, but it was fun, going back to Eighties-style, gonzo horror movie-making. Gabe Bartalos designed all this crazy creature stuff and we just made it look as cool as we could. Like this demon made of a hodgepodge of musical instruments. We figured out on the spot how to paint it, and it wound up being one of the coolest-looking make-ups in the movie.

It was a busy couple of weeks, but I had the best time!

Bill Corso

7

FROM THE LAND BEYOND BEYOND

Back in those halcyon days before everything was instantly achievable, Ray Harryhausen gave us our first peeks at the impossible. Of roaring, stomping prehistoric beasts and exotic, hypnotic mythological creatures.

Telling spellbinding tales of long ago and far away, Ray was the star of the movies he made, an artist and technician: a magician, really, who breathed patient, artful life into his distinctive, charismatic creations.

It is with love, respect and gratitude that we devote the following chapter to the Godfather of Stop Motion Animation.

> Frankly, my films are more appreciated today than they were in their heyday. I can't explain it, but I'm not complaining.
>
> Ray Harryhausen

The Beast from 20,000 Fathoms (1953) was one of the big blockbusters of the Fifties because it revived the monster-on-the-loose theme. It also started a cycle of movies about the atomic bomb.

We cashed in on the fact that the atomic bomb was an unknown element. Nobody knew what radiation would do, what kind of horrors it might bring about. It was in all the newspapers that the scientists were worried about blowing up the world, and the beast symbolized our fears. Then the Japanese got in on the act and copied our picture, making Godzilla (1954), which was just a man in a rubber suit.

I gave a lecture at the National Film Theatre a few years ago, and someone in the audience asked, "Why do you go to all the trouble of stop motion? Why don't you just put a man in a suit?"

I didn't know what to say. What do you say to a person like that? I felt like wringing his neck. People who can't see the difference between Godzilla and what I do shouldn't be allowed to see my films. They should only be allowed to watch Attack of the Killer Tomatoes! (1978) and rubbish like that.

Ray Harryhausen

"WE CASHED IN ON THE FACT THAT THE ATOMIC BOMB WAS AN UNKNOWN ELEMENT."

Preceding Spread: The Great Gwangi roams his valley courtesy of Ray Harryhausen's Dynamation, the magical process that brought scores of dreams and nightmares to life on the big screen.

Opposite: They say don't meet your heroes, but for 19-year-old Marshall Julius, interviewing Ray Harryhausen in his home office was an experience no less magical than his movies. "Surrounded by art and props from his incredible films," remembers Marshall, "I felt like Sinbad in a cave of wondrous, exotic treasures."

Right: Ray's Venusian Ymir whispers sweet nothings into his master's ear while shooting *20 Million Miles to Earth* (1957).

Below: Ray's mighty Rhedosaurus pounds New York city streets in the film that inspired Godzilla, *The Beast from 20,000 Fathoms* (1953).

I was at a screening of *The 7th Voyage of Sinbad* (1958) with some friends, and Ray Harryhausen was there. Kevin Haney went up to him and said, "I've been watching your movies on TV since I was a little kid, and you've been such a positive influence in my life."

Harryhausen looked at him, eyes like daggers, and he really wasn't kidding when he boomed, "You can't watch my movies on the boob tube. They're big stories for a big theatre!"

Gerry Quist

Kerwin Matthews was very convincing in *The 7th Voyage of Sinbad* (1958), because he had a direct line where he looked. A lot of actors tend to look through what they should be looking at, and you can always tell that in their eyes. We rehearsed with Kerwin and a stuntman standing in for the skeleton. The whole thing was choreographed like a ballet, by counts, so they could repeat it each shot. The final repeat was without the stuntman and I put the skeleton in his place.

I would analyze the action frame-by-frame and then animate in relation to what was happening on the screen. When Sinbad put his sword up, I had to have the skeleton get there ahead of him so it didn't look silly. That's one of the problems we had with *Jason and the Argonauts* (1963) – trying to time three men swinging their swords with seven skeletons swinging theirs. That one scene took months to film as I couldn't shoot more than 13 frames a day. That's only half a second of film!

Ray Harryhausen

Above: Ray's beloved Cyclops from *The 7th Voyage of Sinbad* (1958) remains the go-to creature for demonstrating perfect monster movement.
Below: Working alone, Ray Harryhausen spent 4½ months animating Jason (Todd Armstrong) and his Argonauts' blistering battle with the Children of the Hydra's Teeth.
Opposite: A trio of international posters for Ray's exotic, enchanting *Sinbad* trilogy.

"THAT FIRST TURN OF TALOS'S HEAD WAS MAYBE THE MOST DECISIVE MOMENT OF MY LIFE."

The first movie I ever saw in a theatre was *Jason and the Argonauts* (1963). That first turn of Talos's head was maybe the most decisive moment of my life. Certainly, of my career. I was riveted. I didn't know what I was looking at, but inside I told myself, "I need to be a part of this." And that was it. That never changed.

Chris Walas

The sound effect when Talos turns his head. It's as subtle as Ray Harryhausen's animation gets. Not a roaring, rending noise, but a creak. Just enough to catch your attention. Then he fixes you with those dead eyes and whoa, I just got goosebumps thinking about it!

Kirk Thatcher

Jason and the Argonauts (1963): the instant Talos turns his head to look at Hercules and Pelias. Oh my God! My head exploded. I wanted to be a comicbook artist right up until that moment, and then I wanted to do special effects.

Books at the time had a rough description of stop motion animation, so I had a basic understanding of the pose-and-shoot, 24-frames-a-second dynamic, and it seemed accessible. Like something I could do.

Then you try it, working hours and hours for maybe a second-and-a-half of a thing moving its arm, and that either fires you up to do more, or you're like, "Not for me."

I was the latter, but having a go definitely gave me a deeper appreciation of Ray's superhuman patience, his work ethic and artistry.

Mark Tavares

Above: Big, bronze and bursting to beat a band of baffled Argonauts, Talos inspired countless monster kids to go build brilliant bruisers of their own.

Most people celebrate Ray Harryhausen for his stop motion skills, but I don't think he gets enough credit for designing and sculpting his creatures, too. There's a godlike power in creating something that didn't exist a moment ago. A thrill in putting pen to paper, or sculpting a lump of clay, and willing something new to life. Ray was a master of that and a huge inspiration.

Damien Leone

Years ago in Japan, there'd be midnight screenings of Ray Harryhausen movies on TV, so I'd sneak out of bed in the middle of the night to watch them. They were worth the risk of getting caught. My parents would yell at me, but what choice did I have?

I was born in 1964, the Year of the Dragon. Maybe that's why I've always been drawn to dragons. Certainly the seven-headed Hydra from *Jason and the Argonauts* (1963) is my favourite Harryhausen monster. All those heads and snapping beaks!

The way Ray's creatures moved, though not quite true to life, made them so much more real to me than other creations of the time.

Takashi Yamazaki

The Ray Harryhausen film that always stood out for me was *The Valley of Gwangi* (1969). The whole idea of dinosaurs in an apparent spaghetti western was so bizarre, but intriguing and exciting. The music's great too, and the animation is fantastic. As much as I love *King Kong* (1933), the stop motion seemed less obvious in *Gwangi*.

Graham Humphreys

The Valley of Gwangi (1969) is my favourite Ray Harryhausen film, because what could be cooler than cowboys versus dinosaurs? The story is so fun, and the cast is so great, even when there aren't any monsters about, it's still really entertaining. And when the dinosaurs do show up, they're so well integrated into the action, it's magical.

I sat my kids down to watch it when they were little, and I remember they cried at the end. When Gwangi died, Kelsey was almost inconsolable. That's when I knew I had the perfect daughter.

Howard Berger

Right: Like Kong before him, Gwangi the allosaurus is snatched from his home and, quite reasonably running rampage in a cathedral, murdered by humans who just should have left him alone, in *The Valley of Gwangi* (1969).
Below: Ray lines up a shot of one of his dinosaurs at an exhibit showcasing his brilliance.
Opposite (left): Stealing scenes as well as hearts as the beautiful Margiana in *The Golden Voyage of Sinbad* (1973), Caroline Munro is one of the most memorable human characters in any of Ray's films.
Opposite (right): The battle of the Cyclopean Centaur and the Griffin in *The Golden Voyage of Sinbad* (1973) was a breathtaking display of stop motion animation.

Ray Harryhausen was my dear, dear friend. A lovely man. Warm and funny with a wonderful sense of humour. He took a chance on me. A big chance. No one helped my career more and, still, whenever I go to festivals, The Golden Voyage of Sinbad (1973) is usually the first thing anyone asks me about. After all, Ray was the greatest special effects person of his time. He raised the bar and changed cinema itself.

Brian Clements was a bit of a mentor for me. We'd just made Captain Kronos: Vampire Hunter (1974) for Hammer, and he'd written the screenplay for Golden Voyage. He told Ray and his producer, Charles H. Schneer, about me, and showed them some footage. Though they were mostly auditioning American ladies, and really wanted someone well known like Raquel Welch, they agreed to meet me. Honestly, I didn't expect to get the part, but I went for the experience of meeting them.

Ray did most of the talking. He had a wonderful, warm voice. Loud, but very beautiful. Charles was more business-like and mostly observed. We had a nice, interesting chat and when it was over, I left with no expectations. Then lo and behold, I got the part!

We shot the film in Spain and even though the budget was less than £1 million, which was middle-ish for the time, we seemed to have the best of everything. I stayed in a beautiful apartment and had my own driver. The catering was fantastic and I was looked after very well. The crew was wonderful too. Great make-up people. Outstanding costume designers. Ted Moore was our D.P. – he'd won an Oscar for shooting A Man for All Seasons (1966) and a BAFTA for From Russia With Love (1963) – and his work was extraordinary. I don't think I was ever better lit.

Before we shot anything that would eventually involve one of his amazing creatures – because he'd always call them creatures, never monsters – Ray would explain to us what we were dealing with. Though he hadn't animated anything yet, he'd show us his beautiful artwork and that would really set the scene. Even if he hadn't become a filmmaker, he would have been a famous artist instead. He drew. He painted. He sculpted. I don't think anything was beyond him.

Whenever the time came to shoot a scene that would eventually involve one of Ray's creatures, Gordon Hessler, our director, would step away, and then Ray would tell us exactly what to do. He always knew precisely what he wanted from us. How we should be feeling. How we should react. And to make sure we'd look precisely where we needed to. Say, for the Centaur scene, Ray held up a big cardboard eye on a stick. To my mind, after all his wonderful prep, I could really see the creature! Ray made it come alive. He was fascinating.

For Ray, of course, the real work began when the shoot was over. He'd return to his London studio, upstairs at the top of his house. Just Ray and his models, almost always alone, painstakingly animating them one frame at a time. Just Ray, the Centaur, little Margiana and the rest, for a year or more. When I finally saw the film I remember being amazed because I had no idea how lusciously beautiful it would look.

I'm so happy that fans and filmmakers today appreciate and love Ray's films. They were like his babies, so I'm always happy to look in on them, and talk about them. His creations, they had the human touch, I think. It elevated them above normal effects.

Ray may not have invented the process of the stop motion, but he elevated it into something special. Something higher than art, even. His creatures lived and breathed. They had character. Ray put so much love into his characters, and the stories they were part of, they became timeless. I know he was thrilled that years after his films were shown in the cinema, people still watched them and loved them and were inspired by them. Whenever I meet his fans at screenings or conventions, they bring their children, their grandchildren... They're movies that span generations.

Caroline Munro

Ray Harryhausen's creatures weren't just models. They were actors. They didn't just move. They gave performances. You didn't just see them. You could feel them.

Stephan Dupuis

Ray Harryhausen's creatures were great because they had their own weird personality traits. It was almost as if Ray put on the suits and played them himself. Maybe one had a limp, or moved a certain way because they'd hurt their shoulder. He infused each creature with its own internal life, which went a long way towards making them all feel so much more real.

I don't know if he did that intentionally or if the choices he made were more instinctive, but certainly it drew a hard line between his creations and everyone else's since.

Michael Giacchino

My dad managed our local ODEON and used to take me to special screenings. Once I was lucky enough to meet Ray Harryhausen at a press show of *Sinbad and the Eye of the Tiger* (1977). Ray had brought all the models from the film, and I ended up in the *Daily Mail* newspaper, age four, hugging Trog.

So many images from the film remain engraved in my head: those ghoulish skeletons, that huge wasp and the witch with the gull's foot. I went back to see the film over and over again, and never passed up the chance to watch other Ray Harryhausen films on the telly.

Ray was the ultimate one-man band, a pioneer whose designs were as original as his stop motion animation was unmistakable.

Barrie Gower

Ray Harryhausen didn't try to hide his monsters. He didn't cloak them in shadow or tease the audience with brief flashes of fangs or claws. He loved them and he wanted you to marvel at them, study them... With the exception of Medusa from *Clash of the Titans* (1981), which is probably the moodiest of all his creatures, he put his monsters front and centre. Boom! There's Kali. Boom! The Hydra.

It's not like *Alien* (1979). Obviously that movie scared the hell out of me, but even after I saw it, I still didn't really know what the monster looked like. With Ray, though, it was like he was telling you, "Look. It took me three months to animate this scene. So you're gonna watch it, and I hope you're gonna love it like I do."

How much of the monster you show is a personal choice, of course, but I personally land on Ray's side of the fence. When we were doing *Creepshow* (2019–present), we had a monster in every episode. It's a bit frustrating to spend so much time building something, only for it to end up on screen for just five or six seconds, so I always leaned on adding more shots of the creatures.

Greg Nicotero

Ray didn't just create monsters. He created characters. Though obviously some were mainly focused on destroying things, there was also Medusa; there was the Cyclops: fully formed characters you could relate to.

What I loved about his stuff was there was always emotional content. Even when it was just a Big Bad Monster, it wasn't just moving around, doing things. You could somehow feel the life of that being.

Roger Ebert put it perfectly when he said that while CGI looks real but feels fake, stop motion looks fake but feels real.

Chris Walas

I was maybe six when I first saw Ray Harryhausen's movies. They were my introduction to monsters in cinema: Talos, the Cyclops, Trog and the Children of the Hydra's Teeth... I have a tattoo of those skeletons now, so clearly Ray's films had a huge impact on me.

When you look at his work now, as beautiful and incredibly artistic and skilful and amazing as it is, obviously it's not as photoreal as the stuff today. But that never was an issue for me. I never questioned the authenticity of it because, as a kid with imagination, I had the capacity to suspend my disbelief.

I didn't consider the technicalities of stop motion animation, and I don't ever remember thinking that it didn't look very real, because it did to me. That wasn't part of the agreement, you know? It was like, "I'm going to get lost in this world and I'm going to believe it and I'm going to love it."

Simon Pegg

Opposite (top): Make-up maestro Tom Savini visits Ray Harryhausen.

Opposite (bottom): A young and enthusiastic Phil Tippett chats with his hero, Ray, about the magic of stop motion animation.

Top: The Children of the Hydra's Teeth join Ray Harryhausen for tea! Mike Hill's beautiful tribute sculpture captures the essence of Ray's playful heart, and his love for his creations.

Above: Ray surrounded by fanboys at a convention in 1989. From left to right: Howard Berger, Michael Trcic, Brian Rae, Wayne Toth and Greg Nicotero. The joy that day was overwhelming!

Right: *Jason and the Argonauts* (1963) superfan Tom Hanks cherishes the memory of presenting Ray Harryhausen with his honorary Oscar in 1992.

8

SLICE 'N' QUEASY

Like Timex watches of old, the stars of our next chapter can take a licking, and damn, but they keep on ticking. Who's that by the hedge? Who's that in your dreams? It's the Boogeyman, kids: masked, stabby and inescapable as death.

Best not catch their eyes by having sex, going to camp or, well, taking a nap. Like the make-up effects folks whose practical gags make you practically gag, they're artists, and their medium is your blood.

For me, it was the music that made *Halloween* (1978). What John [Carpenter] did really sold it.

Kevin Wasner

I grew up in a household with music, so my father decided I was going to play the violin. The only problems were I had no talent whatsoever, and I hated it. I'd walk to school, carrying my violin like a sign around my neck saying 'GEEK'. It made me a mark: "There's that kid..." BAM!

When I couldn't take it any more, I moved on to guitar, piano and keyboard. I wasn't great at keyboard, but I could fake it. For a while I was in a rock 'n' roll band called The Kaleidoscopes. I was making pretty good money, meeting girls, and it was fun. I could have stayed with them, but I decided to go to college and get into movies because that's what I'd wanted to do since I was a kid. I wanted to direct.

Writing music for movies started as a necessity. You don't have any money when you're making student movies, so you can do needle drops, from records, but that's cheating. So I started writing my own film scores, for my movies and other people's. I enjoyed it. It came pretty easily to me.

I was inspired by great movie composers like Bernard Herrmann and

"I HAD THREE DAYS TO WRITE AND RECORD THE MUSIC FOR *HALLOWEEN*, BECAUSE THAT'S ALL WE COULD AFFORD."

Dimitri Tiomkin. I especially loved Bebe and Louis Barron's electronic soundtrack for *Forbidden Planet* (1956). It was so alien, and made me fall in love with synthesizers. You can get a big sound out of those, for track after track, without an expensive orchestra.

I had three days to write and record the music for *Halloween* (1978), because it was a $200,000 movie and that's all we could afford. When I was 13, my dad bought me a pair of bongos and taught me 5/4 time, and that's the main theme! Simple as that. Just doing it on octaves,

over and over, and always minor, because that's darker. Major's more hopeful.

I wrote five themes for Halloween and just dropped them into the movie. There was lots of guesswork, but it worked out. So every film, I kept writing the music. It was a trap! But I did get to work with Ennio Morricone on The Thing (1982), and God, I loved that.

Ennio was an experimental musician and even though we had to work through translators – as he didn't speak any English, and I didn't speak Italian – we found a way to make it work. He wrote some beautiful piano pieces, but they weren't quite right for the movie. For the opening title, I suggested he write something with fewer notes, for synthesizer. That's exactly what he did and it was fantastic.

These days I'm mainly doing music, which is great. It's the purest art form we have as human beings, because it doesn't require any talk. Just music that comes out of you easily and cheaply.

John Carpenter

We'd just shot a bunch of hookers getting murdered in a hotel room, then we broke for lunch. That was a pretty typical day on Vampires (1998)! I had to go back to set to gather some equipment, and as I got close I could hear someone playing the Halloween (1978) theme on the piano there.

Not just someone, but as I got closer, I saw it was John Carpenter, sitting alone, taking a moment for himself. I didn't want to interrupt. I listened for a bit then sneaked away, feeling very privileged. What a thing to stumble upon!

Tami Lane

Preceding Spread: Tyler Mane peers through Michael Myers' iconic mask, reimagined by Wayne Toth for Rob Zombie's Halloween (2007).
Opposite: Director John Carpenter and fledgling Scream Queen Jamie Lee Curtis take five on the set of Halloween (1978).
Above: John Carpenter – working with longtime collaborator Alan Howarth – proves less is more with stark, sparing keystrokes as pointed and uncompromising as Michael Myers' slashing butcher blade.

Opposite (top): Rob Zombie, Tyler Mane and Wayne Toth on the set of *Halloween* (2007).

Opposite (bottom left): Wayne Toth fits Tyler Mane with Michael Myers' transformative terror mask on the set of *Halloween* (2007).

Opposite (bottom right): Michael Myers (Tyler Mane) prepares to make a point in *Halloween* (2007).

Left: Working beside a wall of inspirational Michaels, Wayne Toth paints a Myers mask for *Halloween* (2007).

Below: The Mane Man playing the Main Man in *Halloween* (2007).

Rob Zombie was directing, so I was ready for *Halloween* (2007) to be intense. I did my research. I read a lot about serial killers and watched all the old *Halloween* movies. Thought a lot about Boris Karloff. About creating a character with just movement.

But when you're shooting, you don't think about any of that. You don't decide how you're going to tilt your head. From the first time I wore the mask and jumpsuit, and especially when they handed me the butcher knife, it all just came together. I was in the zone.

Once, the editor asked me how many different masks we used. He said, "It looks like you're showing different expressions every time."

We had a few masks, of course, but they were actually all the same. It all just came from how I moved in every scene, and how I was shot, of course. He was surprised, and that was such a great compliment.

Over the years, often at conventions, I've met all the other Michael Myers actors. I'm so grateful to Rob. So lucky and blessed to be part of such a great brotherhood.

Tyler Mane

One night during reshoots for Rob Zombie's *Halloween* (2007), I got some popcorn from the craft service truck and sat on the steps outside the Myers' house. That was already pretty cool, but then along comes Rob with Dee Wallace and Tyler Mane, who's in his full Michael Myers outfit, mask and all. Dee's talking about *Cujo* (1983) and *E.T.* (1982), and I'm just sitting there, eating my popcorn, chatting with these guys and thinking, this is the best nerd moment I could ever ask for!

Silvi Knight

It was an honour, designing a new Michael Myers mask for Rob Zombie's *Halloween* (2007), but I didn't want to do anything drastic. In the story, it's been buried for years, so when Michael digs it up, it's already weathered. Just following the physics of the storyline got me started.

I didn't do a lot of designs. I never do. I just went ahead and sculpted it as your first instincts are almost always the best.

Wayne Toth

I was like a kid in a candy store on David Gordon Green's *Halloween* (2018). Lots of pinch me moments, like spending a night in the Myers' house with Nick Castle, the original Michael, just helping him take his mask on and off. He told me there's no way he could have known the original would be so successful. He just thought it was a helping a friend out kind of thing.

Another time, I'm standing with Jamie Lee Curtis. Just me and her, and she tells me a story about the first *Halloween* (1978). She said John [Carpenter] told her to run around the house and scream. And she told him, "I've never screamed in my whole life. I don't even know how, or where it would come from."

She was freaking out. Afraid of mustering the energy required to really let rip. But in the end, she said the fear of having to scream made her scream!

Kevin Wasner

"I'VE NEVER SCREAMED IN MY WHOLE LIFE. I DON'T EVEN KNOW HOW."

Top: Smiling like a kid in a candy store, Kevin Wasner hangs with original Michael Nick Castle in the Myers' house during the production of David Gordon Green's *Halloween* (2018).

Bottom: Dead, and loving it, actress Jillian Kramer takes a happy snap with John Carpenter, Kerrin Jackson and Kevin Wasner on the set of *The Ward* (2010).

Opposite (top): Betsy Palmer's fake head enjoys a brush with greatness, fine-tuned by Tom Savini for *Friday the 13th* (1980).

Opposite (bottom): Tom Savini reassures Jason that he's never been more handsome ahead of his fleeting but memorable appearance in *Friday the 13th* (1980).

The script for *Friday the 13th* (1980) originally ended with Alice (Adrienne King) in the hospital. But I'd just seen *Carrie* (1976), and right at the end of that, when the music was playing and it felt like the credits were gonna roll any second, that fucking hand came out of the grave and scared everyone to death. So I suggested we do something like that. That Jason burst out of the water and drag Alice, screaming, back down with him.

Sean [S. Cunningham] was like, "Jason's dead!"

So I suggested we make it a dream, and the audience bought it completely. I was inspired by Charles Laughton's Hunchback make-up to give young Jason one low ear and eye, along with weird teeth and a hydrocephalic dome on his head.

It was a great way to end the movie. A really effective jump scare.

Tom Savini

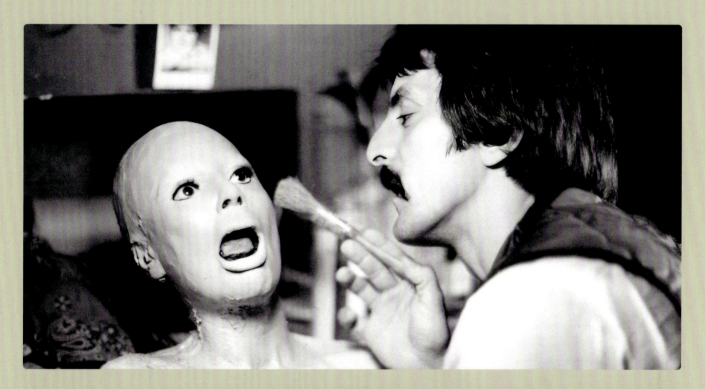

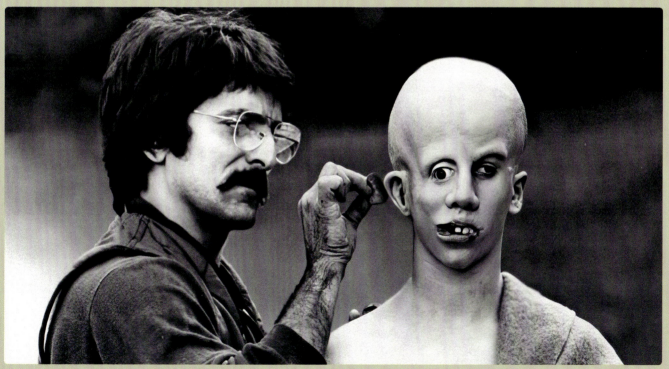

When the producers of *Jason X* (2001) first approached me to design Jason's new suit, they explained the 'Jason in Space' concept and I laughed! We had a good time making the movie, though.

Kane Hodder was easy-going and well versed in make-up, so very professional and a real pleasure to work with. He was especially happy with the suit as it came all in one piece and easily zippered up around him, with pieces of flesh and armour that just velcroed on. So, wham, bam, thank-you ma'am – and out of the trailer!

Stephan Dupuis

Ted White was my favourite Jason. He was John Wayne's stunt double and a total badass. Almost 60 when he played the part in *Friday the 13th: The Final Chapter* (1984), which at the time we really thought was going to be the last one. He lived to almost 100 and we did a lot of conventions together. Even in his nineties he could still kick everyone's ass in the room.

In interviews he'd always say how much he enjoyed playing Jason, but no, in reality he hated it, and only played him once. He also only wore the make-up once. One time, Alec Gillis, Kevin Yagher and I gathered around Ted to explain how a hacksaw gag was going to work, but he cut us off, saying, "Look. You do the effects. I'll do the stunts."

Then he got up and walked away. I'd been reading a lot of self-help books at the time and felt emboldened to stick up for myself, so I chased after him. He whipped around and pointed his finger at me. I grabbed it and told him he'd hurt my feelings. Instead of punching a hole through my face, Ted seemed to appreciate my honesty and backed down.

Later, when we were putting the make-up on him, he was back to his old self and complaining about the bald cap. I screamed, "Ted! You do the stunts. We'll do the make-up."

And he laughed. "Oh," he said, "I guess I had that coming to me."

Tom Savini

"YOU DO THE STUNTS. WE'LL DO THE MAKE-UP."

They asked me, "Do you want to do a *Friday the 13th* movie?" Of course I did!

You have to be respectful of what fans love about the series. If you shit on their good time, you're gonna hear about it. So it can be unnerving, taking on a project like that. But I'm a fan too. I love those movies too.

For the remake, I got to follow in the footsteps of Tom Savini, Kevin Yagher and Carl Fullerton. Carl's deformed hillbilly design was definitely in my Jason's DNA. First thing I did, though, was make the hockey mask. You really feel you're a part of film history when you make something like that.

Soon as I'd finished, the plan was to fly out to Texas to show the mask to producer Brad Fuller and director Marcus Nispel. There was no way I was going to check it into luggage though, so I put it in a pelican case and carried it with me. Going through security, they scanned it, then told me, "Come with us."

They took me to a back room, told me to open the case, and asked, "Is this what we think it is?"

I'm like, "It's just a hockey mask. I play hockey."

That, they didn't believe. Maybe I don't look like the hockey type. Anyway, I admitted it was a prop from a movie, and right away they guessed it was for *Friday the 13th* (2009). They asked if they could touch it, and suddenly everyone's grabbing it. They were all so excited, I almost missed my plane!

Later, I told Brad the story, and he just lit up. He's like, "This is gonna be great!"

Scott Stoddard

Right: The puppet and his master, Jason Vorhees and Tom Savini, take a breather during the filming of *Friday the 13th: The Final Chapter* (1984).

Opposite (anti-clockwise from top right): Scott Stoddard's designs, sculpture and finished make-up for Jason in director Marcus Nispel's *Friday the 13th* (2009).

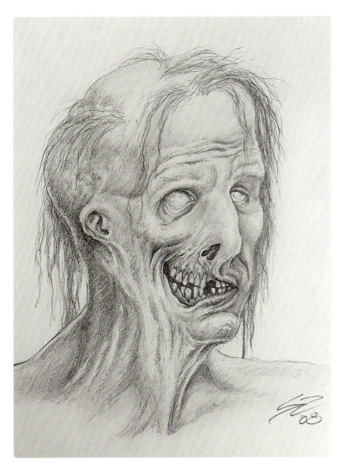
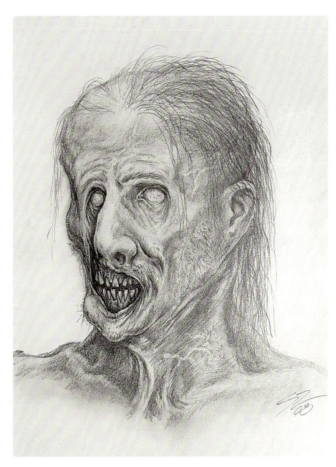

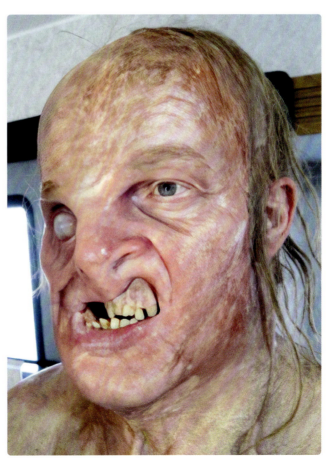

W hile we were shooting *Friday the 13th* (2009), Derek Mears kept to himself. He's a big guy. The perfect Jason. But also one of the sweetest people you could ever hope to meet. Because of that, he avoided the other cast members as he didn't want them to get to know him. To come to like him. Just in case that took the edge off their scenes with him.

Scott Stoddard

Above (left): Derek Mears lurks like a champ in *Friday the 13th* (2009).
Above (right): Derek Mears unmasked.
Right: Jason (Derek Mears) gets to grips with Scott Stoddard as the make-up master bravely adjusts the big man's hockey mask on the set of *Friday the 13th* (2009).
Opposite: The Holy Grail of Horror: Jason's hockey mask from *Friday the 13th* (2009).

I have *alopecia universalis*, a disorder where my body sees hair as a foreign obstacle and rejects it. I grew up feeling like an outcast and gravitated towards the monstrous. With my hair falling out in patches, I looked exactly like Corey Feldman when he shaves his head to mimic Jason in *Friday the 13th: The Final Chapter* (1984). It was with a serious sense of symmetry, then, that years later I auditioned to play Jason in Marcus Nispel's *Friday the 13th* (2009) reboot.

Lisa Fields, the casting director, admitted that she was unsure how to audition me. She said, "There's no dialogue, so you can't really read for the part. I know this time around, they want a professional actor. Not just a big guy with a mask. What do you make of that?"

I told her, "I'd approach the role as if I had dialogue. I'd do the same thing as any normal actor, breaking down the script, figuring out my beats and understanding my arc. No one watching the film will see the choices I make, but they'll help make my character more believable."

No matter how hidden you are in mask, a make-up or a suit, you have to avoid consciously expressing how you're feeling via exaggerated physical gestures. That's called indicating, and it's bad acting. Instead, you have to feel your character, commit to the moment and trust that energy will be transferred through the mask and captured on camera.

Anyway, I got the part!

I met with Scott Stoddard to talk about the under-the-mask make-ups he'd designed for the movie. Scott's a wonderful human being and a creative genius. We were in his workshop, standing on this raised little island section in the middle, when he picked up a metal case and popped it open. Inside were three Jason masks – The Holy Grails of Horror – and just looking at them made me tingle. He handed me one and said, "Since you're here, you should try this on."

Suddenly, everyone in the workshop below stopped working and looked up at me. It sounds like such a cliché, but surely the best, most wonderful kind, that as I put on the mask for the first time, first a few people spontaneously applauded, and then everyone joined in. It was a perfect, once-in-a-lifetime moment.

Months later, after being nominated for Best Villain at the MTV Movie Awards, I was on the red carpet doing interviews, and everyone had this jokey perception of what Jason was. They're like, "Hey Derek, what was your process, coming up with Jason? Did you party a lot, get drunk and chase girls with their boobs out?"

I told them, "No. I actually did a lot of research on child development. Jason had already been rejected by society when his mother – his only tie to love – was murdered right in front of him. He was only eight at the time, or thereabouts, so I imagined how that might have affected him.

"I also studied the psychological effects of loneliness, of how sadness might lead to Jason feeling empty inside, and how he'd maybe fill that void with rage. So Jason's attacks weren't simple murders, but emotional releases from someone who only knew love from his mother and really just wanted to be left alone. But when the kids in the film infringe on his territory, it sparks his childhood trauma as if they were the ones who killed and took his mother from him."

That's what I carried, I told them, behind Jason's mask. And they were totally bummed out. They said I might be overqualified for the role. But in no way was that the case. I'm a huge horror nerd and Jason's my favourite character. I am incredibly lucky to have been able to play him.

Derek Mears

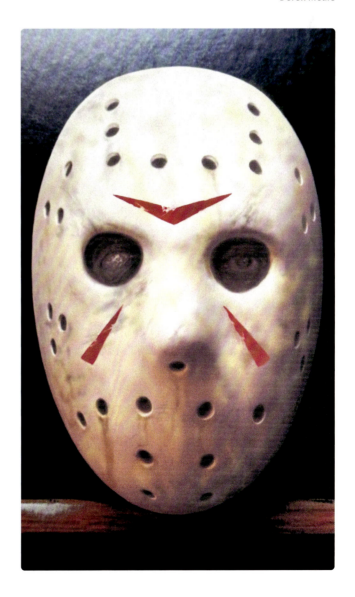

"ULTIMATELY, A MOVIE WILL TELL ME WHO IT IS, WHAT ITS SHORTCOMINGS ARE, AND WHAT IT NEEDS."

Each time I meet a film, it's like meeting a human being. Temp tracks can interfere with that process. It's temporary music a director adds to the soundtrack to give you a sense of what they think the movie needs. But what I want is to meet a movie on its own terms, without a temp track colouring my first impression. Because ultimately, a movie will tell me who it is, what its shortcomings are, and what it needs. The director certainly has the final word, but what the movie itself tells me is just as important.

On *A Nightmare on Elm Street* (1984), and many other films where I felt I contributed something original to the process, there were no temp tracks. Wes Craven was smart, sensitive and without any intellectual static. Open-minded and interested in my musical insights. Three reels into composing the music for the movie, I formed an impression that what it needed was an accessible theme. Something rather more fluid and lyrical than traditional horror themes. Wes told me he loved it, and that I should go for it.

That's the way it always was, working with Wes. He didn't criticize, but he guided. He didn't interfere. He was a man of few words, but those words were always informing, encouraging and supportive. And, without a temp track, I felt free to find a unique voice for the film.

Charles Bernstein

Freddy Krueger's not on screen a great deal in *A Nightmare on Elm Street* (1984), but the music keeps him in the story. You never know when he's going to jump out. Same with *Jaws* (1975). John Williams' score keeps the shark ever-present.

Charles Bernstein

I used to think that if Freddy was in my dreams, we'd probably be friends. We'd hang out. I had a dumb dream once, as a kid, that he gave me flowers. He took them out of his hat, like a magic trick.

I told my mom about it, and she must have told my brother, because 30 minutes later, someone knocked at the door with flowers for me. And there was a little card from Freddy!

Axelle Carolyn

Freddy Krueger's a very solidly constructed character and, if I do say so myself, he was very powerful and original. I don't think anybody had seen anyone quite like him before.

Freddy inhabited a world that had not been properly explored for many years. I can't think of another character who has inhabited nightmares and drawn the characters and the audience into that world of dreams in a coherent, exploratory way. It was the opening of a whole new door, a door that people have gone through for aeons, but which had not been represented in the arts very well.

Wes Craven

Everyone thinks they're safe in bed, but the truth is that's where we're most vulnerable. No one exploits that weakness quite like Freddy Krueger. You can't avoid sleep, or control your dreams, so there's no escaping him, or overpowering him. It's really the freakiest idea, and Freddy's the perfect monster: not a victim of circumstance, or somehow misunderstood – just 100 per cent pure evil. I love that!

Tami Lane

Opposite (top left): One, two, Charles Bernstein's composing for you.
Opposite (top right): Charles Bernstein and his musical hero, John Williams.
Opposite (bottom): Charles Bernstein's original, hand-written score for *A Nightmare on Elm Street* (1984).
Left: Director Axelle Carolyn and actress Kate Siegel enjoy a cheerful moment while shooting polished spookfest *The Haunting of Bly Manor* (2020).
Above: Wouldn't you really rather vote for Freddy? A sticker from Topps' 1988 *Fright Flicks* trading card series has us thinking. "Coming out of the Eighties," recalls filmmaker Jason Reitman, "my version of the 'Biggie or Tupac?' question was, 'Freddy or Jason?' For me, it was Freddy. I loved Freddy."

149

It took us forever to figure out what Ghostface was. Wes [Craven] just didn't approve any of our drawings or sculptures. Then one day, after he'd been out scouting locations, Wes was looking through his photos, and really just randomly, in the window of a house, a Halloween mask caught his eye. And he told us, "That's what I want."

Dimension was worried about copyright, so they had us sculpt lots of variations for the first movie. Eventually, though, they realized that Fun World, the company that created the mask, was happy to work with them as they could make a fortune selling Ghostface merchandise every Halloween. And they still do!

Howard Berger

Above: The Killer from *Scream* (1996) wants to know, what's your favourite scary movie?
Opposite (top left): Tom Holland bravely gives Chucky acting notes during the production of *Child's Play* (1988).
Opposite (top right): Kevin Yagher's cheery Chucky puppeteers gather for a class photo. Along the top, from left to right, there's Marc Tyler, Steve James, Charles Lutkus, producer Barrie Osbourne, Loren Soman and Howard Berger; Along the bottom, left to right, sits Brock Winkles, Bill Byrant, Allan Coulter, producer Laura Moskowitz and Kevin Yagher.
Opposite (bottom): A full house of puppeteers on *Child's Play* (1988) learned it takes an army to move a Chucky.

When I was a little boy, I'd look around at my action figures and think to myself, "Wouldn't it be wonderful if they came to life?"

The thing about killer doll movies before *Child's Play* (1988) was there was always the chance they weren't really alive. That even if you saw them move a little, it might have all been in the character's head. But there was no doubt Chucky was alive. He wasn't coy about it. He was a psychopath in a doll's body and that upped the ante in a way that hadn't been done before.

Before I wrote the screenplay for *Psycho II* (1983), Richard Franklin ran every Hitchcock film for me, picking out the set pieces to show me how Hitchcock built terror, and maintained cascading terror. All of that learning went into *Child's Play*.

Jerry Weintraub at United Artists gave me the go-ahead to make the movie, but then he got fired, and from the moment he was replaced the studio gave me nothing but grief about it. They were like, "Who's going to care about a piece of trash killer doll movie? Make it faster. Get it done."

They wanted me to cut the doll from the third act. Can you imagine? They beat the living hell out of me over it. But I told them, "No Chucky – no movie."

Politically, it was a terrible experience, but creatively, it was wonderful. I was more than halfway through the shoot, and I knew it would work when I cut it together. I just had no clue how to get the rest of the doll stuff we needed, but then that's why you work with good people.

I owe so much to my DP, Bill Butler. He made everything possible. Like, there was this one time I was trying to get Chucky to roll under a couch. I spent two hours trying to get him to roll using fishing wire, but got nowhere. Then Bill suggested we tilt the set, shoot it at an angle so it looked straight, and it worked so well!

Every shot of Chucky in *Child's Play* was realized practically, live on camera, and it all looked so real. I don't care if this sounds conceited, but in the end, despite everything, we made a brilliant film.

Though the studio had no faith in the project until preview audiences went wild for it, everyone always told me there'd be sequels. As far as I was concerned, though, it was a one-off, and I did everything I could to kill that damn doll!

I blew his arm off. I blew a leg off. I took his head off. I burned him. Then right at the end, I shot him in the heart. But in Hollywood, if a movie makes money, no matter how you end it, there are going to be sequels.

I guess you can't keep a good guy down.

Tom Holland

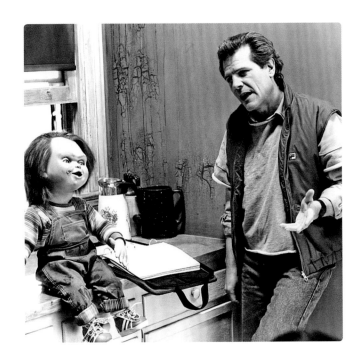

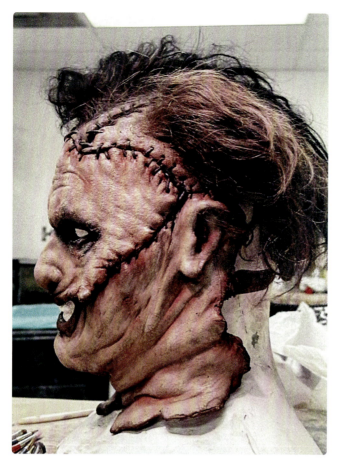

I love horror fans. It's all so meaningful to them. They tell me *Scream* (1996) and the sequels got them through hard times. That they were a comfort. A constant through the years.

Horror's such a healthy outlet for them. It's how they work out their fears, frustrations and any negative feelings they might have. They're really some of the sweetest people you'll ever meet.

David Arquette

Brad [Fuller] and Drew [Form] at Platinum Dunes wanted to remake *The Texas Chainsaw Massacre* (1974). It was their first movie, and they asked me to come do the make-up effects. They're like, "We're going to lean on you because this is your world."

Our 2003 remake was a true collaboration. I met with Marcus Nispel, the director. We talked about the photographer Joel-Peter Witkin, whose work focuses on death, dismemberment and displays of macabre things, so very much Leatherface territory and the direction of the production design. I got to work, designing the make-up, basically a deformed, diseased guy, and also the mask, made from bits and pieces of people he'd killed, and a character in its own right.

On set, it was a 30-minute make-up every morning: big, open syphilis sores, misshapen and missing teeth. One day we did a digital nose removal for the scene where he takes his mask off and you can see that cancer has eaten away part of his face.

That was my 50 per cent of the character. The rest was up to Andrew Bryniarski, who played Leatherface. He's an ominous guy and just absorbed that role. The younger actors were all afraid of him, which was great for the movie. It was more than just a job for him. That meant production sometimes had to rein him in. Like the time he said he wanted to use a real chainsaw.

They're like, "We don't have the insurance for that, man! You're getting the saw without the blade. We're not risking you chopping anyone's legs or arms off."

He certainly brought a lot of passion to the project!

Scott Stoddard

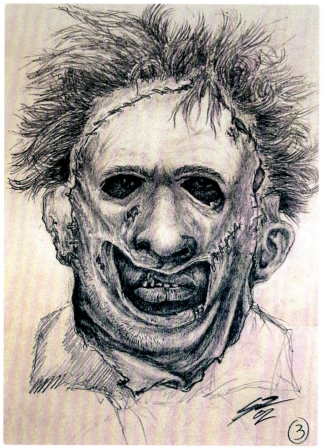

Top: Scott Stoddard's completed Leatherface mask for *The Texas Chainsaw Massacre* (2003).

Bottom: Scott Stoddard's Leatherface concept art for *The Texas Chainsaw Massacre* (2003).

Opposite: Almost as terrifying behind the scenes as he was on screen, Andrew Bryniarski brought Leatherface to life in *The Texas Chainsaw Massacre* (2003).

If you're making your own film, and you finally have control, it's up to you to step up and create something no one's seen before. The first feature I wrote and directed was *Skinned Deep* (2004). There's a scene where Brain (Jay Dugré), who has an enormous external brain, visualizes his yearning to break free by running naked at the busiest time through the busiest place on Earth: Times Square at rush hour.

Years later, Jay told me he only said he'd do it as he never thought I'd pull it off. It was an independent feature that took a couple of years to shoot, and we kept delaying and delaying that scene, but finally I was like, "We're going to New York!"

Jay's like, "Really? This is happening?"

Though we didn't have permission to shoot in Times Square, we had a renegade spirit, two cameras and a pair of vans. With his giant prosthetic brain, hiking boots, and nothing else, Jay had to jump out of one van and skip happily to the second on the other side of Times Square. Which, unbelievably, he did.

My only mistake was I got greedy.

We got a great first take, and while Jay's still hyperventilating in the back of the van, I say, "Let's do it again."

What I didn't know was, right across the street, two undercover cops saw a peachy pale, wiggly dick, big brain thing blur by them. So quickly, they couldn't quite believe their eyes. So they're like, "Let's wait to see if it happens again."

Thanks to me, it did. And halfway through Jay's run... BAM! They take him down. I had no idea they were cops so I ran to Jay's defence and grabbed one of them. They look at me like I'm crazy and show me their badges. I'm like, "Oh, we got a real problem."

They're like, "Yeah, you got a real problem."

Paddy wagon comes and in goes Jay, wearing a robe someone found for him. His brain was too big for him to easily fit in the van, so he had to shimmy right down in the seat, and when he did, his robe fell open. So there he was, handcuffed in the back of a police van, his dick and balls hanging out, seriously questioning his life choices.

They drove him to the station, booked him, took a mug shot of his big brain head and locked him in a cell. Eventually he managed to convince them he wasn't insane, but an actor, and had streaked for a movie. So now they're laughing and taking photos with him. Everyone's having a great time at his expense, and the next day in front of the judge, minus the giant prosthetic brain, he got six months' probation and was sent on his way.

Incredibly, Jay didn't punch me in the nose the instant he saw me. He took it as a great life experience. And I got a truly original scene for my movie.

— Gabe Bartalos

> "RIGHT ACROSS THE STREET, TWO UNDERCOVER COPS SAW A PEACHY PALE, WIGGLY DICK, BIG BRAIN THING BLUR BY THEM."

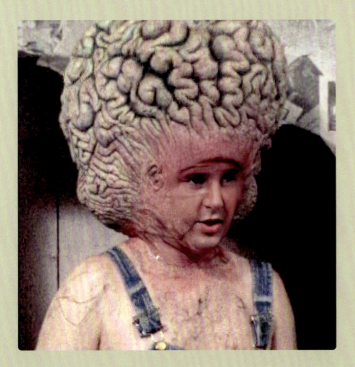

Opposite: The Surgeon General (Aaron Sims) is out for blood in Gabe Bartalos's *Skinned Deep* (2004).
Left: Jay Dugré bared more than his soul for *Skinned Deep* (2004).

As a young, amateur filmmaker, I felt I should make a short film as a calling card. I didn't have the money to go to film school, so the only thing I could do was make something I could hopefully get into festivals. Something that might stand out and get some eyes on me.

I always thought clowns were creepy and had this *Twilight Zone*-y idea about a woman. She's all alone on a city bus in the middle of the night, when out of nowhere a clown sits across from her. He stares at her, silent and playful. She's uncomfortable and the mood intensifies until it becomes sadistic. Then he tries to stick her with a needle.

I thought it was a good, creepy way to kick off the short. Not supernatural, so technically possible, and relatable. The question then became, what does this clown look like? We've seen a million killer clowns. I had to try to do something different. So I didn't make him colourful and I didn't give him hair. Also, I didn't let him speak, as there's something more animal about silent slashers. You can't reason with them.

I wanted him to look like a cross between the devil and a witch, with a pointed nose and chin. I wanted him to be gaunt like a zombie, so I gave him cheekbones and sunken eye sockets. Another big inspiration was the clown in *The Twilight Zone (1959–64)* episode, 'Five Characters in Search of an Exit' [S03, E14]. The Joker from *Batman* was another reference I used when sculpting his face. All those things combined to make Art the Clown.

The original Art was my buddy Mike Giannelli. He isn't an actor, but when I was getting into make-up effects, he was always around, always willing to let me test stuff on him, and probably the first person I ever made prosthetics for. So he was my guinea pig! I told him, "You don't have to act. Just sit and smile and wave a bit."

Basically, I forced him, and it worked. It worked so well! The resounding note I got from that first short, *The 9th Circle* (2008), was that everyone loved the clown at the beginning, and I should make more stuff with him. It was good advice, and I listened to it.

The second short, *Terrifier* (2011), focused solely on Art. I developed his personality and sense of humour, and because I love gore, and slashers, I went all in and turned him into a psychopathic serial killer. That short went down even better than the first, and that's when I knew in my gut there was something there. Art was my North Star, and I just had to keep following him, and get him in front of as many faces as possible.

But by the time I was ready to shoot the movie, *Terrifier* (2016), Mike had had enough. He was like, "I'm not an actor. I can't do all those hours in the make-up chair for months on end."

I begged him to reconsider, but he wouldn't. I couldn't blame him, but I didn't know if Art would work without Mike. Since I had no choice but to start from scratch, though, I looked for a taller, thinner actor, as I knew the make-up would be ten times scarier that way.

"ART WAS MY NORTH STAR, AND I JUST HAD TO KEEP FOLLOWING HIM."

David Howard Thornton was probably the sixth person to audition. As soon as I saw him, I knew he'd look amazing in the make-up. He didn't have any lines. I just told him to act as if he was decapitating somebody, and having a great time doing it. He gave a gleeful performance. Flipped the switch and did this amazing Mr Bean/Jim Carrey's *Mask* sort of thing. It was so theatrical! And the first time I realized that putting a real actor in the costume would take Art to an entirely new level.

As soon as he left, I turned to Phil [Falcone] and said, "Honestly, what else are we looking for?"

Dave's like my brother now, and so great to work with.

As for the gore, sure, I push it further than most people would dare, but you can't go backwards. You have to one-up what came before. Still, I don't want to alienate people. I don't want them leaving my movies feeling depressed, or like they need a shower. That said, *Terrifier 2* (2022) has such a strong fantasy element, it's like a comicbook world, so hopefully that gave me the leeway to push the violence a little further, and get away with it.

My favourite kill so far is the bedroom scene in *Terrifier 2*. There was a lot of pressure to top the hacksaw scene from the first movie, so I knew we had to deliver the goods. The first time we shot it, though, there'd been some delays and upsets, and I really wasn't satisfied with what we had. Then we got hit with the pandemic, and I used that time to reconfigure the entire scene. I wrote a list of the ten worst things I could think of doing to this poor character, then told my producer, "Let's pick five and spend the next couple of months building them to the best of our abilities."

When we finally got out of lockdown, we went back and shot five days of Art mutilating that girl and that's the scene that had people fainting and throwing up. I'm proud of what we achieved!

Damien Leone

Opposite: Art the Clown (David Howard Thornton) and his dad, Damien Leone.

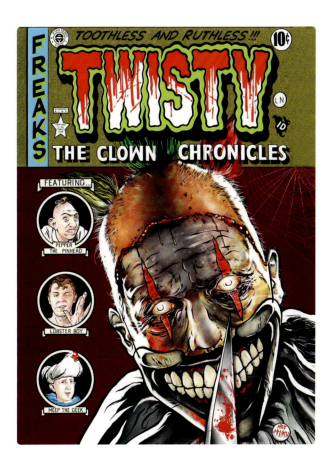

'**THE TWISTY SONG**' by John Carroll Lynch. Sung to the tune of 'The Candy Man'.

Who can kill his maid off?
Stab her with a knife?
Head on out to Twisty's and make Bonnie fear for life?
The Dandy Man! Oh, the Dandy Man can! The Dandy Man can 'cos his mother is indulgent and gives everything to him.
Who is so impatient,
That his Halloween is shot?
Cuts up all clothes and makes his jammies Polka Dot?
The Dandy Man! Oh, the Dandy Man can! The Dandy Man can 'cos his mother is indulgent and gives everything to him.
The Dandy Man takes everything you make and turns it into something evil!
Oh, you talk about someone primeval?
He would even eat a weevil!
Who steals masks from dead clowns?
And terrorizes freaks?
But wishes he were one of them when he and Jimmy speak?
The Dandy Man! Oh, the Dandy Man can! The Dandy Man can 'cos his mother is indulgent and gives everything to him.

Eryn: John Carroll Lynch is such a lovely human. Just the kindest, sweetest, most generous guy. Soon as we made him up as Twisty, though, man, he was something else. First time he got in the make-up, he just walked around, not saying a word, blowing up balloon animals for people.

Mike: It was the creepiest thing ever. Creepier than a creepy-ass mime. But outside of that, yeah, he's a wonderful person. He made us a song! When the season wrapped he gave us 'The Twisty Song'. I loved that.

Eryn: Then the Halloween after *American Horror Story: Freak Show* (2014–15) aired, we were in New Orleans and there were Twisties everywhere. People got totally into that character, and fast.

Mike: It's a shame they never released 'The Twisty Song'. It would have been a hit for sure.

Eryn Krueger Mekash and Mike Mekash

Opposite: John Carroll Lynch doesn't clown around as Twisty in *American Horror Story: Freak Show* (2014–15).
Above: Mike Mekash's nightmarish cover art for the Twisty comicbook featured in *American Horror Story: Freak Show* (2014–15).
Right: Lon Chaney's bitter clown from *He Who Gets Slapped* (1924) was a huge inspiration for Twisty.

The Duffer Brothers were writing season four of *Stranger Things* (2016–25), and finally ready to introduce the main villain of the series, Vecna. In keeping with the *Nightmare on Elm Street* feel of the new season, they wanted a Freddy Kruegeresque type of character and were aiming for nothing less than iconic. They were big fans of our work on *Game of Thrones* (2011–19), and impressed by the horrific, semi-translucent radiation burns we'd created for *Chernobyl* (2019). They basically told us, "We need our own Night King."

No pressure, then!

Barrie Gower

"THE DUFFER BROTHERS BASICALLY TOLD US, 'WE NEED OUR OWN NIGHT KING.' NO PRESSURE, THEN!"

"IN MAKE-UP WE CAN ONLY ADD. WE CAN'T TAKE AWAY."

Above: Barrie Gower adds a finishing touch to Jamie Campbell Bower's Vecna suit for season four of *Stranger Things* (2016–25).

Right: Even incomplete, behind the scenes on *Stranger Things* (2016–25) with make-up artist Joel Hall, Jamie Campbell Bower cuts an imposing figure as the villainous Vecna.

Opposite (top): Vecna (Jamie Campbell Bower) in all his gory glory in *Stranger Things* (2016–25).

Opposite (bottom left): Patt Foad works on Vecna's elaborate sculpture for *Stranger Things* (2016–25).

Opposite (bottom right): Creating Vecna for *Stranger Things* (2016–25) took equal measures of paint and patience. Paula Eden was one of a talented team at BGFX who rose to the challenge of creating an iconic villain.

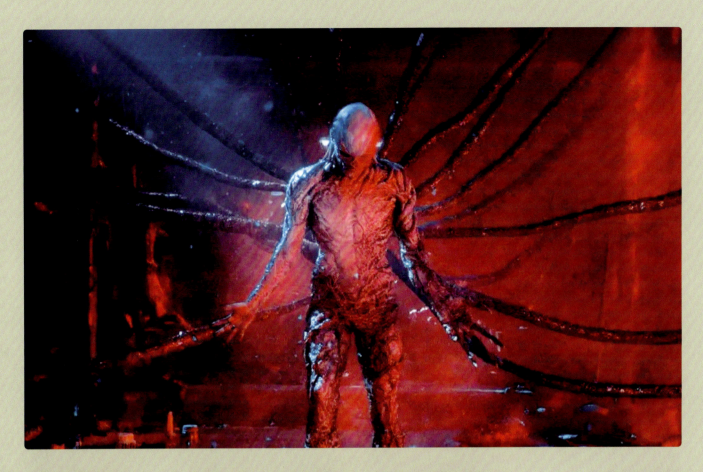

In make-up we can only add. We can't take away. So Barrie [Gower] and I are never precious about collaborating with visual effects. If they can improve on our work simply by us adding a little green on the cheeks or wherever, allowing them to, say, carve something out, we're always happy to oblige. I actually love it when we all work together to make something cool and creative.

For season four of *Stranger Things* (2016–25), we knew from the very first design of Vecna that we'd be collaborating with visual effects. The last thing we wanted was for Jamie [Campbell Bower] to have to sit through seven hours of make-up, only to have his whole body replaced by VFX. So once we understood what Matt and Ross [Duffer] were hoping to see from the character, we got to work figuring out how to best combine practical and digital to bring him to life.

Ultimately we were able to create Vecna almost entirely with prosthetics, but there's this subtle visual effect of vines slithering around him that really adds something. Also we created these beautiful mechanical hands for the character, but when his fingers dart into someone's head, obviously that's VFX too!

Sarah Gower

I'd worked with Jamie Campbell Bower a few times before the Duffer Brothers picked him to play Vecna on *Stranger Things* (2016–25), so I knew he was going to be easy to work with. He's never grumpy about having stuff stuck all over him, and that makes all the difference when you're in a trailer together for hours and hours. His proportions are perfect too – super-skinny with amazing cheekbones. It's a shame he's an actor and not specifically a creature performer, as we'd use him all the time.

Duncan Jarman

Below: The devil's in the details – fine-tuning the Vecna sculpt at BGFX with Patt Foad and Duncan Jarman.

Opposite: Duncan Jarman applies final touches to Vecna (Jamie Campbell Bower) in the make-up room for *Stranger Things* (2016–25).

Overleaf: The gang's all here, via the poison pen of Mark Tavares. From left to right: John Carpenter, Joe Dante, Tom Savini as Sex Machine (1996's *From Dusk Till Dawn*), Simon Pegg as Shaun (2004's *Shaun of the Dead*), Caroline Munro as Laura (1972's *Dracula A.D. 1972*), Robert Englund, Rick Baker, Howard Berger, Ve Neill and Marshall Julius, plus creatures of every shape and size as we're all best fiends in the Monster Kids Clubhouse!

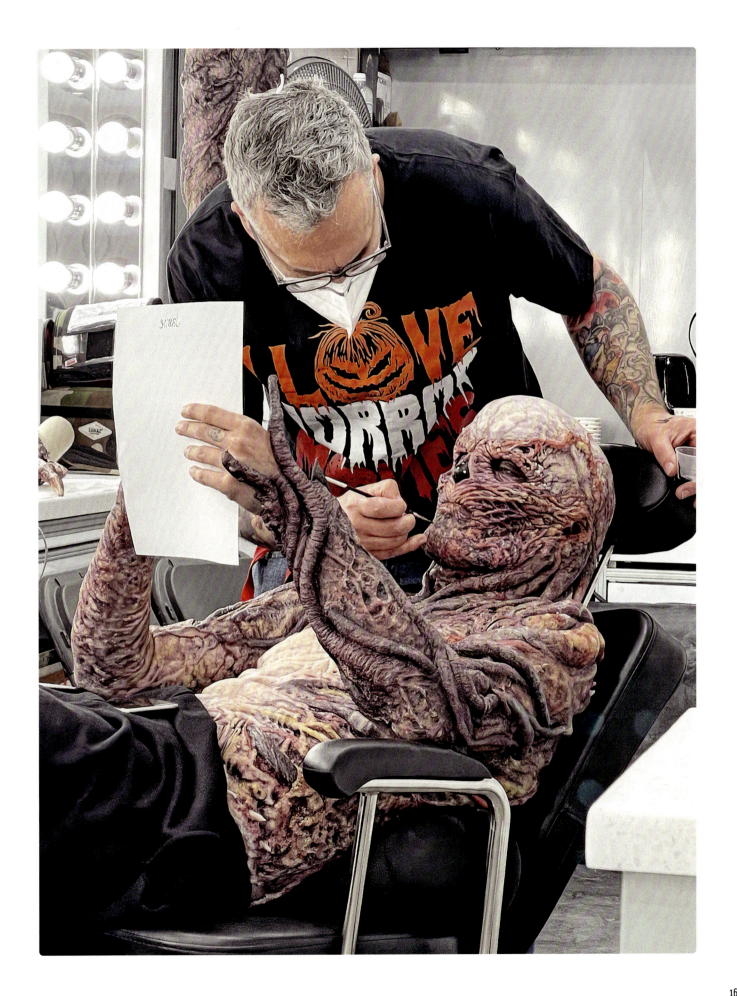

9

GROWLING PAINS

Driven by forces beyond their control, werewolves are no less the protagonists in their stories, than they are the antagonists. Both victim and monster in one furry, fearful package – as deserving of our sympathy, as our dread.

A crimson monster stew of ancient folklore, mythology and literature, synthesized by Hollywood into bloody fables of duel identity and the beast that lurks within us all, werewolves have no more power over their impulses than most of the rest of us, and that makes them weirdly relatable.

> Maybe it's because I had a German Shepherd as a kid, but the Wolf Man's always been my favourite monster.
>
> **Gino Crognale**

I rarely visited the set of *The Munsters* (1964–66). Mostly, I worked in the lab. My main job was to make up Butch Patrick as Eddie Munster. I'd place a wooden plank across the arms of my make-up chair so he could sit at a comfortable height for me to apply his ears and hairpiece. After that, I'd run a new Frankenstein head and bolts for Fred [Gwynne] and fresh ears for Eddie, as at the end of each day they'd just throw the used pieces away.

Years later, on *Star Trek: The Next Generation* (1987–94), I learned that, if you take off the prosthetic pieces very carefully, you can save them to use over and over. Those heads took so long to paint, we'd never have been able to afford making a new one every day.

Michael Westmore

Jeff: The first real monster movie I saw in colour was *The Curse of the Werewolf* (1961). It told the whole history of how Oliver Reed became a werewolf, so you got to know him as a person, before he became a monster. It made everything so much more meaningful, and I've loved that creature ever since. In fact, Reed's werewolf was one of the very first model kits I ever designed.

Howard: I worked with Oliver Reed in the early Nineties. He told me the best time he'd ever had on a movie was *The Curse of the Werewolf*. He just loved being in Roy Ashton's make-up. So I called my wife and got her to ship me your model kit, which I'd built at home, and I gave it to Oliver Reed.

Jeff: Oh my God. Wow!

Howard: I told him you'd sculpted it and he held it like it was gold. He said, "This is the greatest thing I've ever gotten."

Jeff: I've always wondered if he ever got to see it.

Howard: He was out of his mind, he loved it so much. He was like, "I've never seen anything like this before. It's incredible."

Jeff: That's insane. I love it. That makes me so happy!

Jeff Yagher and Howard Berger

Preceding Spread: Created by Rob Bottin for *The Howling* (1981), and later restored by Greg Nicotero, Eddie Quist's lycanthropic alter ego is arguably the most memorable werewolf ever to stalk the silver screen.

Left: Jeff Yagher's classic garage kit model of Oliver Reed, terrifyingly transformed in *The Curse of the Werewolf* (1961). This was the first kit Jeff tried his hand at, and the results speak for themselves.

Top (left): Michael Westmore in his home studio, pictured with some of his most iconic creations.

Top (right): Michael Westmore served his apprenticeship in his Uncle Bud's make-up studio at Universal.

"ROB [BOTTIN] THOUGHT THAT TO MAKE THE WEREWOLVES LEAP, HE COULD MAKE FLYING ROCKET WOLVES."

The entire budget for *The Howling* (1981) was just $1 million, including the special effects. Our original werewolf costume was more like a bear suit. The proportions were all wrong, so we threw out every frame we shot of it. Rob [Bottin] thought that to make the werewolves leap, he could make flying Rocket Wolves. We spent a lot of time and money trying to figure that out, but after you lit their tails, they'd fly with a stream of smoke coming out of their backs, so that didn't work either.

Rob built some werewolf pieces, heads and hands and stuff, but those only worked for close-ups. So we went back to our investor and asked for another $50,000. International Film Investors was the name of the company and for years they sent me plaques celebrating how much money they'd made from my movie. I didn't make anything from it. I wasn't in the Director's Guild and didn't even get residuals. But we did get to build a pretty cool werewolf.

We didn't want to do a Jack Pierce one, though. So Rob's design was based on ancient woodcuts, some of which we put in the movie. He built this big, beautiful beast, but to operate it, you had to stand behind it, which again, limited how we shot it. We realized we couldn't show the werewolf from head to toe, so we built a top half a person could wear, with a great animatronic face, and also werewolf legs we could shoot separately.

Our DP, John Hora, was great with light and shot everything beautifully. Though Rick Baker's work in *An American Werewolf in London* (1981) was technically better than what Rob was able to achieve, John Landis overlit the transformation in his movie, so you could see every little piece of latex. John also threw Rick a curve by shooting from unexpected angles.

We, on the other hand, were well aware of what we were working with, and tried to address the flaws in our monster by how we presented it. Ultimately, we managed to piece the film together in a moderately convincing way that made it look like there was this terrifying lupine creature.

Joe Dante

Top: Make-up effects genius Rob Bottin shows off his insert werewolf puppet to director Joe Dante for *The Howling* (1981).

Above: Director Joe Dante poses with an old friend in Greg Nicotero's office. Greg took it upon himself to restore the original artifact, and it's now so intense and frightening, only the bravest souls would dare turn their backs on it.

"THERE'S SOMETHING ABOUT THAT MOVIE THAT FEELS DIRTY, LIKE YOU SHOULDN'T BE WATCHING IT."

The Howling and An American Werewolf in London both came out the same year: 1981. I have a theory that whichever one you saw first, you like best.

Howard Berger

Opposite Graham Humphreys' striking, dynamic one sheet for *An American Werewolf in London* (1981). Beware the moon, lads!

Below: Director Joe Dante is flanked by a pair of Rob Bottin's werewolves, poised to rocket up a wall for a scene in *The Howling* (1981).

Bottom (left): Actress Belinda Balaski fends off Eddie Quist's fearsome werewolf, here played by make-up artist Steve LaPorte, for a scene from *The Howling* (1981).

An American Werewolf in London (1981) is my favourite werewolf movie. It's fun, with a story and characters that really draw you in. It's clean and perfect. It's so Rick Baker.

My favourite werewolves, though, are in *The Howling* (1981). There's something about that movie that feels dirty, like you shouldn't be watching it. Almost pornographic, in a weird way.

I love the aesthetic of Rob Bottin's werewolves. Those angles! Those thin heads and pointed ears, but also so big and tall, towering over you. Inescapable. They'll tear you apart. That's all they're meant to do.

David (David Naughton) was a lovable guy in *American Werewolf*. To some extent, that took the edge off when he transformed. But in *The Howling*, Eddie Quist (Robert Picardo) was a pervy serial killer, terrifying before he even turned into a werewolf. So when he does, it's horrifying.

Christopher Nelson

"HIS ENTIRE PERFORMANCE WAS BASED ON THE DESPERATION OF BEING INSIDE THAT SUIT."

Joe: Robert Picardo got his part in *The Howling* (1981) as he was the only guy who'd sit still for that make-up! We'd hoped to shoot his scenes quickly, but it took longer than expected, as Rob Bottin spent the whole of his first day doing the make-up. We were all just sitting there waiting to go, running into super golden overtime, but Rob was still trying to get everything exactly right, because he's a perfectionist. Finally we had to send everyone home, and Robert had to wear the make-up all night so we could shoot him the next day. The man's a trooper. Even after all that, he worked with Rob numerous times.

Howard: He can't have anything applied to him any more, though. Not only is he highly allergic, but also I think all those years getting into extremely heavy make-ups gave him PTSD.

Joe: There's a limit, I think, to how much your flesh can stand having that stuff on.

Howard: He said he's done having anything glued to him ever again.

Joe: After what we did to him on *Explorers* (1985), I'm not surprised. I mean, he couldn't even move in the Wak suit. His entire performance was based on the desperation of being inside that suit, sweating bullets.

Joe Dante and Howard Berger

Top: Make-up Master Greg Cannom applies his Eddie Quist transformation make-up on actor Robert Picardo for his role as a psychopathic werewolf in *The Howling* (1981).
Above: One of Rob Bottin's amazing transformation puppets for *The Howling* (1981).

I got to be the werewolf in *Howling V: The Rebirth* (1989), wearing the same suit that Steve Johnson built for Bill Forsch to wear in the previous movie. I was so eager to do it that even though Bill's skull cap was a whole different head shape and horribly uncomfortable, I was like, "It fits. It's great!"

Mike Elizalde

"I WAS SO EAGER TO DO IT."

Below: Before he was a true make-up effects superstar, Mike Elizalde played the werewolf for Steve Johnson in *Howling V: The Rebirth* (1989).

In his script for *Creepshow* (1982), Stephen King described Fluffy as, "A blur of fur and teeth."

That's it! I started with Warner Bros' Tasmanian Devil and took it from there.

The one thing I'd change about Fluffy today is I'd make him skinny, as he was maybe a little too plump for something that hadn't eaten in 150 years.

Tom Savini

Below: Stephen King and Tom Savini talk monsters during production on *Creepshow* (1982) in Tom's home town of Pittsburgh, Pennsylvania, USA.
Bottom (left): Tom Savini sculpts his crate creature, Fluffy, from *Creepshow* (1982).
Bottom (right): Proud dad Tom Savini stands just a swipe away from "Ghoulish" Gary Pullin's epic mural of his iconic beast, Fluffy, from *Creepshow* (1982).
Opposite (left): A memorable moment from Christopher Tucker's groundbreaking transformation from *The Company of Wolves* (1984). The UK's answer to Dick Smith, Christopher consistently stretched the bounds of what was considered possible.
Opposite (right): Tucker gets to the point with a werewolf he created for a 1984 Dr. Pepper ad.
Opposite (bottom): Leanne Podavin and a werewolf chum on the set of *Poltergeist: The Legacy* (1996-99).

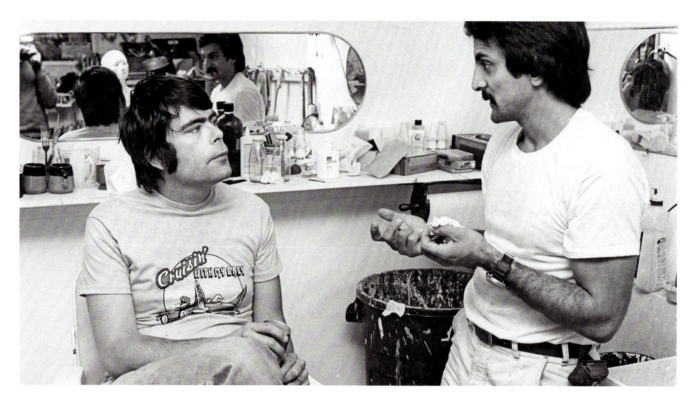

The werewolf transformation in *The Company of Wolves* (1984) had to be unlike anything that had come before. That's what everyone always wants: for you to come up with something completely original, every time!

When they hired me, I asked them what they wanted. And Stephen Woolley, the producer, told me, "We want a scary horror film. Something really frightening."

I came up with this scene where the man's flesh crumbles off, then the wolf's muzzle bursts out of his mouth, so it's born like a big, bloody butterfly. The one thing I wasn't aware of was that the director, Neil Jordan, actually imagined he was making this delicate

"WHO EVEN KNEW HAIRY EYES WAS A THING?"

little child's fantasy film. Certainly that wasn't communicated to me.

So when Neil walked onto the set, and saw this skinned man I'd produced, all bloody and raw, he was absolutely horrified. He cried, "What have you done with my little fillum?!"

Christopher Tucker

We did a werewolf for *Poltergeist: The Legacy* (1996–99), a second season episode called 'Rough Beast' (S02, E09, 1997). We did the hair-growing trick where you punch a bunch of hair into a gelatine piece and then shoot it as it's pulled out. Run the film backwards and it looks like it's growing. Simple! And exactly how Rick Baker did it on *An American Werewolf in London* (1981).

I spent so long punching all that hair, such an enormous amount of hair, one hair at a time, over and over and over again, that for a week afterwards I saw hair in my vision. Hair wherever I looked. Hair on everything. Who even knew hairy eyes was a thing?

Leanne Podavin

I'd gotten to know people on my film course who were into practical make-up effects and I had a pretty good idea of what was achievable on a lower budget. I decided that I wanted my first feature to be a werewolf movie. Everyone said that was way too ambitious, that zombies and vampires were easier to achieve, but it's good to be ambitious. That was the point. That's what drew me to want to make *Dog Soldiers* (2002).

I'm an outdoorsy person, so I get a lot of inspiration from dark, scary woods. That's where I wanted the film to be set, rather than somewhere more urban. Werewolves are rural. They're creatures of the woods. So it was always going to be werewolves for me.

Unlike most werewolf films, though, my film wasn't going to be about a person cursed to turn into a large, feral creature every full moon. When I pitched the story to the cast, I made a point of explaining, "This isn't a werewolf movie with soldiers. It's a soldier movie with werewolves."

We just had to make sure the werewolves were terrifying. As authentic, realistic and plausible as possible. If they'd looked fake or foolish, the cast would have looked like idiots!

A friend of mine, Colin Lang, did some incredible sketches in the pub one day. Turned out my sound recordist had a hidden ability as an artist. He drew this werewolf from behind, and it was this incredibly elegant, almost feminine thing. I thought it would be an interesting way to go with our werewolves, so we followed that design path a bit further, then Dave Bonneywell refined the design.

What I knew from the start was that my werewolves would stand on two legs. Though I liked the transformation in *An American Werewolf in London* (1981) better than the one in *The Howling* (1981), I always thought the werewolf in *The Howling* was scarier. After *Dog Soldiers* came out, I said as much in lots of interviews and that almost got me in trouble with Rick Baker!

Bit of a tangent, this, but I went to visit John [Landis] on the set of *Burke and Hare* (2010) and while I'm sitting at a monitor, John says, "Neil, have you met Rick?"

And there's Rick, who I hadn't met before. The legend himself. And he looks at me and goes, "You're the guy who said werewolves should walk on two legs."

He held my gaze for ages. The pause was endless. And then finally he said, "I agree with you. John wanted it on four, but I'd always wanted it on two."

Bob Keen and his team at Pinewood fabricated, I think, three suits in total for *Dog Soldiers*. Plus one fully animatronic head and a couple of stunt heads. Besides standing on two legs, my werewolves were tall and slender. Rather than putting them on clunky stuntmen, I put three dancers in the suits as I wanted grace and control in their movements. Then I put them on stilts, which meant elegance was rarely achieved, but there were beats, there were moments, that were just beautiful.

The other thing that I did was I specifically designed the werewolves so they wouldn't fit inside the house. The ceiling was just a little bit too low for them. So whenever they came into the house, they had to stoop and ended up pressed against the ceiling. It gave them a real presence inside the house and made them all the more creepy. It helped the dancers, too, as they supported themselves on the stilts by holding onto the roof. And it looked great in the film.

Sometimes when you have a guy in a suit, if you linger on it too long, you'll give away the fact that it's a man in a suit. Audiences can only suspend so much disbelief. So when I edited the film, I used lots of fast cuts, and while we shot it, lighting was key. We used a lot of backlighting.

There's one shot in *Dog Soldiers* which I absolutely love. It's just a werewolf in silhouette. You can't see anything beyond the shape and its hot breath. In that moment, you totally believe it.

Neil Marshall

Opposite: A snarling werewolf looms large in *Dog Soldiers* (2002).
Below: *Dog Soldiers* (2002) director Neil Marshall took great inspiration from Colin Lang and Dave Bonneywell's evocative concept art.

"I GET A LOT OF INSPIRATION FROM DARK, SCARY WOODS."

The tricky thing on *The Wolfman* (2010) was coming up with a design that everyone approved of. Before Joe Johnston took over, the original director just kept telling me, "Do another one… Do another one… Do another one…"

I was like, "What would you like different?"

He'd say, "I don't know. Just do something else."

It was sucking out my soul, you know? Eventually, I did a make-up test on myself, as I thought maybe he just wasn't visualizing what these Photoshops would look like in reality. But he didn't like that either. This was just seven months before we were supposed to start filming, and we kept on playing the "Do another" game for months and months and months.

When they eventually got rid of the original director, just a month before we were supposed to start filming, as I still didn't have an approved design, I told the producers, "I'm just going to make what I think it has to be, because we don't have the time for any more discussion."

So I went back to what I'd done seven months before, which was in part a homage to Jack Pierce's original Wolf Man make-up, with the lower underbite. But because we'd spent so much time screwing around, instead of having a room full of everything I needed, perfectly finished off and ready to go, every day we were pulling pieces out of the mould, hoping they were good, and using them straight away.

Though it was frustrating in lots of ways, Benicio [Del Toro] was a lot of fun to work with. He's a monster kid, and we bonded over that. When he was young, he told me he'd had a poster of Lon Chaney Jr over his bed, and so like me, he wanted his Wolfman to look like the Wolf Man.

Anthony Hopkins was a great guy, too. Ate his lunch with the crew. Very down-to-earth. And I loved working with Dave and Lou Elsey on that film. So even though it was difficult in many different ways, we still had fun. We got to be in the forest with gypsy wagons, a full moon and a Wolf Man, and it doesn't get much cooler than that.

Rick Baker

"THE ORIGINAL DIRECTOR JUST KEPT TELLING ME, 'DO ANOTHER ONE… DO ANOTHER ONE… DO ANOTHER ONE…'"

Göran: When I was on *The Wolfman* (2010) with Rick [Baker], he told me he changes his make-ups all the time. His attitude was like, "What's the use of keeping continuity if it didn't look great previously? Always improve it if you can, then that weak shot was just one bad day."

Howard: Rick also does that to keep it interesting. I'd get bored too, doing the same make-up over and over. So in some small way, I change them every day. Eventually you hit it, but no one ever knows or notices the tiny differences along the way.

Göran: When I do my make-ups, I usually just go with what I feel so they rarely look absolutely the same. I'll have an idea of what colours I'll use and where I need to reach, but I seldom plan the journey.

Göran Lundström and Howard Berger

Opposite (clockwise from top left): Benicio Del Toro dwarfs Rick Baker in a striking make-up that earned the legendary artist an Academy Award; Benicio Del Toro had a howling good time playing The Wolf Man; Anthony Hopkins in magnificent, monstrous form for *The Wolfman* (2010); ever the monster kid, Benicio Del Toro was thrilled to follow in the pawprints of his acting heroes.

Right: Lou Elsey helps Rick Baker ready Benicio Del Toro as *The Wolfman* (2010).

I grew up making movies. That's all I ever did from when I was nine. Then my career took all these crazy turns and next thing you know, I'm scoring video games, TV shows and movies. Which was wonderful, of course, but I never stopped wanting to make my own films.

I had this silly idea about a guy who got stuck in Japan and was forced to compete for cash on a game show by dressing like some crazy kaiju monster. My friends at Bad Robot loaned me the equipment and thankfully both Patton Oswalt and Ben Schwartz agreed to wear monster suits and fight each other on this little city we built.

Monster Challenge (2018) was supposed to be this light, fun thing that got the urge to direct out of my system, but after completing it, I just didn't want to stop. I wanted to make more. That led to me chatting with Kevin Feige. He told me they had to make shows for a new thing called Disney+, and asked me what I'd do, given the chance? Immediately I told him, *"Werewolf by Night"* (2022).

He looked at me funny. Most people would ask to do a Spider-Man or Captain America, he said. But they'd already been so well done, and I wanted to make something I'd loved as a kid that only a handful of people in the world knew about. That's how that got started.

Right at the beginning I looked at the budget and there was this really hefty line item. I asked them what that was for, and they said, "That's our digital werewolf. You're going to have him through the whole thing, aren't you?"

And I was like, "No, he's only going to show up at the end for maybe five minutes. And by the way, it's going to be a guy in a suit."

I wanted to make as much practical stuff as we could possibly have on the set with us. I didn't want someone with a tennis ball on the end of a stick getting the actors to try to imagine what they're looking at. If that was me, I'd go nuts. So we built monsters, and it was wonderful to have Carey Jones on the set in KNB's amazing Man-Thing suit. It made such a difference for Gael [García Bernal] to have a proper character to play off, and it definitely helped inform the next layer of visual effects in terms of performance and lighting references.

All around the set we had these amazing monster heads mounted on the walls, as the hunters in the film are the real bad guys, and mounting heads is what bad guys do. I went through the comics and we found some great monsters from them to recreate. We also included Ben and Patton's creatures from my *Monster Challenge* film, which was kind of hilarious. At least to me!

I wanted Bigfoot up there too, because he'd always terrified me as a kid. I had no reason to be scared of him, as I lived in a suburban little town in New Jersey, but I'd seen Bigfoot on *In Search Of...* (1977–82), and Leonard Nimoy had me absolutely believing that thing could be living in my backyard. So I washed Bigfoot from the trauma centre of my brain by mounting him on the wall, and when the film was finished, Marvel gave me his head to keep. Not his actual head, though. The one from the show. Obviously I'd never hunt or display a REAL monster.

Michael Giacchino

Left: Director and musical maestro Michael Giacchino with Ted the Man-Thing from *Werewolf by Night* (2022). Ted was a combination of actor Carey Jones in the KNB EFX-created suit, and a CGI version based on KNB's final design.

Above: Stunt actor Luis Valladares doubled for Gael García Bernal on *Werewolf by Night* (2022).

Opposite: Graham Humphreys celebrates a quartet of classic howlers in this werewolf tribute art created especially for *Making Monsters*. Graham is a master of his craft and we're thrilled to be able to debut this evocative, moonlit portrait.

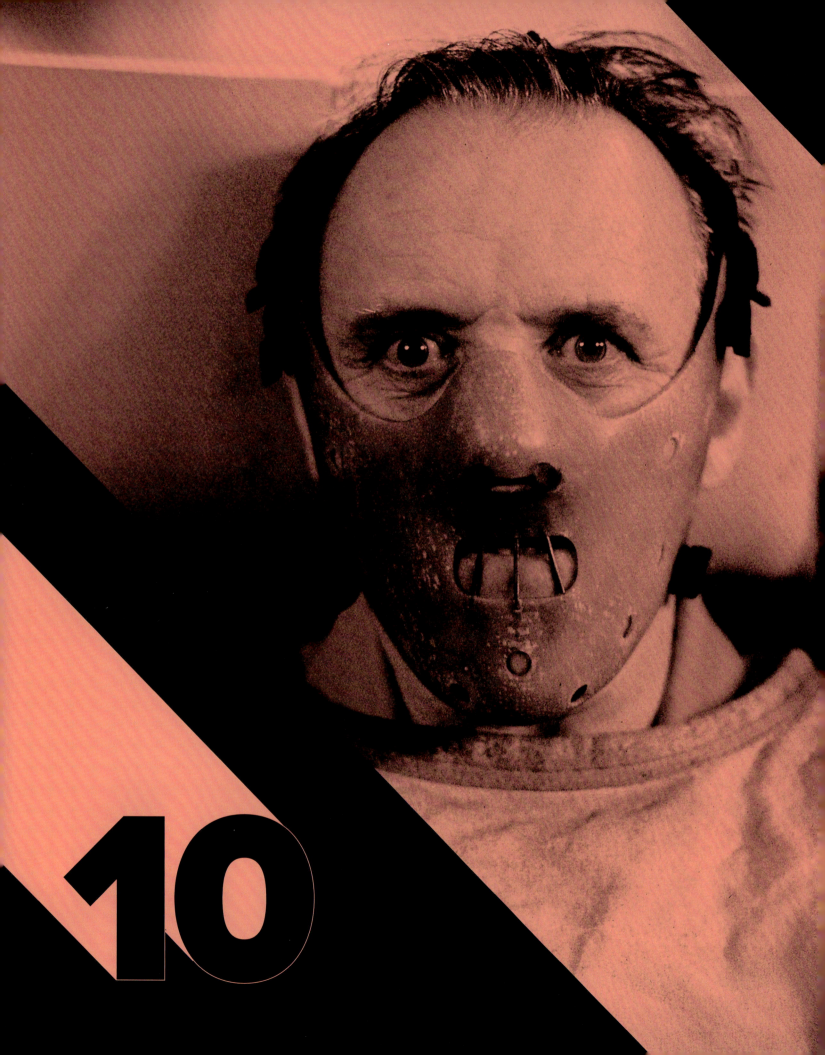

TO SCARE IS HUMAN

Though we're not in the business of pointing fingers, certainly we couldn't write a book about monsters without including the worst of the lot: you.

OK, maybe not specifically you, but humans in general. Because people are the worst, you know? People are henchmen. People are serial killers. People are Nazis.

Humans don't need to be comprised of reanimated corpse bits to be a menace, and there's no escaping us. Run for the hills if you like, but we'll be there too. Hell, look in a mirror… Boo!

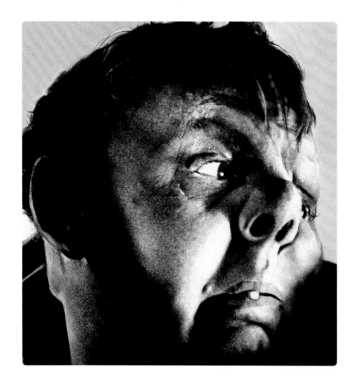

RKO brought my Uncle Perc over from Warner Bros. to create and apply Charles Laughton's Quasimodo make-up for *The Hunchback of Notre Dame* (1939). The two weren't exactly friends. The root of the problem was, Perc was ultra-clean. He wore white to work and always kept things tidy and hygienic. Laughton meanwhile... Let's just say he wasn't the most wonderful-smelling person in the world.

At the end of every long, hot, sweaty day, Laughton got down on his hands and knees so Perc could unbuckle his hunchback suit and pull him out. It was the most challenging part of Perc's day, and by the end of the shoot, he'd had enough. While Laughton was still down on all fours, Perc poured a bottle of seltzer water over him and kicked him in the butt. He yelled, "Take a shower, you son of a bitch."

Perc got away with it because he didn't work at RKO. He just went back to Warners. Obviously he and Laughton never talked after that. Perc loved telling that story!

Michael Westmore

I've always been fascinated by people who make a living out of being ugly. When I watch Three Stooges movies, I feel great sympathy for the weird-looking fat lady they make fun of. I imagine her going home after being cast and saying, "Honey, I got the part!"

Her husband asks who she's playing, and she tells him, "I'm the scary fat lady the Three Scrooges run away from."

Rondo Hatton has one of the most intriguing Hollywood stories of all time, because he wasn't just ugly – he looked like a monster. Here's a guy with a horrible, disfiguring disease [acromegaly] who heads out to Hollywood for the heat, only to get discovered like a starlet.

Universal was having some kind of contract dispute with Karloff, I think, when they spotted Hatton. I guess they thought, "This guy could be a monster without sitting in a make-up chair for six hours a day."

He was so ugly, they realized they could save money by putting him in movies. Films like *House of Horrors* (1946), where he played The Creeper. Let's just say, it was a very different time.

Larry Karaszewski

The shark in *Jaws* (1975) scares the hell out of me because it's mindlessly indiscriminate. Its next victim might just as easily be a guy in a rowboat as a little boy on a raft. All are equal in the eyes of the shark and that's horrifying.

That said, the shark's only doing his job. Terrifying and toothsome and obviously very dangerous, but that's as nature intended.

Really the scariest thing in *Jaws* is Mayor Vaughn (Murray Hamilton). There's a guy with a conscience, a man with friends, family and love in his life, yet keeping the beaches open is the best decision he can manage. And boy, does he stand by that decision. He's so oblivious and uncaring, it's chilling.

Gerry Quist

Preceding Spread: Anthony Hopkins in his Oscar-winning role as Hannibal Lecter from *The Silence of the Lambs* (1991).
Above: Charles Laughton as Quasimodo (left) and make-up maestro Percy Westmore (right) had the hump with one another during production on *The Hunchback of Notre Dame* (1939).
Opposite: No make-up required for Rondo Hatton, Hollywood's instant monster man.

When Cubby Broccoli first interviewed me for the role of Jaws, I told him I wanted to give the character some human characteristics, things like perseverance and frustration that everyone could identify with. No matter what, we all have to carry on, and Jaws became a role model for that. Like Wile E. Coyote in the *Road Runner* cartoons, Jaws would just straighten his tie, brush off his clothes, and keep going.

Roger Moore was very kind to me, and very supportive. His heart's much bigger than his ego. When I stole scenes he didn't complain; a real team player kind of guy, and best of all, he doesn't take it too seriously. I've worked with a lot of movie stars who are real jerks. They wouldn't let you steal scenes and become an icon like I did with Jaws.

Cubby let Jaws survive *The Spy Who Loved Me* (1977), as he suspected the character was going to be a hit. That suited me! After the movie came out, I remember the director's grandson, who was a big Jaws fan, asked why he had to be a bad guy. That's why, in *Moonraker (1979)*, they turned me into a good guy.

Jaws switching sides was a little controversial, but really it was only the die-hard Bond fans who took it so seriously. The proof of the pudding, as they say, was that *Moonraker* was the highest-grossing Bond film for many, many years after that. It appealed to young children and old people, as well as the normal 18–30 year-old audience. It was a huge success.

Richard Kiel

We'd just filmed Toht's head melting, Belloq's head exploding and Dietrich's head imploding for *Raiders of the Lost Ark* (1981). We sat with George [Lucas], watching the dailies, and they were brutal! Steven [Spielberg] was worried about the ratings so he asked us to tone it down a bit. We shot some fire elements and sandwiched the deaths between them.

When the movie went to be rated, we were all so paranoid, but we needn't have worried. There was a scene at the beginning they made us trim, a grisly shot of Satipo impaled on those spikes, but the bad guys getting it at the end? They loved it!

You can do anything to a Nazi.

Richard Edlund

 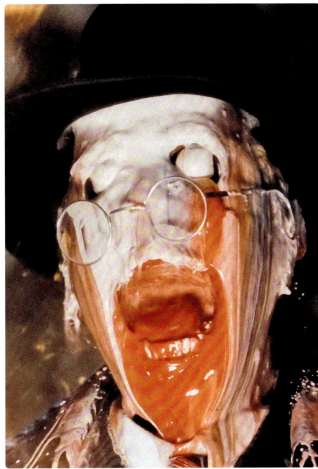

Originally, at the end of *Raiders of the Lost Ark* (1981), they were going to make three plaster heads and just blow them up. Richard Edlund stopped me in the hall one day and asked if I could think of anything more interesting to do with them.

"I know I'll have to blow up one for Steven," he said, "but then we can do other stuff. Any ideas?"

I'd always wanted to do a melting person, so I suggested that, and a shrivelling one, and Dennis [Muren] gave me the thumbs up. I didn't have access to the actors, but I'd gotten moulds I could use from the English make-up artist, Tom Smith. For the melting head I used gelatine, which I'd worked with a fair bit before, and felt comfortable with. We did a rough test with different layers of gelatine, and that convinced everyone it could work. The mix I used was extremely delicate, though, and once it was cast it only had a lifespan of four or five hours before it started deteriorating. Normal gelatine would have been too gloopy, though. With my special mix, we got that nice, even flow.

On the day of the shoot, I got started around 1am, laying everything in the mould and getting the head ready. Unfortunately, that day, *Life* magazine was visiting ILM and Richard wanted to give them a bit more of a show, so we had to wait until they arrived. Plus the electronics guys still had to come down and set up the motion control rig. By the time we finally shot the scene, the head was only, like, 20 minutes away from falling apart, and if we'd waited any longer, I'd have had to start again from scratch.

But we got it first take! One take was all it took. We had two big propane heaters on either side, and I was underneath with a heat gun, keeping it all nice and even, with hot gelatine dripping all over me. It was messy, but fun!

Chris Walas

"I'D ALWAYS WANTED TO DO A MELTING PERSON."

Opposite (top): Richard Kiel gets to grips with Roger Moore on the set of *The Spy Who Loved Me* (1977).

Opposite (bottom): Richard Kiel treats a surprised Marshall Julius to his signature move.

Above (left and right): Toht gets what he deserves at the hands of a vengeful God – and a resourceful Chris Walas – in *Raiders of the Lost Ark* (1981).

For the scene where Jordy Verrill (Stephen King) blows his head off in *Creepshow* (1982), Darryl [Ferrucci] was in the suit, lying flat through the set. We put electric matches in the shotgun, and I set off blood squibs as I yanked off the top of his head. It was a great effect! But every time we did it, the suit caught on fire. Barbara Anderson was always ready with a fire extinguisher to put it out, so no real harm done, but at the time, Darryl had no idea that he was continually bursting into flames.

Tom Savini

The best exploding head scene in a movie, at least for my money, is the one we shot for *Scanners* (1981) where Michael Ironside uses his powers on Louis Del Grande. We tried three different heads. The first was made of plaster, but it just looked like a plaster head exploding. The second was made of wax, but again, it just looked like a wax head exploding. Finally we made a gelatine head and filled it with all sorts of gross stuff: burger meat, rabbit livers, syrup and even dog food.

Later, when we tried to blow it up, first we used pyrotechnics, but sparks flew everywhere, so it was more like a *Star Wars* (1977) spaceship exploding. Then we used air pressure, which just made the head blow up like this crazy balloon. Finally Gary Zeller, the special effects guy, told everyone to get out of the way, pulled a double-barrelled shotgun, pointed it at the back of the head and just blew the shit out of it. And that's what you see in the movie!

Stephan Dupuis

Robert Bloch wrote a sequel to his novel *Psycho* (1959). It was published in 1982, but there was no way Universal were going to turn that into a movie. They hated it! Bloch's book really stuck the knife into gory Hollywood horror. Plus he killed off Norman Bates in the first 30 pages.

The studio didn't want our sequel to be anything like the book and wouldn't even let me read it before writing the screenplay for *Psycho II* (1983). They were that paranoid about Bloch suing them. In fact, I wasn't even allowed to talk to him.

Much to everyone's shock and amazement, including me and the director, Richard Franklin, the movie was an enormous success. I did a symposium at the Writers Guild, and Bloch was there. So finally we met.

He criticized me for the film's gratuitous violence, and he was right, of course. But there was no avoiding that, as we'd felt commercially committed to a certain level of gore. But fair's fair, Bloch had Norman strangling a nun with a rosary, so his novel wasn't all flowers and sunshine either.

Tom Holland

We had to film a head exploding for *MaXXXine* (2024). That one gag, more than anything else in the movie, is what kept me up at night. To me, there have only been two truly great head explosions: the best of all was in *Scanners* (1981), and the runner-up was in *Maniac* (1980). There have been thousands of others, but nothing else has come close.

There's just something about the organic nature of that effect in *Scanners*, and that's probably down to them blowing apart the head with a shotgun. Same as they did with the head in *Maniac*. You just can't beat old-school solutions! So I suggested we clear the set and do it the same way, but everyone was like, "You're out of your mind."

In the end, we created a pressurized head with lines we could pull, so when it exploded it splayed out exactly how I wanted. It took three attempts, though, and in the end, only by comping all three together did we finally make it work. And all the time I'm thinking, "A shotgun would have solved this problem."

Ti West

Above: Jordy Verrill's bitter end, from artist Bernie Wrightson and colorist Michelle Wrightson, in the gloriously graphic *Creepshow* (1982) comicbook adaptation.

Opposite (top and bottom): New-fangled effects are all well and good, but nothing beats a shotgun when a head needs exploding, as can clearly be seen in these shots from *Scanners* (1981).

Scott Alexander and I were stuck writing these studio comedies and not terribly happy about it, so we wrote *Ed Wood* (1994). It was the film that changed our lives. We thought it was going to be this little independent thing, but when Tim Burton decided he wanted to make it, and on a larger scale than we'd ever imagined, it was a dream come true.

After Martin Landau was cast as Bela Lugosi, Rick Baker and his team designed and applied what eventually became an Oscar-winning make-up. On the day of the camera test, though, no matter what angles they shot him from, or however much make-up they added, Martin just didn't look as tired and haggard as Bela did in his final days.

Everyone's looking at old pictures of Bela, when Stefan Czapsky, the DP, walks over to the monitor and turns off the colour. Just to see how their shots compared with those original photos, and suddenly – BAM! – Martin Landau became Bela Lugosi. It was just one of those magical moments and I'm getting chills just thinking of it now.

Tim realized he'd never seen a colour photo of Bela Lugosi. That he, Ed Wood and the others were black-and-white people in a black-and-white world, and from that moment on, Tim couldn't imagine shooting the movie in colour. It had to be black and white.

Larry Karaszewski

It was so hard, and really against my nature, doing deliberately shitty make-ups on *Ed Wood* (1994). But shitty make-ups are what Tor Johnson had in those crazy old movies, so I ignored my instincts and applied these big, ugly rubber scars. The worse George Steele looked as Tor, the happier Tim [Burton] was. It was an unsettling job, but I'll admit, kinda fun too.

Ve Neill

Right: *Ed Wood* (1994) screenwriting duo Larry Karaszewski (left) and Scott Alexander (right), all dressed up with Jeffrey Jones as The Amazing Criswell and Martin Landau, who won an Oscar for his role as Bela Lugosi.

Below: Alongside Rick Baker and Yolanda Toussieng, Ve Neill won the Best Make-Up Oscar for *Ed Wood* (1994). Here she is, flanked by longtime collaborator Johnny Depp and a fangful Martin Landau.

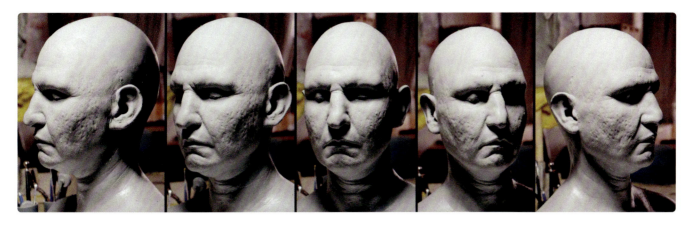

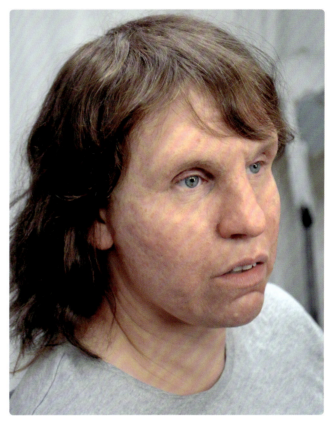

I'm surprised how many directors don't understand the limitations of what we do. They think we can turn anyone into anything, and of course we always do our best, but give me a cool face I can do something interesting with, and it'll always come out better.

Eva Melander has such a sweet face, it wasn't easy transforming her into a troll for *Border* (2018). Another actress had previously been considered, and looked far more like she'd suit the role, but I didn't get a say in casting.

The director, Ali Abbasi, suggested a neanderthal look, which was fine as a kicking-off point, but I felt we needed to tone that look way down. I wanted to create something unusual that was still realistic enough that Eva could walk down the street without people turning around.

Usually when I'm making a monster, like a lot of sculptors, I judge my work by seeking a payoff. Some feeling of satisfaction whenever I create an interesting shape or angle. For *Border*, though, I tried doing the opposite. Every time I got too attached to a wrinkle or got a kick out of something, I threw it out. It had to look real, and not excite me, so the feeling I was chasing was feeling nothing. Which felt like a really weird way to do things.

Ultimately what I did was, well... I've always thought Eddie Marsan looks a bit like a fairy tale person, with pointy ears and sleepy eyes. Everything's just a little bit wonky on him, but in a great way, like you could put him in *Legend* (1985) and he'd fit right in. So I used him as a reference for Eva's new face, but with a wider nose and her co-star Eero Milonoff's chin. He already had a bit more of a neanderthal look, so it was a lot easier turning him into a troll.

Göran Lundström

Top: Göran Lundström's sculpt for Eva Melander's prosthetic make-up as Tina the troll from *Border* (2018).
Above (left): Göran Lundström puts the finishing touches on his Tina sculpture for *Border* (2018).
Above (right): Eva Melander as Tina in her final make-up applied by Göran Lundström and Pamela Goldammer for *Border* (2018).

Creating and designing the Crawlers for *The Descent* (2005) came, in part, as a reaction to how difficult it was to shoot the werewolves in *Dog Soldiers* (2002), and how awkward it was for the people inside the suits. I wanted to strip these creatures back to the bare bones of what they could be, and once I figured out that they were just differently evolved humans, it was simply a case of figuring out what they'd look like having evolved underground.

People often say the Crawlers remind them of Gollum, but the starting point for me was the head of the Master (Reggie Nalder) from *Salem's Lot* (1979), and the body of Iggy Pop.

How the Crawlers moved, and how we shot them, was most important. I wanted them to imitate spiders in the sense that spiders hold very still for ages, and then suddenly they'll scuttle away. So we practised fast, jerky movements. Then we filmed them at 18 frames-per-second, with a 45- or 90-degree shutter that gave them a kind of staccato look, moving ever so slightly faster than they should. Little tricks like that can be the making of a monster.

What's most interesting about *The Descent* is, if you consider it from the creatures' point-of-view, it's a home invasion movie. They're perfectly happy, living underground with their family and kids, occasionally going up to grab a deer for their dinner. They're just doing what people do when, suddenly, this bunch of girls burst into their world and start killing them. Really they're just defending their territory. I actually have a lot of sympathy for them.

Neil Marshall

I saw Anthony Hopkins at the Oscars, the year he won for *The Silence of the Lambs* (1991). I said, "Mr Hopkins, I just want to say you scared the heck out of me as Hannibal Lecter."

He went, "Really?"

Then he came in close and made that hissing, lip-smacking noise in my ear. I almost wet my pants! He's such a cool guy.

Ve Neill

I love the idea of a ghost who seems terrifying but is actually on your side. The scary thing in *The Devil's Backbone* (2001) is not the little boy with the floating blood and the skin like cracked porcelain. It's the good-looking guy who's a threatening piece of shit.

Axelle Carolyn

"LITTLE TRICKS LIKE THAT CAN BE THE MAKING OF A MONSTER."

Below: From the darkest corners of director Neil Marshall's imagination came the underground-dwelling Crawlers from *The Descent* (2005).

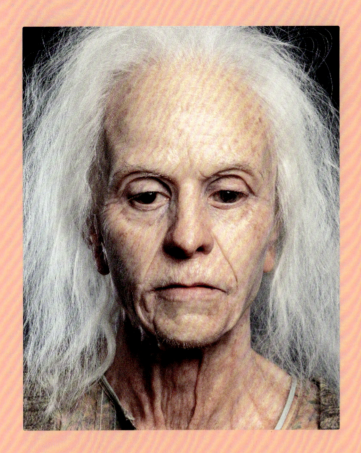

"FIRST IT WAS TOO MONSTERY, THEN IT WASN'T MONSTERY ENOUGH."

I hadn't made a movie in a while. I wondered why I wanted to put myself through two years of trauma again.

What I love most about movies is the craft of filmmaking. Not only the writing and directing, but also the acting, the costume design, the music, and the special effects make-up. All those things. Everything. So I decided I wanted to make a film that was very craft forward, with a crew who'd all shine in their own departments.

Next, I asked myself what I originally liked about horror movies. As a kid, what really appealed to me was the stuff I wasn't supposed to see: violent, salacious exploitation films. My goal, then, was to come up with a low-brow idea, but approach it like high-brow craft. That's the challenge that got me up every morning, and eventually led me to *X* (2022).

Pearl and Howard were essentially my monsters, so I thought it would be interesting to have whoever played the young wannabe star, Maxine, to also play Pearl. That was a challenge from a performance standpoint, a make-up standpoint and a directing standpoint. If I could pull that off, and people didn't realize it was the same actress, that seemed like the sort of achievement that, if I were watching the movie, I'd be excited and inspired by.

I thought it might be a bit of a struggle, finding the perfect actor to play the two roles. So we lined up a ton of meetings, but, actually, Mia [Goth] was the second person I met. So I told A24, "We're good. I've found her."

When we first met, she thought we were just talking about her playing Maxine. She didn't know it would be double duty as I hadn't told anyone I was considering that. Finally, when I told her that, ideally, I'd like her to play Pearl too, she froze. I could see the wheels turning. Then she was like, "I could crush that."

I believed her! She said, "I don't care what it takes. If it's six hours in the chair, I'm fully down to do this."

A technical challenge like that can kick an actor's ass, but Mia couldn't wait to get started. She was exactly who I'd been looking for: a partner in crime for the movie.

For the make-ups, I worked closely with Jason Docherty at Weta to design age make-ups for Mia as Pearl and Stephen Ure as Howard. The trickiest part was to find the perfect line between realistic and creepy. It took a lot of R&D. First it was too monstery, then it wasn't monstery enough. We just kept incrementally moving the designs forward until we nailed it.

I remember the first time I saw Mia in the full make-up. Sarah Rubano and Kevin Wasner applied it, and it had been so meticulously designed, that it looked great and fitted perfectly. You never know what you're going to get till you make it through that first test, but it was an amazing transformation. Mia was unrecognizable.

I was like, "This is going to work."

My main worry, when we started the process, was that Mia might not be able to properly enunciate through the make-up, or that it might prevent her from gesturing in a way that you could follow her emotions. But the appliances were super-thin. I think just 2mm. So you could always hear her clearly, and see every expression on her face.

I felt for her. For Sarah and Kevin too. I don't know when they ever went home. But Mia was true to her word. She was up for everything. And she crushed it!

Ti West

Above: Hidden beneath Weta Workshop's incredible old age prosthetic make-up – applied by Sarah Rubano and Kevin Wasner – Mia Goth embraced the challenge of both physically and mentally inhabiting the character of elderly psychotic Pearl in Ti West's craft-forward horror hit *X* (2022).

Eryn: For the first season of *Feud* (2017–24), *Bette and Joan* (2017), Ryan Murphy wanted to feature Joan Crawford's *Trog* (1970), a low-budget British film about a scientist who bonds with a caveman. Vincent Van Dyke created the prosthetics, and while out with the Van Dykes for drinks one Saturday, Mike joked he should play Trog. He's a hairy guy. He has the body shape. I thought he'd be great and Ryan did too, so by Monday he had the gig!

Mike: Then the script arrived and there was dialogue!

Eryn: Yeah, we were just expecting a bit of roaring.

Mike: It wasn't just that there were lines – I had to deliver them in a Cockney accent. Fortunately, my friend Mat Fraser, who's English and played Paul the Illustrated Seal on *American Horror Story: Freak Show* (S04, 2014–15), recorded a tape of the dialogue for me to memorize.

So I'm in the trailer, getting my make-up done, when in walks Jessica Lange. And I can't help myself. I stop her and say, "Correct me if I'm wrong, Jessica, but aren't I the second ape you've worked with?"

Eryn: She was like, "Oh, Mike!"

Eryn Krueger Mekash and Mike Mekash

Above (left): Silvi Knight prepares make-up artist Mike Mekash for his close-up as Trog in *Feud: Bette and Joan* (2017).
Above (right): Mike Mekash in all his shaggy, primal glory as Trog in *Feud: Bette and Joan* (2017).
Opposite (top left): For her final feature, *Trog* (1970), Joan Crawford shared the screen with an actor (Joe Cornelius) wearing a leftover mechanical ape head from *2001: A Space Odyssey* (1968).
Opposite (top right): Jessica Lange and Mike Mekash stand in for the original stars of *Trog* (1970) in this pitch perfect recreation from *Feud: Bette and Joan* (2017).
Opposite (bottom): Trog (Joe Cornelius) grabs a handful in this dynamic lobby card from his eponymous movie.

"CORRECT ME IF I'M WRONG, JESSICA, BUT AREN'T I THE SECOND APE YOU'VE WORKED WITH?"

DO THE RIGHT THING

Though the jury's out about intelligent life on this planet, certainly we're convinced that out there in the infinite cosmos, minds immeasurably superior to ours are slowly and surely drawing their plans against us. It's just common sense.

Have you not seen all the movies? All the shows? Either they kill, conquer or impregnate us, or hunt us for food and sport. Even friendly ones like E.T. look diseased and infectious. In short, beware the alarming aliens ahead.

Doctor Who (1963–89) was such a huge staple on British television. When you look at those early episodes now, of course, the monsters are incredibly makeshift and hilarious, but my God, they scared us when we were kids.

Davros was obviously terrifying, as were the Sea Devils and the Daleks, and when that guy turned into a big insect in 'The Ark in Space' (S12, E5–8, 1975)… I haven't seen it for 45 years, but I remember it so clearly. I was horrified!

In some bizarre way, though, the lo-fi, thrown-together nature of those monsters made them scarier. Maybe because our imaginations had to do a lot of the work, back before it was all done for you in a very realistic way. You had to engage a little more, and that engagement saw you being more active as a viewer. Not to decry CG, which is an incredible tool that's enabled us to do so much, but there's something to be said for artificiality.

Simon Pegg

As soon as we started Doctor Who (2005–present), the first monsters I wanted to bring back were the Daleks. My absolute favourites! There was a lot of wild concept art floating around, lots of modern, exciting shapes, but I was very strict about not changing the design at all.

I brought in my toy Daleks and literally sat there going, "Every element of this has got to stay the same. We can improve the colours and the texture, burnish it and make surface additions, but the design has endured for decades. It's a work of genius and not to be sniffed at."

People thought I was mad. They said traditional Daleks wouldn't work in the modern world, and I admit, I had doubts. How much of my

"IT WAS THE MOST RIGHT I'VE EVER BEEN IN MY ENTIRE CAREER."

opinion was I basing on my terror of the Daleks as a three-year-old? How would a new audience react to them? I don't think anyone else thought they'd work, but I absolutely stuck to my guns, and it was the most right I've ever been in my entire career.

As soon as the Daleks were back on the telly, my lovely old clumsy Daleks, lo and behold, they were the number one toy that Christmas. It was the greatest triumph of my entire professional life and I'm still happy about it!

Though I've focused more over the years on refreshing the old monsters, I invented the Ood and think they're delightful! Very calm, but also horrifying, and I love that contrast.

They were the by-product of a bigger story, an episode of Doctor Who (2005–present) called The Satan Pit (S02, E09, 2006). We needed some monsters, a slave race, and the Ood were born. That episode cost a fortune, so we only had enough room in the budget to create and replicate one Ood mask. That sameness, and their servitude, got into my head, and inspired stories of their own. I'm very proud of them.

Russell T. Davies

I love honouring the Seventies stuff on Doctor Who (2005–present), and I'm a big believer in if it ain't broke, don't fix it. I'm all for improving designs, tidying them up and making them more actor-friendly, but I'll always fight change just for the sake of change.

Why update the Sontarans? Their helmet-shaped potato heads are brilliant! I was utterly fascinated by them when I was six, so why deviate now? Yes, I polished the look and made it more flexible, but why mess with something so freaky, weird and brilliant?

Neill Gorton

Preceding Spread: As a lifelong fan of Doctor Who (1963-1989 & 2005-present), Neill Gorton didn't want to reinvent the wheel with his designs for the modern incarnation of the show. As you can see in his updated Cybermen, and really all the legacy monsters he's helped usher back, they're very much like they always were, only with nods to the present that make them perfectly contemporary too.

Left: "Long before I worked on Doctor Who (2005-Present)," said Russell T. Davies, "I had my own Dalek built for my house!"

Right: Of his many creations for Doctor Who (2005-Present), showrunner Russell T. Davies is especially proud of his "delightful" Ood.

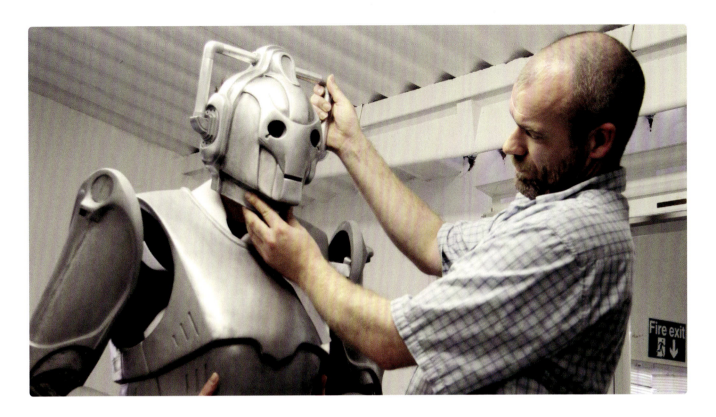

I often look at monster design from a child's point-of-view. If it's something they want to draw, you've cracked it. Pick anything from *Doctor Who* (2005–present). Say, the Cybermen. They have handles for ears and that's mad! There's no logic to them, but they're fun to draw. And when you've got them drawing, you're in their heads, and you've won. Hopefully then, in 30 years' time, they'll be doing our jobs!

Russell T. Davies

I enjoy working with Russell T. Davies on *Doctor Who* (2005–present), as it's a true collaboration. Often he's happy for me to just go off and do stuff. Other times he has more specific ideas, because he's actually a brilliant illustrator himself, but even then, he never foists them on me. It makes all the difference in the world when your boss respects your opinion and your craft. Honestly, if I had to choose only one person to work with for the rest of my career, it would be Russell. He's the perfect exec producer.

Neill Gorton

What you realize with Neill Gorton, is how lucky you are to be working with someone with such a vast breadth of experience. Though there's never enough money, and never enough time, no matter what last-minute thing comes up, he's always ready for it.

Gugu Mbatha-Raw plays a homo-amphibian in *The War Between the Land and the Sea* (2025), a *Doctor Who* (2005–present) spin-off series featuring Neill's gorgeously re-designed Sea Devils. Gugu's a human/Sea Devil hybrid and every inch of her is in prosthetics. After our first day of shooting, yes, she looked wonderful, but still I asked Neill if he could add a little definition to the bottom of her eyes, and move the scales down onto her cheeks.

There was a mild panic, a general sense of, "You can't do that. She's already been on camera."

I told them, "You can do that. You can actually change things as you go along. She's in a different lighting set-up on every angle. You do it with humans. Go less heavy on the make-up. More heavy on the make-up. Pull the hair back. So you can do it with human/Sea Devil hybrids."

The one person who was completely calm during that conversation was Neill. He said, "Of course we can do that. I'll do it tomorrow."

Then there he was, at 5am the next morning, altering the eye make-up, shifting the scales, and it looked wonderful. We were done! We've worked together for more than 20 years now, and become proper mates. I absolutely adore him.

Russell T. Davies

Opposite: The many faces of *Doctor Who* (2005–present) showrunner Russell T. Davies, and friends (clockwise, from top left): the Slitheen, the Goblin King, a Wrarth Warrior and Jimbo.

Above: Make-up Master and Creator of Cool things Neill Gorton gives a *Doctor Who* (2005–present) Cyberman his final fitting.

George [Lucas] asked John Berg and I to do the chess set for *Star Wars* (1977). He said, "Make as many stop motion space aliens as you can in two weeks."

Dennis [Muren] and Ken [Ralston] helped us set it up. We asked George what he wanted. He was like a kid playing with toys! Making it up on the spot, he told us, "Get this blue guy to walk in, then the yellow guy hops up, then have the green guy pick him up and throw him to the ground."

We shot it in a couple of days. ILM had their wrap party while we were doing it.

For *The Empire Strikes Back* (1980), George asked me to design the Tauntaun. I was never that invested in my own designs as I saw myself as more of a craftsman than an artist. But in the script the Tauntaun was described as a snow lizard, and I reckoned I could do better than that. George was always open to suggestions and changing stuff, with his one caveat being, "Do it, as long as it doesn't take you longer."

I was totally on George's wavelength in terms of wanting to do things as quickly and cheaply as possible, and he pretty much left me alone to get on with it.

There was a line in the script for *Return of the Jedi* (1983) that read, "There's a big monster party going on in Jabba's palace."

George said it should be, "Like the cantina scene, only bigger."

I collected a half dozen local sculptors and once a week we'd show George three or four new maquettes. He always responded better to those than drawings. As a rule, filmmakers respond to sketches by suggesting endless combinations and variations. But a maquette that they can pick up, move into the light and consider what angles they'd shoot it from, they're much more likely to approve.

As he studied each maquette, George would decide if they were background or featured creatures. For instance, I showed him this bust one day and he asked, "What's this?"

I said, "That's a calamari man."

Then George says, "That's going to be Admiral Ackbar. And this little blue guy is going to play the organ."

George made most of his decisions like that. I'm still appalled at some of the stuff in *Jedi*, though. I did some things I thought were really questionable, but everyone had different ideas about what's good or bad, and oddball stuff I suggested for deep in the background ended up getting pulled up front.

I also wish I hadn't shown George what Dave Carson came up with for the Gamorrean Guards, but of course I had to show him everything. I just thought it looked too much like something from a Disney movie, and could have been a lot better.

Working on *Star Wars*, though, man, we were in Pig Heaven! Having a boss who was just a few years older than us, who'd grown up on all the same movies and loved all the same cool stuff as us, it was a miracle. Just the perfect recipe and we lucked out.

Phil Tippett

Post-*Star Wars* (1977), everybody wanted a cantina sequence. No matter what sort of film or show it was – *Little House on the Prairie* (1974–83) or anything else – everyone was like, "We need that. We need those aliens."

Chris Walas

Above (left): Phil Tippett and John Berg sit down to a game of Dejarik – created in record time for *Star Wars* (1977) and better known as holochess – though of course they'll have to let the wookiee win.

Above (right): George Lucas practises his moves with a selection of stop motion holochess aliens created by Phil Tippett and John Berg for *Star Wars* (1977).

Top (left): Phil Tippett fine-tunes his Admiral Ackbar sculpture for *Return of the Jedi* (1983).

Top (right): Phil Tippett helps Admiral Ackbar run his lines on the set of *Return of the Jedi* (1983). "It's a trap!"

Above: Flanked by a shoal of Mon Calamari, Kirk Thatcher's first job was at ILM on *Return of the Jedi* (1983), and surely you'd be just as happy?

Far left: A trio of crazy critters created for *Return of the Jedi* (1983), in sticker form.

Left: Obi-Wan and Luke are surrounded by scum and villainy in Marvel's fanciful take on the cantina scuffle from *Star Wars* (1977).

The first movie I ever worked on was *Return of the Jedi* (1983). It was part luck and part preparation. The preparation was I'd been making monsters and movies and plaster moulds and painting latex since I could afford an airbrush at around 14. The luck was, when I was 15, I met Joe Johnston.

It was 1977, the Summer of *Star Wars*, and it turned out ILM was just a mile-and-a-half from where I lived in Van Nuys [LA]. I met Joe, he gave me a tour and I told him I wanted to work there. A year later they moved to Marin County [San Francisco]. I was like, "Nooooooo! There goes my Summer dream job!"

But Joe was very kind, and we stayed in touch. When I graduated high school in 1980, I went on a road trip with my brother and his friends, and got a tour of the new ILM. I brought a creature I'd made for one of my high school movies, a fat gobliny thing with glass eyes, and I gave it to the guys as a present and portfolio piece. They kept it in the Rubber Room, as they called it, where all the creatures were made.

I started UCLA and wanted to be a film major, but it would have been two years before I could even touch a camera there. Before that it was all theory. So when it was announced they were making a new *Star Wars* film, around January '81, I called Joe and told him I'd do anything for a job there: make coffee, run the Xerox machine, sweep the floors...

He asked, "Who did you talk to?"

I'm like, "What?"

He said, "I just gave them your name. They're looking for people to come work at the creature shop, and I know that's what you want to do."

I interviewed, and it turned out I had the perfect set of job skills: I knew how to run urethane and latex. I knew how to mix rubber cement paint and how to make plaster moulds. Not great ones, but they held up. Plus, I was happy to work for $80 a day. I was 19 when I moved to Marin County and got started on *Jedi*. I did everything from build shelves to mould, cast and paint most of the creatures in the movie.

The Gamorrean Guards were one of Dave Carson's coolest designs. They were these brutish, gorilla-sized, pig-faced green beasts, really textured and detailed, like I'd always pictured orcs. The original maquette was just a bust, but it was gnarly. When Dave sculpted the finished suit, though, he used water-based clay that was faster to pull out of a mould, but smoother and not as textured or cool. I asked him why he'd done it that way, and he said, sort of defensively, "I don't want it to be too hard for you guys to mould."

He also said it needed to be simpler as it was going to be a toy, but man, I felt it was a cop out. Still a cool design, but not as amazing as he'd originally envisaged.

Later, in Yuma, Kit West, the physical effects guy, had built this crazy, vibrating Chevy engine-powered Sarlacc tentacle. I didn't really understand it. Kit was a guy who liked to build things and blow things up. He'd spent a lot of time and money on this bizarre thing, and was really proud of it.

George [Lucas], though, wasn't the least bit convinced. He's like, "We're just going to do the old reverse technique where we take a rubber tentacle, wrap it around the leg, and let it unravel."

That worked great! Reverse shots always do. So simple. But I felt bad for Kit.

Maybe the coolest thing I got to do on the movie, and certainly the most physically demanding, was play the Rancor for two days. Rather than do it as a stop motion puppet, George had the idea to put a guy in a suit. We were all, like, "What?!"

And George said, "Come on – show those Toho guys how to do it!"

Tony McVey sculpted a Rancor suit that we built over a backpack. You'd have a 12lb TV strapped to your chest as without it you'd be blind, but it made you very front heavy, so soon as you got in, you'd fall over. Your right hand worked the head and the jaw and your left hand worked the left arm. It was very ungainly and difficult to manoeuvre in.

Phil [Tippett] and I took turns wearing the suit. We built a cave set and shot the test film at high speed. Tony sculpted a two-foot tall Gamorrean Guard that I moulded and cast out of gelatine, so it could be torn apart. We spent a couple of months trying to do it, we shot a number of tests, but it always looked like exactly what it was: a guy in a rubber suit. Eventually, George acquiesced and let Phil do it his way. Though we all expected him to take the go motion route, he actually ended up doing the Rancor as a hand and rod puppet. People are often shocked to discover the Rancor was the size of Kermit the Frog, and basically the same technology, but shot at high speed.

That's how I got my start. I learned more on *Return of the Jedi* than I would have in four years at UCLA. And I never looked back.

Kirk Thatcher

"GEORGE SAID, 'COME ON – SHOW THOSE TOHO GUYS HOW TO DO IT!'"

Opposite (left): Ably hoisted by Phil Tippett, Kirk Thatcher gives his Rancor legs a spin for *Return of the Jedi* (1983).

Opposite (above right): Kirk Thatcher in a mockup Rancor costume for *Return of the Jedi* (1983).

Opposite (below right): A panel from Marvel's *Return of the Jedi* (1983) adaptation featuring the terrifying Rancor.

Left: Dennis Muren (left) lines up a shot on the Rancor suit worn by Kirk Thatcher for *Return of the Jedi* (1983).

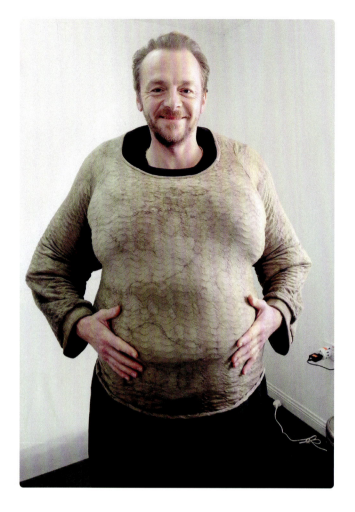

J. J. [Abrams] took me out to dinner and said, "I want you to play Unkar Plutt in *The Force Awakens* (2015). He's a Blobfish!"

I was like, "OK."

I remembered as a kid, in those *Star Wars* (1977) making-ofs, watching the actors boiling in their alien suits, getting cold air blown down their snouts. Then there I was in Abu Dhabi, 50-degree heat, wearing a big, fat, silicone suit. It was so much fun!

I was like, "This is what it was like in Tunisia. This is how it's supposed to be."

It felt to me like the *Star Wars* I'd grown up with. Even when I wasn't working, I used to walk around the creature shop and visit the set. It was all so magical.

Simon Pegg

As much as *The Thing From Another World* (1951) scared me, the thought of making my own version scared me even more. Nothing wrong with being scared though, so fuck it: I made *The Thing* (1982).

I loved Rob Bottin. He was nuts. He had a great team of artists, always drawing monsters, making monsters, and figuring out how to make them work. All that rubber! That head sprouting legs was something else.

Everything had to be perfect with Rob, so you could never rush him. Of course, we went way over budget. I'd just pace around, waiting for him to be done, giving him the stink eye. But he was a good kid.

In his book *Danse Macabre* (1981), Stephen King wrote that if you have a great monster, you should show it. It inspired me to show as much of the Thing as I could get away with. It was a big-time tightrope, figuring out how much to reveal, and how much to hide in the shadows, but I had the best cameraman I've ever worked with, Dean Cundey, and he did an amazing job.

When the movie first came out, it was hated. The director of the original, Christian Nyby, acted like I'd raped the Madonna. He really piled on the scorn. The open ending also seemed to really upset people. At a research screening, this teenage girl asked me, "In the end, who was the Thing?"

I told her, "You have to use your imagination."

She moaned, "God, I hate that."

Now that's what I call scary.

It's all in the past, though. I survived. From all my films, it's one of my favourites and I wouldn't change a thing.

John Carpenter

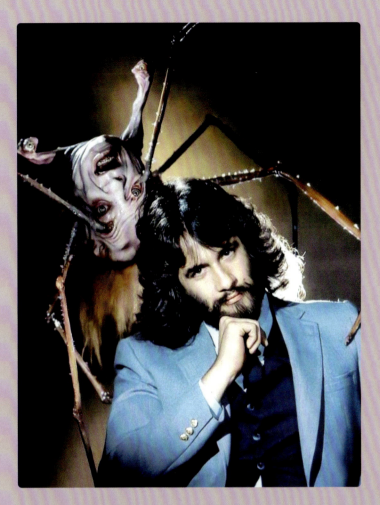

"I LOVED ROB BOTTIN. HE WAS NUTS… THAT HEAD SPROUTING LEGS WAS SOMETHING ELSE."

Preceding spread: ILM's remarkable *Return of the Jedi* (1983) Creature Crew.

Opposite (top and bottom): Simon Pegg embraced the rigours of baking in the Abu Dhabi sun as that's what you do when you play an alien in a *Star Wars* movie. Here he is, trying on his Unkar Plutt suit ahead of shooting J.J. Abrams' *The Force Awakens* (2015).

Left: Look behind you! Make-up effects wunderkind Rob Bottin strikes a pose with one of his most iconic creations, the Norris Spider Head, from John Carpenter's *The Thing* (1982).

Below: John Carpenter's favourite effects sequence in *The Thing* (1982) was the multi-stage Norris transformation.

I played a lot of sports growing up. Yeah, I was this monster kid, but also I played football, basketball and ran track. I even did some kickboxing, so physically I felt like I could do anything.

When I got out to LA, if ever anyone needed someone to get in a suit, I'd be like, "I'll do it!"

I liked the challenge. The feeling of achieving a goal. So on *Invaders from Mars* (1986), my hand shot up the second Alec [Gillis] asked, "Who wants to get in this suit?"

I played the snake brain thing with the croissant flippers. The Supreme Intelligence! There wasn't much to it. I was inside this fibreglass dome with a mechanical face, mainly operating the croissants, plus I had to move a little, just to undulate it and give it some life.

So we get to the scene where the soldiers break in and shoot the Supreme Intelligence. Tobe [Hooper] wanted me to do a reverse sit-up in the suit so it would lift up when it gets shot. They duct-taped me to a board from the waist down, I'm wearing a headset with a mic and an earpiece, and I'm looking at a monitor so I'll be able to move in time with the soldiers' shots.

As soon as Tobe yells "Action," the first move I make, the monitor falls forward and my headset flies off. So I'm in there blind and I can't hear anything but the squibs going off, and every time one does, blood's squirting all over me. But fine. I close my eyes and just try to time my movements to the sound of the squibs going off.

So I'm doing it, but God, it was taking forever. My back's starting to fatigue, I'm sweating, covered in blood and I can't see, but I keep going. And going. It felt like I was doing it for ten minutes, but I'm like, "Dude, you can't quit on this!"

Next thing I know, I feel people pulling the board that my legs are strapped to. Even then I kept trying to do my reverse sit-ups! I'm wondering what the fuck's going on when suddenly, through a little hole in the suit where I got in, a hand with a knife bursts through and starts cutting me free from the duct tape. Then I feel these arms grab me and pull me out.

It was Everett Burrell and Dave Nelson. Then Dave yells at me, "Gino, we've got to go. The set's on fire!"

I looked up and the roof's a furnace. Flaming chunks of the set's falling all around us, smoke's everywhere, and we run for our lives.

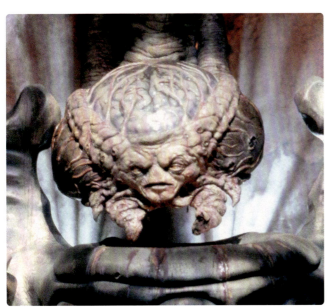

Howard: Sam Raimi took the entire cast and crew of *Evil Dead II* (1987) to see *Aliens* (1986). He bought out the entire theatre and we all watched it together, for the first time. Bob Kurtzman cried. He said it was the most beautiful film he'd ever seen.

Mike: There's a synchronicity to that because I remember hearing Bill Paxton tell a story about how James Cameron once called him to say there was a movie they both had to see. And he immediately picked him up and took him to a theatre to see *Evil Dead II*!

Howard Berger and Mike Mendez

"WE'VE GOT TO GO. THE SET'S ON FIRE!"

What happened was, the pellets the soldiers were firing ignited the polyfoam set. When the fire broke out, everyone was told to evacuate. Obviously I was still in the suit, doing my reverse sit-ups, and the reason I was covered in blood was, on top of everything else, the squibs had been loaded backwards. It was only after everyone had run out, luckily Everett and Dave remembered they'd left a man behind and rushed in to rescue me.

Of course, once we rebuilt everything, I was back in the suit doing my reverse sit-ups, but it went a little smoother, second time around. That was a crazy ass movie.

Gino Crognale

Opposite: Stan Winston's Martian Drones await their orders from the Supreme Intelligence in Tobe Hooper's *Invaders From Mars* (1986).
Top (left): Gino Crognale jumped at every chance to play a creature. Here he is as a Martian Drone in *Invaders From Mars* (1986).
Middle (left): The Supreme Intelligence in Tobe Hooper's *Invaders From Mars* (1986).
Above: Bruce Campbell was blind as a bat for his role as Evil Ash in Sam Raimi's horror classic *Evil Dead II* (1987).

John Chambers was trained as a cosmetic dental technician in the army, so his expertise was fake teeth. He was generally very open to sharing his techniques, but teeth he kept to himself. Teeth, he said, were his bread and butter. When I was his apprentice, though, he taught me how to sculpt, mould and cast them. It meant a lot, him confiding in me.

My whole *Star Trek* career I made every pair of Klingon and Ferengi teeth. Actually, for years, I made fake teeth for every alien on *Star Trek* that needed them. I made them light, I made them fast, and no two sets were ever the same. There was a lot of room for creativity, and it was always a lot of fun.

Michael Westmore

Michael Westmore gave so many people opportunities they wouldn't normally have had. And he has the best way of critiquing your work without making you feel bad about yourself. He's an amazing artist and so well organized! I learned a lot of craft from him, and how to head a department too. He was the perfect mentor.

Eryn Krueger Mekash

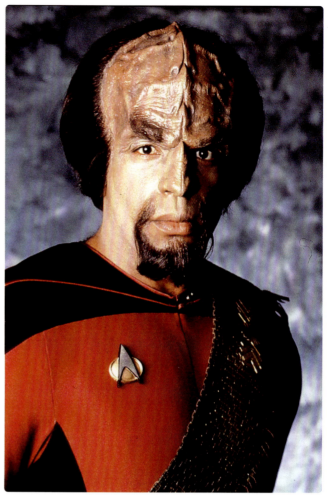

"I WANTED EVERY KLINGON TO BE DIFFERENT. SO EVERY ONE HAS A DIFFERENT DINOSAUR FOREHEAD."

Left: When you're as accomplished as legendary make-up artist Michael Westmore, you can grow your nails as long as you like.

Above: Michael Dorn strikes a characteristically stoic pose as Starfleet's own Mr Worf, a Klingon and proud of it in *Star Trek: The Next Generation* (1987-1994).

Opposite (top left): Michael Westmore surrounded by a selection of alien artefacts that he created for *Star Trek: The Next Generation* (1987-1994).

Opposite (middle left): Ferengi bartender Quark (Armin Shimerman) and his brother Rom (Max Grodénchik) from *Star Trek: Deep Space Nine* (1993–1999).

Opposite (bottom right): Tasked with creating placeholder dialogue for the Martians from Tim Burton's *Mars Attacks!* (1996), Larry Karaszewski and Scott Alexander started by mashing random keys and never looked ack.

From *The Next Generation* (1987–94) to *Enterprise* (2001–05), I did about 625 episodes of *Star Trek*. Not once, in all that time, did anyone describe what any of the aliens should look like. Every script would just say, "The alien," and the rest was up to me, though Gene Roddenberry did ask me to avoid covering the actors' eyes and mouths. Contacts and fake teeth were fine.

First thing I'd consider was, where's the episode set? Desert, jungle, underwater... Once I knew that, I'd search for things on Earth indigenous to those environments. If it was a dry planet, for example, I'd look to lizards, snakes and gila monsters for inspiration. I'd take pieces of each and put them together to create something new.

In the original *Star Trek* (1966–69) series, Klingons were just dark brown. From *The Motion Picture* (1979) on, they had forehead ridges. But for *The Next Generation*, for Mr Worf (Michael Dorn) and every Klingon after him, I wanted to do more. I found a book with incredible cross-sections of dinosaur vertebrae. No two were alike and that appealed to me as I wanted every Klingon to be different. So every Klingon has a different dinosaur forehead, a matching nose and jagged, brown upper teeth. That's how we did it for 18 years.

The first *Hellraiser* (1987) I thought was brilliant. Everything from the make-up to the music came together so well. The Cenobites were a great source of inspiration on *Star Trek* whenever I wanted to create meaner, scarier aliens. There's a reptilian race of Xindi in *Star Trek: Enterprise* (2001–05), and certainly Pinhead inspired me to give them mohawks made of porcupine quills.

Michael Westmore

Scott Alexander and I were brought in to do rewrites, from time to time, on *Mars Attacks!* (1996). The Martians just weren't popping on the page. It was all scene description, with no flourish. There was no sense of who the Martians were. And it was impossible to tell how long their scenes were, as they literally had no dialogue.

We thought, eventually, Tim Burton would bring in some college guy to invent a Martian language, but until then, we needed placeholder dialogue. So Scott starts typing ACK, ACK, ACK. Just three random keys that Scott could type quickly and wouldn't be mistaken for a proper word. Sort of like Charlie Brown's teacher saying WAH WAH WAH.

Sometimes there'd be 15 ACKs, other times just three. We quickly found that just by adding a question mark, or three exclamations, you could get a sense of what the conversation was. But we never, not for one second, thought they'd use that dialogue in the movie.

It wasn't until the film was finished, till we went to a screening and a Martian came on saying "ACK ACK ACK!" that we realized they'd used our ACKs! We just grabbed each other and laughed. It was unbelievable.

Larry Karaszewski

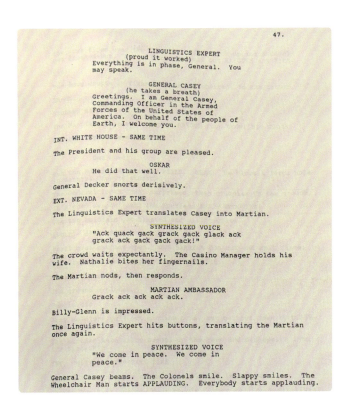

Left: ILM VFX supervisor Jim Mitchell (right) pops his head through the miniature set of the Martian ship interior created for Tim Burton's *Mars Attacks!* (1996).

Below: The interior of the Martian spaceship as it appears in *Mars Attacks!* (1996).

The Martians in *Mars Attacks!* (1996) were going to be stop motion, but the glass helmets presented lots of problems. Fingerprints, for one, and reflections for another. So Larry Franco, the producer, asked if we could composite CG glass helmets on top of the Martian puppets.

Just like when we took the initiative on *Jurassic Park* (1993), though, I felt we could do more. So as an extra test, we built a complete Martian in the computer but then animated it to move more like stop motion, and that did the trick, convincing Tim [Burton] he could still get the characters he wanted, but more easily with CG. There were still lots of practical elements in the movies, but the Martians were CG and their helmets were always spotless!

Jim Mitchell

The further something is from our experience, the harder it is to accept. Even with monsters, we can't help seeking something to relate to. When I first saw the aliens on the set of *Independence Day* (1996), I knew I had to keep them in the shadows, to give them mystery and menace. Too much light and they'd have lost their credibility and power.

Ultimately, every scene is sculpted with light, and particularly with creatures, I learned early on that proper lighting is crucial. You can flatten them out, or give them greater depth. You can make them look cheap, or hide their seams and give them character by adding more top light to cast shadows into the lines. It really all depends on where your main light source is, and where you put your emphasis.

Karl Walter Lindenlaub

The Faculty (1998) was the first time we got to work with Bernie Wrightson. We were so excited. His creature designs were so cool. Every single drawing he did could have been the monster.

Howard Berger

Top left & right: Commissioned by KNB EFX, Bernie Wrightson helped design the creatures for Robert Rodriguez's *The Faculty* (1998). Here are two examples of his utterly fantastic concept art.

Above: Bernie Wrightson's creature designs for *The Faculty* (1998) were stunningly translated by the artists at KNB EFX under the supervision of Greg Nicotero.

People ask me, "Derek, what are you looking for in a character?" I tell them, "Ultimately, to find their truth or humanity."

If I'm being honest, though, it's all about action figures. If there's even a possibility of my character having an action figure, oh yeah, I'm on board! So obviously I was excited to play the Classic Predator in *Predators* (2010). I mean, he's the best one!

The director, Nimród Antal, and I used to get in trouble for talking too much. I'd idly play with my arm bomb while chatting with him about comicbooks, because that's what you do when you make a friend who's into all the same stuff as you. But then the AD would come over, going, "Hey guys, I know you're having a really good time being nerds right now, but we have a multi-million dollar feature that you need to direct and act in."

It wasn't all fun and games. Once I was tied to an altar and leaning forward, so the sweat in my helmet was pooling around my mouth and nose. It wasn't draining away and I was struggling to breathe. I didn't want to ruin the scene, though. It took so long to get into position and for everything to roll. So I pressed my lips against the mesh of my helmet, tried to blow out the liquid and suck in the air. It was gross and I guess maybe I looked like I was struggling a bit.

Eventually Greg [Nicotero] comes over and asks if I'm ok. I mumbled something back as no way could I speak clearly. And he's like, "Are you drowning in your own sweat?"

He pulls out a knife, slashes the mesh and as the sweat pours out, I gasped, "I could have made it!"

He's like, "Derek, dude, no."

Swings and roundabouts then. Most days I get to live out my wildest childhood dreams. But other days, yeah, I'm sort of waterboarded in my own sweat.

Derek Mears

I'm less interested in literal monsters than I am in exploring the monstrous realities of life. So whether it's Navy SEALs getting shot to shit in *Lone Survivor* (2013), civilians devastated by homemade explosives in *Patriots Day* (2016) or Kobe Tai getting impaled on a towel hook in *Very Bad Things* (1998), I'm focusing on the real-life monsters of war, terrorism and bad life choices.

The one time I worked with literal rather than figurative monsters was *Battleship* (2012). It was so much fun creating alien invaders as I could really let my imagination go. For instance, I remember wanting them to have spiky calcified whiskers, like porcupine bristles. It was such a rush, the first time I saw visualizations of the creatures that up until then had only lived in my head.

That film was a lot of work, but so much fun. Before we'd even shot a frame, though, James Cameron ripped us for having the nerve to make a movie of a board game. It didn't help having someone at that level shit on the project. He created this cynicism which didn't help at the box office or with the critics, but over the years it's done very well financially, and people seem to really love it now.

Peter Berg

"OTHER DAYS... I'M SORT OF WATERBOARDED IN MY OWN SWEAT."

Opposite: Derek Mears was thrilled to play the Classic Predator in Nimród Antal's *Predators* (2010).
Top: Make-up effects supervisor Greg Nicotero gets Derek Mears suited up under the watchful eye of *Predators* (2010) director Nimród Antal.
Above: Taylor Kitsch squares off against an alien in director Peter Berg's *Battleship* (2012).

My parents were quite religious and wouldn't let me watch horror movies at home, but I had a fun auntie who'd let me rent anything I wanted from the video store. From the moment I first saw *Alien* (1979) I was obsessed with the life cycle of the xenomorph. It just seemed so plausible, you know?

When you grow up in Australia, surrounded by poisonous spiders, you're not easily freaked out by creatures. But the facehuggers were something else. Something primal. The way they scurried. The way they jumped. The way they'd latch onto you, forcing themselves down your throat, choking you but keeping you alive long enough for their eggs to incubate. That's all so grim!

Decades later, I was approached to be the creature effects supervisor on *Alien: Covenant* (2017). Ridley Scott was back directing, and there was a new species to create, the neomorph. I was so worried about doing the film justice, though. Part of me was like, how could I bring anything to this perfect, sacred world? But then my normal excitement and joy took over and I jumped aboard.

By his own admission, if Ridley wasn't directing, he'd be in the creature shop. He always knows exactly what he wants, and as he's one of the best artists I've ever seen, he can draw it for you. Once we'd locked down the neomorph design, Ridley had us build a ton of different practical effects for it. Even if it didn't all end up in the movie, he liked everything built. So we built hand puppets, rod puppets and animatronic puppets. Make-up effects and prosthetics. Really everything we could to make the movie as in-camera as possible, as Ridley likes to have something to put in front of his actors.

Of all the things I worked on and created for the movie, David's lab, his trophy room, was my favourite. We shot it at the end of the schedule, and had worked so long and hard, I wanted to celebrate that by giving everyone on the team a chance to make something cool for that room. It ended up being one of the most amazing sets I've ever been on. I created three things for it myself, including a sliced cross-section of an adult neomorph head that Ridley later took for his office.

Working with Ridley was a total career highlight. Like, hearing him talk about all the low-tech, practical solutions he came up with for *Alien*, using condoms in the original xenomorph build, and then watching him dumping yogurt on the neomorph to get it good and slimy. Sights like that are what dreams are made of!

Ridley asks a lot of his crew, but sometimes things aren't possible. It can be scary saying no, but if you're straight with him, he's not like some up-and-comer who'll stomp up and down and make a scene. He'll just be like, "OK, fuck it, let's do it this way…"

It was inspiring to work with a filmmaker who could handle curveballs so calmly and confidently. Because getting upset won't get you anywhere. Much better to just look at a problem, and like Ridley always said, "We'll make it work."

Adam Johansen

It took four more people to help me make-up Robert Bobroczkyi as the Offspring on *Alien: Romulus* (2024) for Legacy FX. It wasn't a suit – mainly prosthetics and paint – so a huge application job.

He's so tall! 7' 7" and really skinny, with a chest so thin you wondered how he could even breathe. He was actually taller than me sitting down than I was standing up. So tall that to pop his black vacuum-formed eyes in on set, I asked him if I should get a ladder or if he wouldn't mind bending down to help me out!

His silhouette was amazing for this role. So unusual and thin. He looks incredible in the film.

Göran Lundström

Below (left): Odd Studio's Adam Johansen works on one of the many alien sculptures created for Ridley Scott's *Alien: Covenant* (2017).

Below (right): Adam Johansen sculpts a xenomorph body for *Alien: Covenant* (2017).

Opposite: A xenomorph wonders why Odd Studio's Adam Johansen isn't fleeing in terror on the set of *Alien: Covenant* (2017).

Tyler: I loved playing Blackstar in *Jupiter's Legacy* (2021). It's my favourite role, by far the most layered, and the suit was the best I've ever worn. It was seamless and didn't stifle my performance at all. Every wink, every snicker came through, and I could move in it without having to think about what I was doing. But it was hell to get into, and when you wear a suit that substantial, it wears you down after a while.

Howard: Originally the plan was to go digital on the suit, for KNB to just do the head and hands, but when I first talked to Steven S. DeKnight about it, I told him I thought that would be a mistake. That we could build a practical rubber suit, and it worked really well – it was beautiful – but I know it was torture to wear.

Tyler: I was 53 when we shot that, and at that age, as soon as you put a suit on, the clock's ticking. Physically and psychologically, it takes a toll. You have to let production know they have to make the most of you quickly, and not leave you till the end of the day, then say, "OK, we're going to do this ten-page scene now."

Even when you're young, a suit like that is exhausting. My stunt double was great, but it was his first big show and he was excited about looking so badass. I told him to stay hydrated, to use the cooling suit and just generally pace himself, but he was like, "It's fine. I'll be fine."

So we're shooting our first big scene. I step out, he steps in. They yell action and he falls flat on his face. A little oxygen and he was back with us. I didn't have to do the whole fight scene myself! After that, he was a lot more careful.

Tyler Mane and Howard Berger

Left (top and bottom): Kevin Wasner applies Dave Grasso's Blackstar make-up to actor Tyler Mane for *Jupiter's Legacy* (2021).

Opposite (top left): Tyler Mane suits up in his Blackstar costume, courtesy of KNB EFX for *Jupiter's Legacy* (2021).

Opposite (top right): Kevin Wasner applies final touches to Tyler Mane's Blackstar on the set of *Jupiter's Legacy* (2021).

Opposite (bottom): Tyler Mane brought Blackstar to life in *Jupiter's Legacy* (2021).

Tyler Mane was such a pro on *Jupiter's Legacy* (2021). So much of what we did every day was try to keep him comfortable in that suit. We told production it took 25 minutes to get him into it, but they didn't want to have to wait, so he had to wear the whole thing all the time. Some days he just sat in a chair, in a cooling suit, ready to go but not doing anything for ten hours.

It's not easy to endure that sort of thing and not be drained by it, but Tyler's a trooper. A great performer too. He loved his character and really brought Blackstar to life. As we'd put on the make-up, he'd start talking to the mirror. Getting into character. Not a method thing, exactly, but he definitely carried himself differently when he was in the make-up. It gave him a certain kind of attitude and he poured all that into his performance.

Kevin Wasner

"AS SOON AS YOU PUT A SUIT ON, THE CLOCK'S TICKING."

I love working with real stuff. Tennis balls on sticks can't compete. On *Halo* (2022–24) there were these incredible, practical aliens called 'Prophets' on large, floating thrones. The puppeteers hid behind them and the effect was incredible.

CG added another layer of perfection, animating their eyes and mouths, but they were real enough for us on the set, and so much easier to work with than big, empty spaces.

Karl Walter Lindenlaub

Above: Karl Walter Lindenlaub's breathtaking cinematography helped bring the *Halo* (2022-2024) universe to life. A cinematographer can either make or break a creature, and Karl Walter masterfully paints light onto his subjects to enhance their realism.

Opposite: Puppeteers operate the Prophets in *Halo* (2022-2024).

"I LOVE WORKING WITH REAL STUFF. TENNIS BALLS ON STICKS CAN'T COMPETE."

12

CREEPY, CRABBY CRITTERS

How to define the undefinable? How to describe the oddities in the chapter ahead?

How about, if it looks like you could kill it with fire, a harpoon or a hefty spray of Raid, it's here. If it's green, and/or gooey, and/or gross, it's here. If it's half man/half fly, half fish/half person or half swamp vegetable/half human consciousness, it's here.

But if you still can't picture the unfathomable entities ahead, just take a breath and turn the page.

Aesthetically, nothing beats the Creature from the Black Lagoon. It's a suit that's stood the test of time. So beautiful and interesting. The product of an incredible collaboration, but one that's sadly tainted by a terrible, if not uncommon injustice.

Women rarely get the flowers they deserve for work they've done, and Milicent Patrick was no exception. But there's no doubt in my mind she was absolutely instrumental in the design of the Creature. She was a truly gifted artist with a clear vision and style that you can see in everything she did, from *Abbott and Costello Meet Dr. Jekyll and Mr. Hyde* (1953) and *The Mole People* (1956) to the Metaluna Mutant in *This Island Earth* (1955).

When the time came to promote *Creature from the Black Lagoon* (1954), Universal saw an opportunity to appeal to female audiences by showcasing Milicent Patrick's work on the movie. Because no one at the time would ever have expected a woman to be involved in creature design. So they rather progressively sent her on a press tour, dubbing her "The Beauty Who Created the Beast".

Unfortunately, a lot of people in this industry have fragile egos, and things backfired when her boss, angry at the idea of sharing credit, denied her involvement, had her fired from Universal and then blacklisted her from the industry. Let's be honest, though: that shit happens all the time.

It's awful that things went down the way they did because I'm sure Milicent Patrick would have happily given credit where credit was due. It takes a team to make something as perfect and iconic as the Creature from the Black Lagoon, and just because one artist

"WOMEN RARELY GET THE FLOWERS THEY DESERVE FOR WORK THEY'VE DONE, AND MILICENT PATRICK WAS NO EXCEPTION."

is celebrated in a promotional campaign, that doesn't diminish everyone else's contributions. Unfortunately her boss thought otherwise, and it makes me sad to think of all the things she never got to create because the opportunity was taken away from her.

Micheline Pitt

Preceding Spread: They told us to remember the rules, but we didn't listen. A fiendish Rick Baker creation causes chaos in *Gremlins 2: The New Batch* (1990).

Below (left): Bud Westmore and Milicent Patrick share Creature design ideas in this completely natural and unstaged behind-the-scenes photo promoting *Creature from the Black Lagoon* (1954).

Below (right): Milicent Patrick works a few final details into a Gill-man mask for *Creature from the Black Lagoon* (1954).

Opposite: The Ghoul of our Dreams, Vixen's Micheline Pitt looks her beast in this fetching *Creature from the Black Lagoon* (1954) movie poster dress with matching bolero and crossbody bag.

On *Creature from the Black Lagoon* (1954), the first time Ricou Browning wore the suit in the water, his feet floated up in the air. It was a rubber suit, and air got caught inside, so upside down he went. My uncle Bud [Westmore] had to get in the water with him and attach extra lead weights to the bottom of his feet to keep him right way up. After that, they built the weights into the suits themselves.

Michael Westmore

The bestselling character in my store, Dark Delicacies, is the Creature. Action figures, model kits, tiki mugs... Everything featuring the Gill-man sells like hotcakes. You'd think Universal would have made more movies about him over the years.

Del Howison

Above: The great Ricou Browning at home in Florida, surrounded by memories of his adventures playing the Gill-man in *Creature from the Black Lagoon* (1954).
Inset: Howard Berger's autographed photo of Ricou Browning was a gift from Ricou's son.
Opposite: A selection of Gill-man toys from the mad monster kid lair of Marshall Julius.

You look at the Morlocks from *The Time Machine* (1960), and maybe today they don't seem tremendously threatening or scary. But when I was a kid, that shot where they're lumbering towards Rod Taylor, and you can see their glowing eyes through the muslin hanging between them... That scared the hell out of me.

We live in a world, now, where everybody's seen everything, so rather than marvel at a classic monster, often people would rather go online and criticize it. I'd prefer to put myself in the mindset of the audiences who first saw those movies. Back when everything was new.

Can you imagine sitting in a movie theatre and seeing, for the first time, something as magnificent as the Gill-man from *Creature from the Black Lagoon* (1954)? And how must it have felt to see *Day of the Triffids* back in 1963? The scene when the man is first attacked in the greenhouse, you see the whip marks across his face, all lit in red, and then the Triffid wraps itself around him. I don't care how it compares to modern effects, or how it looks to jaded eyes. It's horrifying, and don't try to convince me otherwise.

Greg Nicotero

I saw more stars than I expected on the set of *At the Earth's Core* (1976). There I was, 4,000 miles beneath the Earth in Pinewood Studios, standing in the middle of a huge cave set, surrounded by flames and sharing the scene with dear, sweet Peter Cushing. Suddenly, from ledges maybe 30 feet above, several men in heavy, rubber monster suits came swooping down on us.

On heavy Kirby wires they were, and in rehearsal, these beaky, winged 'Mahars' managed to just about avoid colliding with us. But as soon as we started shooting, of course, one clunked me on the head. I wobbled a bit, but Peter jumped to my rescue and kept me from falling. He was so quick!

I had to keep going till the end of the take, because that's what you do, isn't it? And obviously they used that footage, though they cut the bit where I almost got knocked out. I don't know, though. Maybe they should have kept it in?

Caroline Munro

Below: For George Pal's adaptation of H.G. Wells' *The Time Machine* (1960), make-up pioneer William Tuttle designed and created the creepy, post-human Morlocks.
Opposite: Yvette Mimieux squirms at the touch of a Morlock from *The Time Machine* (1960).

I'm turning the pages of the *Gremlins* (1984) script, thinking, "there's some cool monster stuff in here."

Suddenly there's a horde of Gremlins running through the town. Thousands of the things. And I'm like, "this is not as straightforward as I thought."

Still, it gets bigger, and wilder, and finally Mike Finnell, the producer, calls to ask me what I think.

"It's impossible," I said. "Let's do it!"

Fortunately, during production, we brought things down to reality.

Initially in the script, there was no Gizmo, and the Mogwai played a very small part, more props than characters, so there wasn't a lot of design concern for those. Mainly we were focused on the Gremlins.

Originally Chris [Columbus] described them as armoured, with heavier bodies and horns instead of ears. It was a great starting-point, as there was a tone to it. I started with some simple napkin sketches because you could do that in those days! You didn't need a fully rendered 3D model to sell a concept.

Joe [Dante] kept an eye on my designs, approving some things, suggesting changes to others, and I kept fiddling till I was ready to sculpt a maquette. While I can do graphic stuff, I'm much more comfortable working in 3D, and while I designed it, I was also considering the practical side. Like, the Gremlins have wide, far-back mouths because they're puppets, so I was careful to work that into the design, so they didn't just look like Muppets.

I remember the instant it all came together, and I felt like, yeah, it was going to work. That it was the one. I showed it to Joe, and he was really happy. I was very pleased because of all the designs I've ever done, the Gremlin is my favourite.

It was scary because I'd never done anything remotely on that scale before, and this was Joe's first studio picture, so he was under a lot of pressure too. At first Warner Brothers didn't even seem to want to make the movie. They just wanted to say they had a Spielberg picture on the lot. So, we didn't get greenlit right away. Not at all.

We had to figure out not only how to do everything, but also how to do it with the time we had and the money we were given. Before we'd even moulded anything, Joe told me the studio was insisting on film tests, so literally, I sculpted a Gremlin puppet in a day. I spent an entire day and night, didn't sleep at all, building a very rough Gremlin puppet out of just what we had at the moment. The following morning we did a bunch of video tests showing the kind of set-ups we could work with to give everyone an idea of the practical reality of dealing with puppet monsters. We shot a ton of stuff and somehow Joe managed to cut it into watchable footage. That's when I think the studio said, "These guys seem pretty serious about it. Maybe we should just make the movie."

"'IT'S IMPOSSIBLE,' I SAID. 'LET'S DO IT!'"

It was a long road getting there.

Then Joe comes to me, going, "Steven thinks one of the Mogwais shouldn't turn. He should just stay friendly and be Billy's friend."

But I'm like, "No he shouldn't!"

Anyway, that's how Gizmo was born. Though originally the Mogwai were just a minor aspect of the movie, suddenly one of them becomes the star, and we had another character to develop from scratch. Which not only meant designing how he looked, but once you get into the character puppetry side of things, you have to come up with a style of movement that supports the character. It took a whole bunch of puppets with different mechanisms to achieve what we needed, and while we were shooting, those mechanisms needed adjusting, sometimes on an hourly basis. So, it was a real challenge and a huge addition to the workload on the picture.

And his part just kept growing and growing! The more we figured things out, the more Joe wanted us to do. Then suddenly he puts up a list for the crew, saying, "We're having so much fun with Gizmo. What do you guys think he could do?"

And I'm like, "Don't you do that!"

But they're going, "He could do this, he could do that, he could drive a little car..."

And I thought, "No! He can't!"

Eventually we did, of course, because something great about Joe is he's not one of those insane directors who doesn't understand what you're doing. He understands the process. He told me, "We won't shoot those things yet. We're not making the film in sequence. We'll save that stuff for the end and give you time to get it ready."

That was a lifesaver.

A lot of stuff we came up with, like Stripe blowing his nose on the curtain before jumping out of the window, came from testing what the puppets could do, and just from playing around during rehearsal, or between shots when we were filming. Joe would see us playing and say, "Let's put that in the movie."

Opposite (top): Chris Walas and his merry band of *Gremlins* (1984) puppeteers, ready for action.

Opposite (bottom): Team *Gremlins* (1984) work their puppet magic for the scene where Billy (Zach Galligan) introduces his science teacher (Glynn Turman) to Gizmo the Mogwai (voiced by Howie Mandel).

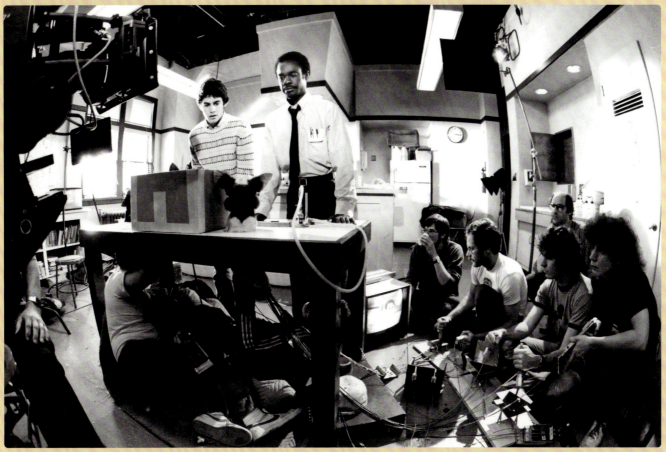

CHAPTER 12 - CREEPY, CRABBY CRITTERS

We developed some amazing things for *Gremlins*, like Stripe's super-arms, which was a slave system where mechanical arms on the puppet were linked to mechanical arms on an operator, with another set of small levers for fine finger control. It was quite elaborate but allowed us to quickly do all sorts of cool things like Stripe picking up stuff and throwing it over his shoulder.

I was in a mad panic from the word go on that picture. All I could think about was getting through the next day. But I remember Joe coming to me one morning and saying, "I don't know who's going to watch this movie, but it sure is fun making it."

And it was kind of fun, but it was also a nightmare, as the project just kept constantly growing and changing and I was always playing catch-up. I never put up with that kind of insanity again on another film.

Chris Walas

Opposite: A cosy family portrait with *Gremlins* (1984) genius Chris Walas, his firstborn Stripe, and unplanned child Gizmo.

Left: "Rub 'em here! Rub 'em there! Rub 'em EVERYWHERE!" A set of *Gremlins* (1984) Rub 'N' Play Transfers, from Colorforms.

Below: Chris Walas reviews the final Stripe sculpture at his Bay Area studio, for *Gremlins* (1984).

Gremlins (1984) was originally going to be an R-rated horror film, but Warner Bros insisted we make something at least pseudo family-friendly, so a lot of stuff from Chris Columbus's original script didn't make it to the screen. Like, the dog wasn't eaten, and the mother's head didn't end up bouncing down the stairs.

Gizmo was supposed to turn into a gremlin after about 25 minutes. He was a small puppet, designed with just enough tech inside of him to make it through the first act, but then Steven [Spielberg] decided, dangerously late in production, that he wanted Gizmo to stick around and be the hero's pal for the whole movie.

We were frantic. We didn't know how we could possibly turn this little bucket of bolts into something people would respond to for 90 minutes. It took a lot of R&D. We built a giant Gizmo head for close-ups, so he could show emotion. And because he couldn't walk, or barely move, we put him in Billy's backpack so he could get around.

We were one step ahead of the sheriff the whole time. Lots of gags in the script didn't end up working, so we improvised a lot to make the most of what the puppet was actually capable of. Much of the movie came out of that restriction, but I don't mind saying it was a gruelling experience. Incredible that Chris [Walas] managed to somehow not lose his marbles while doing it.

The reward was that it was an unexpected hit that, because there was no publicity, seemed to come from nowhere. Suddenly it was the talk of the town!

Chris was off, being a director, when *Gremlins 2: The New Batch* (1990) rolled around. But Rick [Baker] didn't want to do it either. He said, "Chris already did everything. What am I going to do?"

To tempt Rick aboard, we invented a subplot with the genetics lab creating different varieties of gremlin. We were like, "Come work on the script. What kind of gremlins would you like to see?"

That did the trick. Rick and his team built our gremlins, and they did a terrific job. The technology between the first movie and the second had advanced so dramatically, suddenly we were able to do everything that had been impossible just six years earlier. Gizmo could walk and talk! And given the success of the first film, for the sequel, Warner Bros were like, "This time, you guys can do whatever you want."

The experience was so much more positive and personal than the first. It was actually fun!

Joe Dante

Below: Chris Walas kept Stripe's teeth looking their whitest for *Gremlins* (1984).

Opposite (top): Chris Walas's hand-drawn design for Gizmo's mechanical eyes. This was back in the days of pens and paper, kids.

Opposite (bottom): "Bye, Billy." Gizmo turned out to be the star of *Gremlins* (1984), and even today is considered one of the greatest puppets in film.

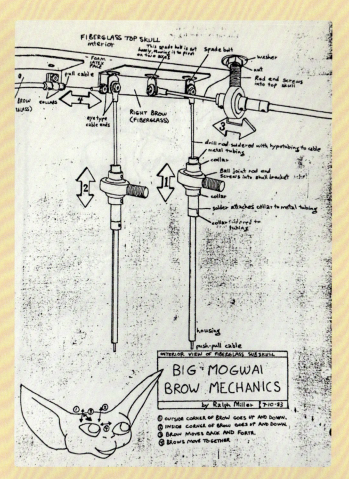

"WE BUILT A GIANT GIZMO HEAD FOR CLOSE-UPS, SO HE COULD SHOW EMOTION. AND BECAUSE HE COULDN'T WALK, OR BARELY MOVE, WE PUT HIM IN BILLY'S BACKPACK SO HE COULD GET AROUND."

"WE DIDN'T KNOW HOW WE COULD POSSIBLY TURN THIS LITTLE BUCKET OF BOLTS INTO SOMETHING PEOPLE WOULD RESPOND TO FOR 90 MINUTES."

Above: *Gremlins* (1984) star Stripe hitches a ride on director Joe Dante's shoulders.

Right: Rick Baker interrupts a quiet moment between Joe Dante and Greta the sexy Gremlin on the set of *Gremlins 2: The New Batch* (1990).

I turned down *Gremlins 2: The New Batch* (1990) numerous times. The first one practically killed Chris [Walas]. I visited him when he was working on the film, and at the time, he was on crutches as he'd fallen out of the trailer. He looked like death warmed over, and I thought, "I don't want to be that guy."

On the first film, they'd only had the time to make one Gremlin sculpt, adding a mohawk on one to make it different and identifiable. As you can't make one puppet that does everything, you have to make three or four from the same mould, and give each one different abilities. If they'd wanted every Gremlin to be a different character, they'd have had to make four puppets of each one of those characters, and that's a hell of a lot more work.

But that's what I wanted to do. I told them, "If you let me make them as individual characters, I'd be more interested."

I also wanted to do a little redesign on Gizmo to make him softer and more realistic. And they said, "OK!"

They were still writing the movie, so we had time to do everything. We contributed ideas and worked on storyboards at my shop. It ended up being a very collaborative film and actually a lot of fun.

Rick Baker

> Looking back, it's amazing how much room Rick [Baker] gave people on his team if he trusted them. He'd pass you an effect and be like, "Just go with it." Obviously he had guard rails in place, but it was cool that he wanted to see how each person might problem-solve an effect all the way through. He saw in people where they could go, given the chance, and the sense of confidence you'd get from that would be significant.
>
> Rick asked me to design the vegetable gremlin for *Gremlins 2: The New Batch* (1990). He said it was my kind of crazy. I took inspiration from the great Italian artist Arcimboldo, who painted people made of vegetables. For the brows I used split pea pods. Cabbages for ears and a carrot beard. It was exciting to create a gremlin from start to finish and see him in the movie.
>
> **Gabe Bartalos**

Opposite (top): Rick Baker's Daffy Gremlin makes a mess in *Gremlins 2: The New Batch* (1990). Rick was eager to create a number of Gremlins with discernible features and personalities as that struck him as a more interesting gig.

Opposite (middle): The Vegetable Gremlin created by Gabe Bartalos, under the supervision of Rick Baker, for *Gremlins 2: The New Batch* (1990).

Opposite (bottom): Surrounded by a menagerie of study sculptures, monster kids Norman Cabrera and Rick Baker stop for a snap while crafting creatures for *Gremlins 2: The New Batch* (1990).

Above: Rick Baker's Brain Gremlin leads a rousing rendition of New York, New York in *Gremlins 2: The New Batch* (1990). The tremendous scope of the sequence is a testament to the boldness and brilliance of Rick Baker's Cinovation Studios.

Right: Rick Baker and Marc Tyler puppeteer Cinovation's Gizmo puppet for *Gremlins 2: The New Batch* (1990).

It took a while to crack the different stages of make-up for *The Fly* (1986). For starters, in the original script, they seemed a little out of order. Like there was a scene quite early in the movie where Brundle spits his acid vomit on an old lady in a dumpster. I suggested that David [Cronenberg] save the more extreme stuff for further down the line, and he agreed. Actually, he cut that scene entirely, which made things easier.

When we started designing the different stages of Brundle's transformation, we worked forwards, adding something at every stage, but it didn't feel organic, like a natural progression. It wasn't until we designed the final incarnation of the character, the creature I called Space Bug, that things fell into place, as then we had something to work backwards from.

Once, say, we knew how big the bulge around his eyes was going to be in the final stage, we could make the stage before a little less extreme, and the stage before that, smaller still. So, working backwards was the trick that made it work for us.

David asked ahead of casting if there was anything he should look for in an actor that would help us with the make-ups. I told him, "Small ears and small nose, because we can add, but we can't take away."

Sure enough, a while later he calls to tell me, "Chris, I think I found my guy, but I don't know if he's going to work for you. It's Jeff Goldblum."

I honestly think he wouldn't have gone with Jeff if I'd said no. But Stephan Dupuis and I were huge fans of his, so I told David, "It's not going to be easy, but he's the right guy. I promise we'll make this work."

And it was great. Jeff was magnificent to work with. The best.

Chris Walas

Below: Jeff Goldblum's in a pensive mood while being transformed by Stephan Dupuis for *The Fly* (1986).

Opposite (top): Chris Walas applies goo to a Seth Brundle puppet on the set of David Cronenberg's *The Fly* (1986).

Opposite (bottom): Jeff Goldblum is poised to do something gross in one of the multiple stages of Seth Brundle make-up created by Chris Walas and applied by Stephan Dupuis, both of whom won Oscars for their incredible artistry.

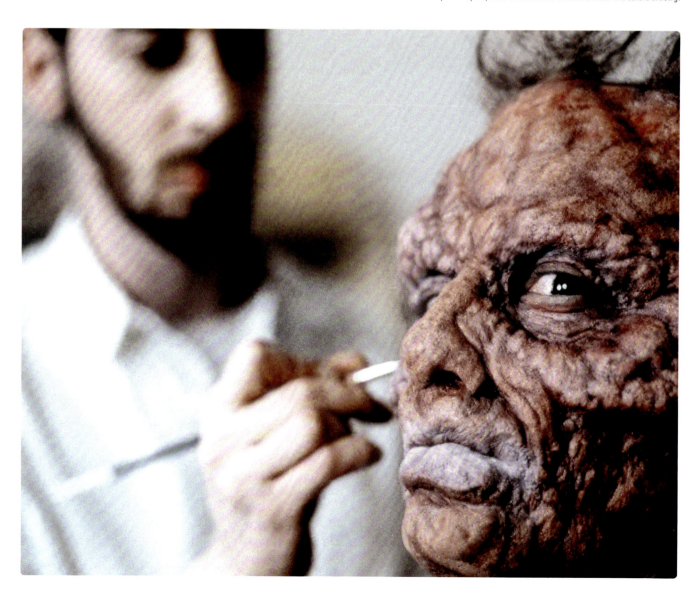

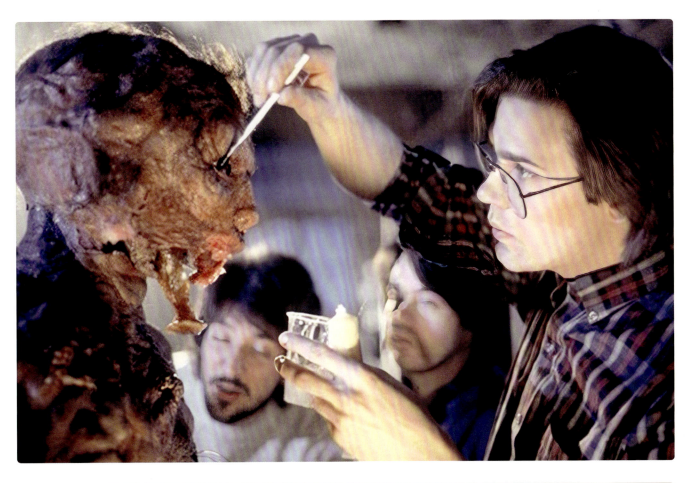

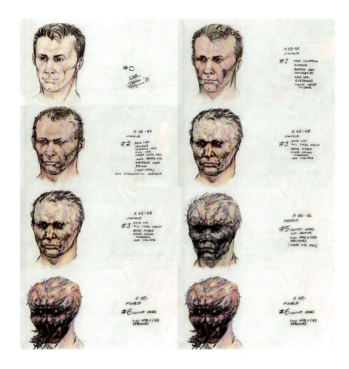

The Fly (1986) was an incredible yet highly stressful learning experience. I was nearly let go on a couple of occasions. Once for talking back to director David Cronenberg, when questioned for not matching the vomit on Jeff Goldblum's hand during resets. Then later, for accidentally picking up the prop man's spray bottle instead of mine, and spraying Jeff Goldblum with vinegar instead of water! I realized the mix-up when he yelled, "I smell like a salad."

I wanted to die at that moment, and spent most of the night feeling sorry for myself, washing the foam latex suit in a bathtub of dish soap. Stephan Dupuis always stood up for me and I'm forever grateful.

The film itself is very much linked in my mind to the AIDS epidemic. A crew member was the first person I ever heard of who had HIV/AIDS. I remember looking at them during the shoot, knowing that by the end of the film, they'd be dead. What Jeff's character goes through in the film, his sickness and deterioration, feels like a direct analogy to me, of what so many other people experienced back then.

When Stephan and Chris Walas won their Academy Awards for *The Fly*, Stephan thanked Margaret Prentice and myself in his acceptance speech. Millions of people heard that and suddenly I was a legitimate make-up artist.

Donald Mowat

The Fly II (1989) featured a much more viable lifeform than the first film. Not the warped and twisted mix of biologies that Space Bug was. I wanted to make him more active, more agile, and fortunately, it was all pretty much there in the script.

Eric Stoltz was fine with all the make-ups. We used gelatine on that show, which is heavier and not as comfortable as foam, but Eric was very good. Very tolerant.

There was a last-minute change to the mutant dog. Originally, the puppet had a full armature with lots of mechanisms in it. But when my crew showed me what it could do, I told them, "It looks too healthy. It looks too strong."

I needed it to look pitiable, so we ripped all that stuff out and basically made it a hand and rod puppet. To this day, I still get a lot of comments about that poor creature.

Chris Walas

"I REALIZED THE MIX-UP WHEN JEFF GOLDBLUM YELLED, 'I SMELL LIKE A SALAD.'"

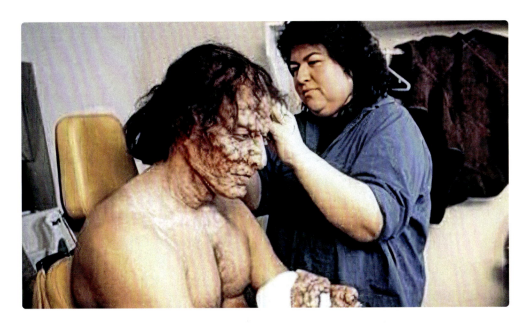

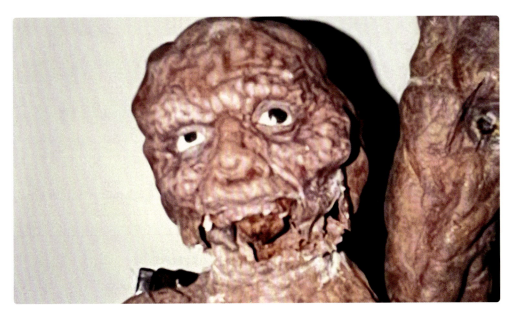

Opposite (left and right): Beautifully illustrated designs by Stephan Dupuis documenting Seth Brundle's gradual transformation into *The Fly* (1986).

Top: Margaret Beserra applies one of the many stages of Seth Brundle make-ups to Jeff Goldblum for *The Fly* (1986).

Middle: Chris Walas and David Cronenberg flank Jeff Goldblum as *The Fly* (1986).

Bottom: A Brundlefly puppet takes five on the set of *The Fly* (1986).

I was cast as the Minotaur on *Legion* (2017–19). From what I understood of the character, it was very sick, so to develop an idea of how I'd move, I researched shell-shocked soldiers, starving cattle and dying horses.

It was a very restrictive character. My lower half was tied into a cart, and I had a head on, so there was no emoting. Still, I had all these ideas of how to bring the character to life, but once I got on set, they told me to just stand still.

It's important to prepare, but you have to be open to throwing everything away because, of course, it's the director's vision, you have to believe in it, and you're his colour to paint with.

Dirk Rogers

"IT'S IMPORTANT TO PREPARE, BUT YOU HAVE TO BE OPEN TO THROWING EVERYTHING AWAY."

Above: Dirk Rogers as the Crippled Minotaur from Noah Hawley's *Legion* (2017-2019).

Opposite (top): Michael Broom's design for the Crippled Minotaur, courtesy of KNB EFX.

Opposite (bottom): Another design for the Crippled Minotaur, this time from KNB EFX's John Wheaton.

It was just the most wonderful opportunity, making a *Swamp Thing* (2019) show with a Bernie Wrightson design aesthetic, an Alan Moore sensibility and a proper, grown-up, hard R-vibe. I was very excited.

Working closely with the illustrator, Luca Nemolato, and inspired by Wrightson's textured, earthy style, we produced a maquette that was part of the final pitch meeting at Warner Bros TV. It helped seal the deal and we got the green light. Walking out of the meeting, James [Wan] nudges me. He's like, "Better make sure it looks like that!"

Fortunately, we had almost six months to spend on initial development, which is unusual for a TV show, and even most movies. It was just as well we had that time, as creating the Swamp Thing suit was a huge technical challenge across the board.

Building a suit that was comfortable, fast to apply, didn't buckle and worked in water was a tall order. Beyond which, it had to survive a six-month shoot. But it did! We all did. Everyone put in blood, sweat and tears because we knew what we were doing was cool, and we loved being a part of it.

I'm so grateful they picked Derek Mears to play Swamp Thing, as he was the perfect choice for that character. So much more than just a creature suit stunt guy, he's a great actor who took the role very seriously. He came prepared, with Swamp Thing's physicality and personality mapped out. I can't tell you how much of a difference that makes. We made the suit, and it was great, sure, but it was Derek who brought it to life.

Besides Swamp Thing we had a whole slew of puppets to build, gore gags to prepare, creature suits to make and six stages of transformation for Kevin Durand's Floronic Man to create. Sadly, we were ten episodes into filming, with three to go, when the studio cut the season short. It was just so disembowelling not to be able to tell the whole story.

In the end, the Floronic Man's final stage was the only one we shot, and that was just the test make-up, for one day. A bunch of cool transformation elements, and two major creature suits we'd built for the show, never came to light.

Still, it was a gratifying experience. Really one of my favourite shows to work on. The entire cast and crew were wonderful. And we're so proud of what we made. But after the first episode aired, the show was cancelled. We were supposed to have five seasons, but all of that disappeared.

Justin Raleigh

Above: Justin Raleigh's make-up effects company, Fractured FX, created an array of Bernie Wrightson and Alan Moore-inspired characters for the sadly short-lived *Swamp Thing* (2019) series. Here, Kevin Durand looks splendid in his final stage Floronic Man make-up.

Opposite (top and bottom): Derek Mears was a living work of art as Swamp Thing. "Not a lot of people get to do what we do," said Derek, "and honestly it's an honour to serve my fellow nerds."

I got to do all the things I love on *Swamp Thing* (2019). I got to wear prosthetics so beautiful, they're art. As an actor, I got a brilliantly written arc for my character. And on the physical side, I got to be part of a team that pulled off a lot of demanding days.

Most mornings I'd get up, stare in the mirror and go, "You can do this."

Four hours it took, every day, to put on that make-up. At least at the beginning. Thankfully, my talented friends, Ozzy Alvarez and Kevin Kirkpatrick, made a game of it and got it down to two. Then of course, at the end of every day, it took another two hours to take it all off.

We had an amazing team on that show with Fractured FX, but the days were hot and long. It was physically and psychologically tough. My character in the show was going through an existential crisis where I played manic day after day for about eight months. Your body doesn't know you're acting and reacts as if it's real. At one point I felt like I was mentally falling through a dark void, trying to grab, like, a tree branch or something for stability. It was wild.

In the end, it was all worth it, though. Every second of effort. Every ounce of energy. Every ache and emotional black hole. Because we made something great. Something we're proud of.

Derek Mears

IT'S ALIVE!

You don't have to look too far in this world for a monster. Mostly, it just depends on your point of view. Dogs can be monsters. Cats, obviously. Pretty much everything in the water is a monster. And did you ever accidentally travel 2,000 years into the future and get yourself captured by damn, dirty, chatty apes? They must have seemed pretty monstrous too. Claws crossed, our animals chapter won't be too triggering for you.

Planet of the Apes (1968) was the first movie that took me to another place. I loved the idea that in this intelligently conceived and incredibly realistic world, man was the beast, and it was the apes who were civilized. Such an amazing flip! That was the first time I sided with the other, the monster, as I had so much more sympathy for Zira (Kim Hunter) and Cornelius (Roddy McDowall) than I did for Taylor (Charlton Heston).

Larry Karaszewski

I was six when I saw a commercial for *Escape from the Planet of the Apes* (1971). I climbed up on our coffee table, looked my parents in the eyes and told them, "We are going to see that movie!"

Years later my therapist suggested the reason the *Apes* movies spoke to me as a kid was because I felt so different from everyone around me. I was like, "Yeah, but maybe it's because they had King Kongs dressed like Fonzie."

Gorillas in leather jackets, man! Honestly, that's what did it for me.

Dana Gould

Dana Gould as Dr Zaius may be the funniest thing on Earth.

Larry Karaszewski

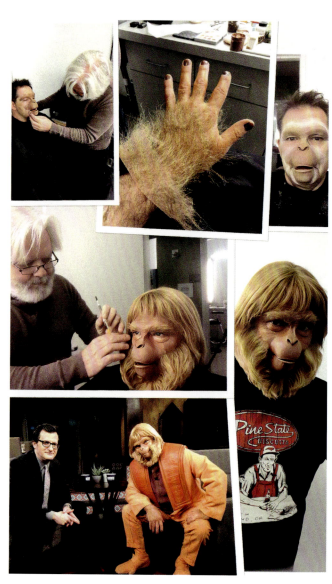

Preceding Spread: Behind the scenes on Steven Spielberg's *Jaws* (1975), arguably the best and most horrifying monster movie of all time, and perhaps even the greatest film ever made.
Top: Fans went bananas over Roddy McDowall's performance as Cornelius in *Planet of the Apes* (1968), sporting groundbreaking make-up from masters of the art John Chambers and Dan Striepeke.
Right: Make-up artist Andy Schoneberg applies his re-creation of Dr. Zaius to Dana Gould for another hilarious performance as Dr. Z.

In 1992, I was a writer on *The Ben Stiller Show* (1992–95), and I had this idea for *Planet of the Apes: The Musical*. This was before they did a much better job on *The Simpsons* (1989–present) than I'd have ever done. Honestly I only wrote it because I wanted to wear an *Apes* make-up.

Because it would have cost a lot to make, I had to come up with a second sketch that we could shoot using the same set and everything else. So I thought, for the second act of the show, we could do, "From the producers of the *Planet of the Apes* musical, Dr Zaius is *Mark Twain Tonight!*"

I only chose Dr Zaius because he's more iconic than Cornelius, more bombastic, and there's gravity to him, so comedically there's more to do with him. Sadly, we got cancelled before I had the chance to do it, but years later I was invited to do it live at Sketch Fest. Andy Schoneberg did my make-up and it built from there.

Next thing I know, someone from TCM calls to ask if I'd like to be interviewed as Dr Z for a *Planet of the Apes* Fathom Event. The angle was, Zaius is an ape who just happened to be in that movie, and like Orson Welles on Merv Griffin, really he's just dropping names and telling stories. That seemed more fun to me than playing the character from the movie, and eventually it led to my chat show, *Hanging With Doctor Z* (2012–present).

It's the only thing I've ever done that's greater than the sum of its parts. It's funnier than it should be and people like it way more than I ever thought they would.

Dana Gould

"GORILLAS IN LEATHER JACKETS, MAN! HONESTLY, THAT'S WHAT DID IT FOR ME."

Above: Maila Nurmi, best known as late night horror host Vampira, bewitches Dana Gould. Recalls Dana of his late friend, "I was to Maila what Ed Wood was to Bela Lugosi. She was larger-than-life: acerbic and very funny."

Bottom: Dana Gould as Dr. Z, relaxed and ready to hang.

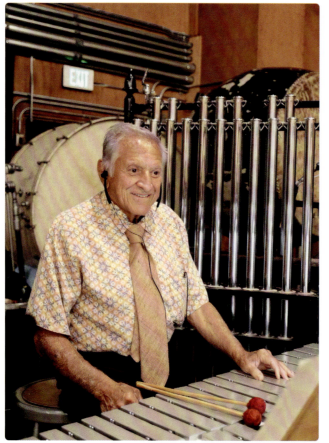

I spent a large part of my childhood pretending to be Cornelius from *Planet of the Apes* (1968). I'd go to the grocery store with my dad and follow him down the aisles, walking like a chimpanzee. They had these large linoleum tiles that were spaced about a foot apart, and if I walked from one to the other it gave me the perfect chimp gait. God knows what my dad thought.

I just wanted to be Cornelius so badly! Everything Roddy McDowall did to bring that character to life was incredible. The way he'd tilt his head, like a dog, to show confusion… You could tell he'd spent a lot of time figuring things out.

Years later, Matt Reeves texted me a picture of Cornelius with a question mark on it. That's how he asked me to score *Dawn of the Planet of the Apes* (2014). I had no idea they were going to make another one, or that he was in the running for it, but I immediately knew what he meant and jumped at the chance.

Matt and I had a similar love for the original movies. We were on different coasts, growing up 3,000 miles apart, but we slowly worked our way towards one another. It's wonderful how you find your friends through your passions.

The first time I heard Jerry Goldsmith's original *Apes* score, I remember thinking, "What are all these sounds? How do you accomplish that?"

It sounded like it had been recorded on an alien planet, and it was years before I figured things out and was able to take those ideas and play with them on shows like *Lost* (2004–10).

One of my percussionists, Emil Richards, played on the original *Apes* scores. He'd spend his time looking for interesting-sounding things. He told me once he'd been in a hardware store and accidentally knocked over a bunch of mixing bowls. He loved the sound they made so he bought them all and used them on *Planet of the Apes*. He gave me one! And we used them on our *Apes* movies, too.

Michael Giacchino

Einstein defined genius as taking the complex and making it simple. I think of that whenever I listen to the powerful brevity of that two-note motif that John Williams conceived for *Jaws* (1975). He did the most with the least.

John Williams is on a planet of his own. Beyond anyone in our field and made out of magic. His ability to write melodies, his taste and technique are all off the map. He is the quintessential film composer.

Charles Bernstein

Opposite (top): Michael Giacchino conducts his score for *Dawn of the Planet of the Apes* (2014) in a monkey mask, aping composer Jerry Goldsmith (inset), who did exactly the same thing while conducting his score for the original *Planet of the Apes* (1968).

Opposite (bottom): Michael Giacchino was thrilled to have percussionist Emil Richards play on his *Dawn of the Planet of the Apes* (2014) score, after Richards had performed the same happy task for Jerry Goldsmith on the soundtrack for *Planet of the Apes* (1968).

Top: Composer Michael Giacchino consults with Caesar on the score for Matt Reeves' *Dawn of the Planet of the Apes* (2014).

Above: Dun-dun, dun-dun... The greatest combination of two notes in all of music history, courtesy of the great John Williams from his immortal score for *Jaws* (1975).

We got the best people we could for *Piranha* (1978). A crew who cared about what they were doing, and could work on a low budget. Making the piranha attacks look like they were actually happening was a particularly daunting task, so there was a lot of designing and figuring things out.

The wide shots we never really got, because the fish were on wires and the groupings looked too uniform. The close-ups worked much better, we found, with puppets ripping off what looked like flesh. There's not a lot of footage of piranha feeding, but ours matched the real thing pretty well. So we figured, let's do more close-ups, and less of what we're struggling with.

The only reason there's any stop motion in the movie is because we had Phil Tippett. Also, because I like stop motion, so I always try to find a way to shoehorn it into anything I'm making. So, even though it wasn't in the script, we added a stop motion creature. Later when he came in to loop the movie, Bradford Dillman asked us what it was. I told him, "Just a little stop motion thing to show people it's the kind of movie where anything can happen."

It was a rather disorganized production. In fact, we almost drowned Phil. He was in the water when Bradford Dillman hit him with the pole he was using to push the raft with. It almost knocked Phil out. Bradford was so angry at how poorly produced the movie was that he went to his trailer and wouldn't come out. We assured him Phil was ok and apologized. A lot. Later, after he saw the film, he sent me a note saying how pleased he was with it, and surprised it turned out so well.

Joe Dante

Joe Dante and Jon Davison were big stop motion fans and wanted it in *Piranha* (1978). Joe said he didn't know how many movies he was going to be able to make, and wanted to fit it in somehow. So we created this odd little piranha creature and had him creeping around Kevin McCarthy's lab.

The original idea was that at the end, there'd be a scene where the sun's going down in Malibu, there are surfers and people picnicking, and from around the bluff of one of the cliffs walks the creature, suddenly hundreds of feet tall, like Talos in *Jason and the Argonauts* (1963).

Sadly, all you ever see of the creature is that tease at the beginning, as the producers killed it off by refusing to give us any more money.

Phil Tippett

Above: Phil Tippett eyes his creation for Joe Dante's *Piranha* (1978).

Left: A very young Rob Bottin pours latex rubber from a plaster mould while working on *Piranha* (1978).

Opposite (top): Two views of Phil Tippett's "odd little" stop motion creature from *Piranha* (1978).

Opposite (bottom): Allan Apone ensured the mutant bear in *Prophecy* (1979) was always well fed to avoid crew disappearances.

Bob Short had jumped on *Piranha's* (1978) underwater effects team. They needed more people, and he suggested me. At that point I was terrified of water. I'm talking a lifelong fear. I tell them, "Fine, I'll go to the pool. I'll fill the blood tanks, I'll pull all the ropes, but I don't want to get in the water."

They're like, "Yeah, fine, whatever."

So, it's getting more and more intense. That's filmmaking! And they say, "It's too much for us to walk back and forth across the pool to get the blood tanks. Put on a wetsuit and just, like, meet us halfway."

So, by inches, finally I was drawn into the depths of, "Put on the scuba gear. It's really easy. Just don't rise faster than the bubbles, or you'll die."

It was a huge workout, and my introduction to on-set insanity. Unfortunately, it was also very addictive!

Chris Walas

I learned an important lesson on John Frankenheimer's mutant bear movie, *Prophecy* (1979). It was Friday, end of the day, and I was putting stuff away, but I had a date that night and my head wasn't in the game. The following Monday, the first shot of the day was going to be of this effects head we'd made, but when I went to get it out of the trailer, I couldn't find it. It wasn't there.

I figured someone must have grabbed it. But why? Maybe I actually left it on set? So I'm running around, swearing and sweating, scouring the stage in a mad panic when I walk past the prop guy. He says, "What's up? You look frazzled."

I tell him, "I've totally screwed up. I don't think I locked the head away. I may have left it out on the set, but now it's not there and I don't know what to do."

He's like, "That's a bad situation. You know everyone's counting on that head being there? They're going to say, why didn't the effects guy put it away?"

He was really rubbing salt in the wound, but he was right. I said, "I'm just going to have to tell them I screwed up, apologize, and keep looking till I find it."

Finally, he says, "I have it. I took it when you left it out last week. When you left Friday night without putting it safely away."

Then he gives it to me. "I hope you learned something from this."

I assured him I had, and after that, I never left for the day without making sure everything was safely in its place. It's a lesson that stuck with me: do your whole job; not just a part of it.

Allan Apone

I've done so many animal things. I was the personal make-up artist to a sea lion for six months on *The Golden Seal* (1983). I turned forty dachshunds into giant rats for *Deadly Eyes* (1982). And I did all the initial tests on Sparky for Tim Burton's *Frankenweenie* (1984).

Tim was a great director, even then. He always knew exactly what he wanted. Sparky was a good boy, too. Mostly just laid down, and didn't get into any kind of mischief. A true professional!

Allan Apone

In one sense, scoring a monster movie is much the same as scoring any other sort of movie. Ultimately, you have to find the humanity in any story, so audiences will care about the characters. *Cujo* (1983) had a scary, rabid dog, but still mostly it was about a troubled family, and finally about a mother desperately trying to save her son.

What makes monster movies special, and quite wonderful for music, is that while on one hand, they're anchored in convention, on the other, they're bold, experimental and give composers license to go anywhere and try anything. No genre is more invitational of creativity.

Charles Bernstein

I couldn't think how to make cockroaches come out of E. G. Marshall. *Creepshow* (1982) was five movies, and by the last one – 'They're Creeping Up on You!' - I was mentally exhausted. Completely spent. Then George [A. Romero] says, "Just cut a hole. Cover it with toilet paper, make-up and hair, and the roaches will eat their way through."

So that's exactly what we did. The entomologist pumped roaches out of the dummy mouth and chest, and I put blood tubing in the body so when they skittered out, the roaches left little bloody footprints everywhere.

It was a wonderful effect and George literally screamed with joy. It's amazing what you can achieve with toilet paper!

Tom Savini

I wanted a practical alligator for the pond scenes in *X* (2022). It might have worked with VFX, but more likely there'd be the uncanny valley thing of, "This is a cool shot, but I know it's not real."

Instead, we sculpted a half-fibreglass, half-foam alligator with an articulated tail that we pulled with a winch. That way, the movement in the water was real and the way the light hit it was real. You really can't beat old school practical effects.

The pond was real, too! It was man-made and used for water skiing and other local activities. What we didn't know though, when we started shooting, was it was full of eels. Actual, real eels. One time, Mia [Goth] was in the water, and she said, "There's eels in here."

So we looked in the water and yeah, there were eels, but we still had to shoot. We had no choice. No one, or any eels, got hurt though.

Ti West

Above: Tom Savini and George A. Romero, together again.
Opposite (top left): Kevin Wasner's sculpture for his and his wife Kerrin Jackson's personal Goat Man project.
Opposite (right): Stephen Vining in Kevin Wasner and Kerrin Jackson's completed Goat Man make-up.
Opposite (bottom left): Kerrin Jackson and Kevin Wasner flank Stephen Vining's otherworldly Goat Man.

"I NEED TO KNOW I CAN DO SOMETHING OTHER THAN A ZOMBIE."

I'd done nine seasons on *The Walking Dead* (2010–22), and I'm like, "I need to know I can do something other than a zombie."

It was a personal project I did with my wife Kerrin [Jackson]. We made a Goat Man! We sculpted it in our apartment. I pre-painted it and Kerrin did beautiful work punching in real fur.

We applied it to Stephen Vining on our weekend off. Stephen played Walkers for us on *The Walking Dead* many times. The man's a rail – very thin. And he can take out his teeth so his cheeks sink in, which gave us extra mileage there.

I'm very proud of what we did. It ended up being one of my favourite-ever make-ups and a fun project to do with Kerrin as we worked so well together.

Kevin Wasner

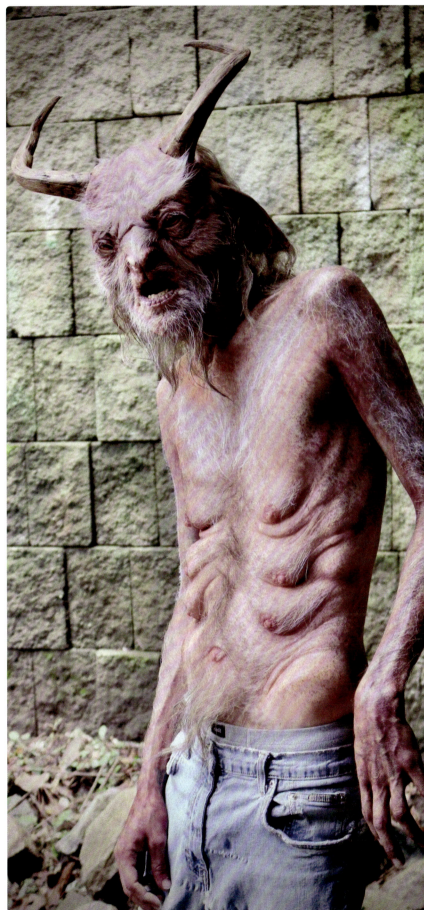

14

TOO GHOUL FOR SCHOOL

Who could have predicted that combining stark, visceral horror with an intense and inescapable atmosphere of dread and hopelessness would create the ultimate audience-pleasing formula? All it took was for hell to fill up, then out they spilled, shuffling into our hearts and hungry for our juicy parts.

We heart zombies!

Seriously, we've built friendships based entirely on discussing what weapon we'd use against the previously deceased. Probably a machete. Best arm yourself, then, for the horde of undead ahead.

There's a moment in Mary Shelley's *Frankenstein* [1818] where Victor looks at the creature objectively for the first time. He's disgusted by the horrendous thing he's created, and after working at it for months, he runs away. It's a feeling most filmmakers can relate to, I think. When you're watching the assembly cut, asking yourself, "What have I done?!"

Axelle Carolyn

Green always struck me as too cartoony a colour for Frankenstein's Monster. I prefer Christopher Lee's look in *The Curse of Frankenstein* (1957): pale, almost yellow, dead skin with deep scarring and a jarring dead eye.

I also like that Lee's performance restored the humanity that Karloff had given the creature in *Frankenstein* (1931), as in the hands of lesser actors, it had become rather caricatured, with the outstretched arms and stiff legs like a wind-up doll.

Sean Sansom

Whenever you dress like Dracula, or do an impression of him, it's Bela Lugosi you're copying. Because Bela was Dracula. That's why he could never get away from the part.

Whenever you do Frankenstein's Monster, grunting and staggering with your arms outstretched, sure it was Karloff who brought that make-up to life, but would you believe that, actually, you're doing Lugosi again?

Though Bela passed on playing the Monster for the first *Frankenstein* (1931), eventually he relented and accepted the role in *Frankenstein Meets the Wolf Man* (1943). What a catastrophe that movie was for him. In Curt Siodmak's original screenplay, Bela's Monster was blind, so it made sense that he walked around with his arms out. But test audiences weren't comfortable that he couldn't see, nor did they like that he could talk, so all of his dialogue was cut, along with any mention that he was blind.

Even though Bela's awkward stumbling made no sense after the cuts, when I was ten, that's how I imitated the Monster, and it's still how most people play him today. It's funny how things work out.

Larry Karaszewski

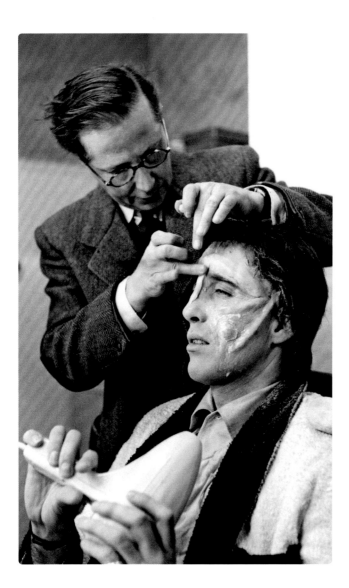

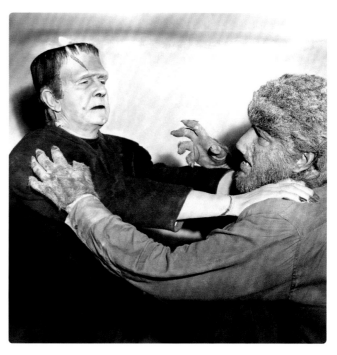

Preceding Spread: When there's no more room in Hell, the dead will walk to Atlanta and get a job on *The Walking Dead* (2010-2022).

Left: Christopher Lee is made up by British make-up master Roy Ashton for his role as Frankenstein's Monster in classic Hammer horror, *The Curse of Frankenstein* (1957).

Above: With great apprehension, Bela Lugosi agreed to play Frankenstein's Monster opposite Lon Chaney Jr's Wolf Man in Universal's *Frankenstein Meets the Wolf Man* (1943).

Opposite: The Monster (Boris Karloff) needs a tailor in *The Bride of Frankenstein* (1935).

"IT'S INSPIRED MUCH MORE DIRECTLY BY MARY SHELLEY'S ORIGINAL TEXT."

Top (left): Artist John Wrightson wrestles with the Monster he created as a homage to his father Bernie's iconic *Frankenstein* graphic novel.

Top (right): John Wrightson's take on Bernie Wrightson's take on Mary Shelley's Frankenstein's Monster.

Above: A frame from Bernie Wrightson's graphic novel adaptation of *Frankenstein*, first published in 1983.

What I love about my father, Bernie Wrightson's rendition of *Frankenstein* (1983), is that while it certainly pays homage to the original Universal monster movies, it's inspired much more directly by Mary Shelley's original text. Dad knew the book backwards and forwards, and embellished every image with his knowledge of it. So for the monster, rather than use the stitching and electrodes from Karloff's incarnation, instead he insinuated burn scars from soldering the elements together, as would have been the case in Shelley's time.

Dad also wanted to challenge himself by making his art feel as though it came from that era, so he didn't use any materials that weren't readily available when Mary Shelley wrote the novel. No airbrushing, for example. Just pens and ink and pencils that rendered his art absolutely timeless.

John Wrightson

Back in 2013, Rick Baker designed three Halloween looks for three different models using MAC Cosmetics. Having been enamoured by his passion and ability since I was young, it was an honour that he chose me to be his Bride of Frankenstein. It was such a privilege to watch him work, and to get to know him, not only as an artist, but as a wonderful man. It's one of my favourite memories and even on my deathbed I'll probably still be talking about it.

Micheline Pitt

When people talk about *The Mummy* (1932), it's Boris Karloff's bandaged make-up they usually praise, but his unbandaged Ardath Bey make-up is really no less iconic. His skin has the texture of parchment with deep lines and sunken, hypnotic eyes. He's so expressive. Karloff had a fantastic face to begin with, and Jack Pierce clearly understood that. It's an elegant and striking make-up that accentuates the angles of his face. A real stroke of genius.

Axelle Carolyn

Top: Looking splendid in a modern take on Elsa Lanchester's look for *Bride of Frankenstein* (1935), Micheline Pitt throttles her creator, Rick Baker, in true monster style.

Right: Boris Karloff was no less creepy as Ardath Bey than he was as the bandaged Imhotep in *The Mummy* (1932).

At first I didn't think of them as zombies. I thought of them as flesh-eaters or ghouls, and never called them zombies in *Night of the Living Dead* (1968). Then people started to write about them, calling them zombies, and all of a sudden that's what they were: the new zombies.

I guess I invented a few rules, like kill the brain and you kill the ghoul, and eventually I surrendered to the idea and called them zombies in *Dawn of the Dead* (1978). But it was never that important to me what they were. Just that they existed.

George A. Romero

You don't really connect with any of the human characters in *Day of the Dead* (1985). Bub's a different story, though. He's the heart of that movie. Between John Vulich's flawless make-up, under Tom Savini's supervision, and Sherman Howard's sympathetic performance, you really feel for him.

It's Bub who drives home the point that, sure, zombies are mindless, flesh-eating monsters now, but once they were kids with parents who loved them, people who had birthdays, and went on holiday. They were us.

Howard Berger

One of the greatest zombie performances of all time was David Emge's in *Dawn of the Dead* (1978), in part because he highlighted everything that happened to him in the movie. He'd been shot in the leg, so that leg hardly worked. His neck was twisted, because that's where he'd been bitten. He was totally committed to being that dead thing. Even the way the gun flipped around on his finger was genius.

Tom Savini

Above: Make-up artist John Vulich enjoys a friendly chat with Sherman Howard's Bub while shooting George A. Romero's *Day of the Dead* (1985).

Below: Tom Savini discusses a scene with George A. Romero on the set of *Day of the Dead* (1985).

Top: George A. Romero's all-time favourite zombie walk was Flyboy's in *Dawn of the Dead* (1978). Apparently, David Emge took inspiration from Lon Chaney Jr's various lurches and stumbles in Universal's vintage *Mummy* sequels.

Above: Howard Berger applies Mark Tierno's Beef Treats make-up under the supervision of Tom Savini for *Day of the Dead* (1985). This was Howard's first location job and he considered it his college days, taking Savini 101.

I got a telegram from George [A. Romero]: "Got another gig. Start thinking of ways to kill people."

That's how I got started on *Dawn of the Dead* (1978).

Tom Savini

Tom [Savini] loved playing Sex Machine in *From Dusk Till Dawn* (1996), but he hated the clean-up because it was oily. I should have handed him a cup of isopropyl myristate and told him to go clean himself, because that's what he used to do to the actors. He was always trying to get out of cleaning them up.

Back on *Day of the Dead* (1985), I'd feel guilty if I didn't do it, despite Tom going, "It's not your job!"

But it was my job! It was his job too. But Tom would try to trick the actors, saying, "Don't you want to wear it home to show your friends?"

We were at the Living Dead Weekend together, in Monroeville, Pennsylvania, and Mark Tierno, who played Beef Treats in the movie, reminded us that Tom would tell them it would all just come off in the shower. But it didn't! And it was painful getting it off.

The thing is, no one likes doing clean-up. Honestly, I hate it just as much as Tom. The difference is, I do it!

Howard Berger

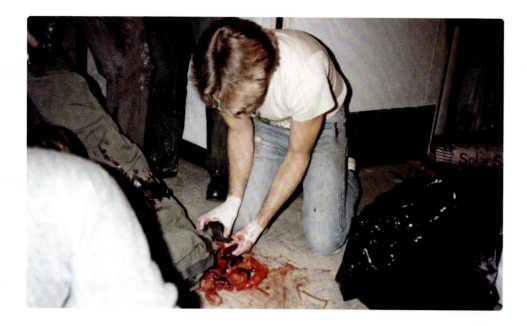

Left: Nicknamed by Tom Savini, Greg "Gut Boy" Nicotero wrangled real pig intestines on *Day of the Dead* (1985).

Below: Tom Savini readies the Taso Stavrakis head-rip gag, while a zombified Greg Nicotero prepares to do the dirty deed. Greg was Tom's go-to guy when filming blood gags, so he ended up playing several zombies in *Day of the Dead* (1985).

Bottom: Joe Pilato squirms at the sight – and smell – of real rotten guts as he's torn limb from limb in *Day of the Dead* (1985). "People swear there's a rubber chicken inside Joe," said Tom Savini. "But there was no rubber chicken."

Opposite: *Shaun of the Dead* (2004) star Simon Pegg and director Edgar Wright got to play zombies for a day in *Land of the Dead* (2005). Here they are – with Simon in a cracking Bub tribute make-up – joined by Greg Nicotero and their hero, George A. Romero.

We had a refrigerator full of guts for the scene in *Day of the Dead* (1985) where Joe Pilato's torn in half. Only somebody unplugged it while we were away for a few weeks in Florida.

So it's 2am and we're about to shoot the scene. We discover a fridge full of rotten pig intestines, but it's too late to go buy fresh guts and we can't delay the shoot. We could have made rubber intestines, but nothing moves and slithers and splatters like the real thing.

So we made do with what we had, but the stench was unbelievable. We had to wear gas masks to get through the scene. But we couldn't protect Joe because you'd see it. So while we were totally protected, Joe writhed around for hours in decomposing innards and it can't have been much less grim than actually being torn apart and eaten by zombies.

Tom Savini

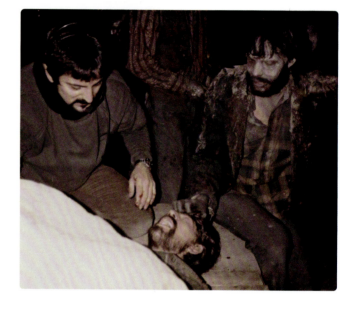

Zombies are interesting monsters because they're the absolute personification of our worst fear: death. They are literally walking death. You couldn't ask for a clearer metaphor for our own mortality. You could be in a room with a Romero zombie and outrun it all day long, but eventually you'd have to sleep and that's when it would get you. It's like in life, you can keep fit, stay off red meat and get lots of sleep, but eventually death will catch up with you anyway.

Dawn of the Dead (1978) wasn't released on VHS until 1989, by which time I'd become obsessed with it. I'd read about it, and look at pictures in books, and really just torture myself about how badly I wanted to see it. When I finally did, it was everything I hoped it would be. Not schlocky at all, but genuinely smart and eerie and sad and funny. Just a fucking great movie.

Edgar Wright had a similar experience with the film, and we bonded over how much we both loved it. We put a little zombie sequence in our TV show, *Spaced* (1999–2001), and that's when the idea of making our own zombie film really took hold. Naivety powered us through the development process. We always just assumed we were going to get it done, and somehow we did.

I have so many fantastic memories of shooting *Shaun of the Dead* (2004), but there's one that's hard to beat. We had about 300 made-up extras for the scene outside the Winchester, where I jump up on the table to distract all the zombies. But the first time we tried to shoot it, and I jumped up on the table, this huge sea of zombies just turned and lurched towards me. I had to yell, "Cut!"

It was just so overwhelming. As a kid I'd had recurring dreams about zombies chasing me, and suddenly it was all too real. I wasn't prepared!

Shaun, of course, was full of references to George A. Romero's zombie films, and we made a point of saying so. I think George appreciated that we made the effort to do that, as so many people still steal from him without ever giving him credit.

I mean, he invented the modern zombie, you know? Prior to George, zombies were all about voodoo and slavery. A whole different creature. But it was George who added the viral communication of vampires, along with all sorts of other bits and pieces to create what people now see as the modern zombie. It's very contemporary, and so many people just nick his ideas and never really thank him for it.

George invited Edgar and me to the set of *Land of the Dead* (2005), and he was so kind. Such a sweetheart. He even wore a *Shaun of the Dead* badge! He was so laid back, so generous and mild mannered. For us, it was the extraordinary culmination of a lifelong admiration for the guy.

We even got to cameo as zombies in the film! Greg [Nicotero] knew I loved Bub from *Day of the Dead* (1985). Sherman Howard's

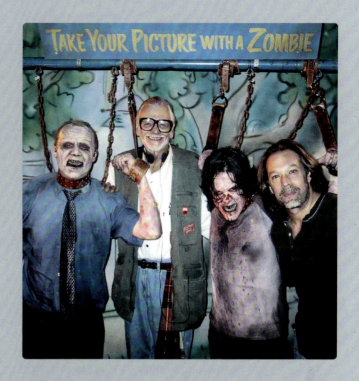

performance is just the most incredibly sensitive and moving portrayal of a zombie ever. He took something as rancid and disgusting as a zombie, and turned it into someone you rooted for, and even kind of loved. So Greg pulls out my appliance, and says, "Look who it is."

It was Bub. I got to play my zombie hero! A dream come true, and when I walked around the set that night, and found myself in a corridor alone, I totally Bubbed out, stumbling around like the big man himself. And, of course, I totally channelled Howard for my performance. Then a few Halloweens ago, I went to a party as Bub. You see, I still haven't gotten him out of my system.

Simon Pegg

"THE FIRST TIME WE TRIED TO SHOOT IT... THIS HUGE SEA OF ZOMBIES JUST TURNED AND LURCHED TOWARDS ME. I HAD TO YELL, 'CUT!'"

The advent of first-person shooter videogames like *Resident Evil* (1996) rejuvenated the zombie genre, and the success of *28 Days Later* (2002) and *Shaun of the Dead* (2004) paved the way for George A. Romero's *Land of the Dead* (2005). George gave me my first job, so running the make-up effects on *Land of the Dead* was my chance to pay him back. Of course, I wanted everything to be perfect, and agonized over every detail.

There's a scene where a girl is grabbed by a zombie (Jake McKinnon) who bites her cheek and rips the skin off. Sean Sansom, Gino Crognale and the guys made her up with a gelatine appliance, blood tubes and a plug. It was a hard shoot – all nights – and we only had one take to get it right.

George says, "Action!"

Jake walks over, bites her on the cheek, and she starts flailing her arms. Right when that big piece of meat gets bitten off, her arm goes up and blocks the effect.

George yells, "Cut!"

I'm standing there, defeated. George asks me what's wrong. I told him the effect got blocked. So he asks me, "If somebody was biting your cheek off, how would you react? Would you flail your arms?"

I told him, "Probably."

"IF SOMEBODY WAS BITING YOUR CHEEK OFF, HOW WOULD YOU REACT?"

George said, "It was real. That's what the actress chose to do at that particular moment and nothing's more important to me than reality."

It was my first lesson in understanding the difference between being a director and being an effects person. Because when you're an effects person, it's all about the effect. But when you're a director, the effect is just one of fifty elements you have to put together.

That's something I've kept in mind whenever I've directed myself: What story are we telling? What's motivating the character? How close should we get with the camera? Not just, the make-up took two hours to apply so we have to make the most of it. That's the biggest challenge in making the transition from make-up effects, or stunts, or director of photography, to directing. Your focus has to dramatically widen, and that's an elusive concept to a lot of people.

Greg Nicotero

Eyes are the windows to the soul, but zombies have no soul, so for my *Night of the Living Dead* (1990) remake, I had John Vulich and Everett Burrell make these milky white lenses that stole the soul right out of them. You could look them in the eye, but you wouldn't see a person.

Tom Savini

The Funeral Home Zombie in Tom Savini's remake of *Night of the Living Dead* (1990) is so damn creepy. His clothes are split up the back, so when he walks, he steps on his pants and everything's pulled down. Then you see his big autopsy scar, because of course, he's fresh out of the casket. Tom's zombies always tell a story. They're scarier because they feel real.

Howard Berger

Opposite: Greg Nicotero enlisted everyone on the crew of *Land of Dead* (2005) to play a zombie or three. Here he is with a grinning Gino Crognale.
Left: Eugene Clark as zombie leader Big Daddy in *Land of the Dead* (2005).
Below: Make-up artist Greg Funk was recruited by director Tom Savini to play the Cemetery Zombie in his remake of *Night of the Living Dead* (1990). The make-up effects were designed and created by John Vulich and Everett Burrell of Optic Nerve Studios.

Stuart Gordon's motto was, "More blood is not enough!" So we kept the blood flowing, and the laughs... Stuart had a grand sense of humour and always found the funny in every situation. I remember he was worried, though, after he saw Lee Percy's first cut of Re-Animator (1985), because the film was funnier than he'd expected. So there was a lot of back-and-forth about the tenor of the piece. Was it a horror movie or a comedy?

In the end, it was both, and more... It was disturbing, and offensive, but really, mainly, just grandly over-the-top, because Stuart came from the theatre, and wanted everything to be BIG. Like, we'd be doing a scene and he'd say, "I'm not quite sure I'm getting enough."

He wanted everything to be heightened. It was his big screen debut and I don't think he realized he didn't have to play to the back of the house. So whatever I was doing, he'd encourage me to "Scream louder, struggle harder..."

That operatic quality worked so well, though. After his next movie, From Beyond (1986), he started to tone things down a bit, but I really loved his first few films. They were strangely beautiful and their tone was just so special. They were the happiest of accidents.

Barbara Crampton

Frank [Henenlotter] just said, "Make her fuckable. But it's a monster." Patty [Mullen] was very pretty, shapely, and wore revealing outfits, so I really only had to take care of the monster part on Frankenhooker (1990). I leaned into the stitching, giving her an African-American arm and an Asian shoulder, hand-sewing the prosthetics every day with playfully loose, baggy thread.

It was a fun make-up!

Gabe Bartalos

"IT WAS DISTURBING, AND OFFENSIVE, BUT REALLY, MAINLY, JUST GRANDLY OVER-THE-TOP."

Left: Barbara Crampton gets a hug from master of horror Stuart Gordon.
Above: Gabe Bartalos had Patty Mullen in stitches on the set of Frankenhooker (1990).
Opposite: The brothers Yagher – Chris, Jeff and Kevin – on the set of Tales from the Crypt (1989-1996), where Jeff played Enoch, The Two-Faced Man.

When we were kids I always played the monsters in the movies we made, so when Kevin got to direct an episode of *Tales from the Crypt* (1989–96), even though at the time I was a leading man and no casting director would have ever considered me for the role of Enoch, The Two-Faced Man, he knew what the role meant to me and gave me the part. It was my dream come true!

The episode was 'Lower Berth' (S02, E14, 1990): I fall in love with a mummy and she gives birth to the Crypt Keeper! Like Karloff's take on Frankenstein's Monster, I played him like a child.

It was a six-hour make-up and we shot seven days straight, so it was gruelling, but I loved every minute. Well... Almost every minute. Kevin was busy directing so he didn't have time to apply my make-up. Instead, one of his assistants did it, but the guy had a shaky hand, and whenever he got near my eyes, he'd poke them with the brushes.

Also I had them put me in a harness to hunch me over, just like Chaney wore for *The Hunchback of Notre Dame* (1923). That was a big mistake, though, as after a while it really hurt my back. Still, none of it really mattered. I was happy as a pig in shit!

Jeff Yagher

> tan [Winston] and Tim [Burton] had already worked on the design for Edward Scissorhands a while. Tim's an artist, so he pretty much designs his characters ahead of time, and Stan had sculpted busts of Johnny [Depp], so they had a good idea of how he'd look in the movie. But as a make-up artist, it was my job to bring it to life. Because you can sit and draw, and sculpt, and paint a stone head all you want, but until it starts moving, it's not a critter.

Ve Neill

> *esident Evil* (2002) was one of those shows where they didn't want to call them zombies. They wanted them subtle, not overly cheekbony, with a more virusy kind of feel. We did some foam latex tests, messing around with different skin tones, but they weren't floating our boat. Then Matthew Smith did a make-up in gelatine, which looked way more real, and everyone loved it.

The interesting thing about gelatine, though, is it doesn't exactly resist moisture. So we're shooting in this industrial complex, with real steam swirling through every scene to give it atmosphere, and the whole place is soaking wet. If our undead got anywhere near it, the gelatine would start to peel and it looked like their faces were swarming with tiny jellyfish. So it was a rather steep learning curve.

Duncan Jarman

Above: Ve Neill works her magic on Johnny Depp for Tim Burton's *Edward Scissorhands* (1990), applying a make-up designed by the great Stan Winston.

Opposite: A bitey, blistered Gino Crognale – peckish for a nice bit of flesh – in a make-up applied by Garrett Immel for *The Walking Dead* (2010-2022).

> o create an emaciated zombie girl for Matthew Barney's *Cremaster 3* (2002), I told production I needed the thinnest person they could find. Someone I could add prosthetics to and still be really thin. If they gave me someone with meat, I'd have nowhere to go. So they found me Nesrin Karanouh, an Indian girl in her early twenties.

Soon after, into our studio comes this 88lb girl, barely able to walk. So fragile, it seemed like her bones were about to splinter. I explained to Nesrin in no uncertain terms how difficult and challenging the job would be. That it required a full-body casting, extensive prosthetic application and lots of detailed airbrushing. Beyond that, her character would be nude, we'd be shooting on an exterior set, and for her resurrection scene, she'd have to claw her way out of the ground.

I painted the job in the worst possible light, but she was up for it, and she was great. She understood I was trying to do something ambitious with a layered make-up effect, and she sat patiently as I worked. Tall and thin, she was the perfect canvas, and when we walked her on set, people didn't know how to react. It wasn't just that they were creeped out, or freaking out. They actually didn't know what they were looking at. Like, was she in her nineties? Or was that maybe a puppet?

Boy, did she set the tone. We shot for three days, and even after people lightened up a little around her, they still didn't really understand what she was, or how to talk to her. It was a remarkably strong reaction.

Gabe Bartalos

"BY THE SIXTH OR SEVENTH TAKE I HAD A NURSE BESIDE ME, FEEDING ME OXYGEN HITS."

I've played in lots of make-ups and suits. They have to be able to function. The performer wearing it has to be comfortable enough to focus on giving a good performance. I've been in some rough suits though, and in those, your mind's more focused on whatever problems you have to overcome.

I've worn stuff that was built for me and it's effortless. But if I'm wearing something we just threw together, if it doesn't fit right, or if you can't breathe or see easily, that's rough.

I played a monster for half a day on *In the Mouth of Madness* (1994). I had a huge shell and tentacle arms, but I'm 5' 10", 160lbs, not a big dude, and that suit wasn't made for me. It wasn't snug, so I was fighting distance.

John [Carpenter] wanted all this crazy motion in it. He kept saying, "Get more animated."

I was doing my best but I was blind, gasping for air and it was so hard trying to move in that thing. By the sixth or seventh take, I had a nurse beside me, feeding me oxygen hits between shots and I swear by that stage they were just fucking with me. Getting me to thrash about, just to see how long I could go.

Of course, a suit has to work aesthetically, but without function, it's not gonna do what you want it to. What you want to aim for is a suit that fits your performer like a second skin.

When I played a zombie in *House of 1000 Corpses* (2003) – that's me on the poster – Wayne Toth did a great lifecast of me, built the pieces to put on me, and everything fitted so snugly, I played the part completely without ever thinking about what I was wearing.

Gino Crognale

I refer to my days on *The Walking Dead* (2010–22) as the toughest and most unglamorous of my career, but with the most wonderful group of people I've ever worked with.

Kerrin Jackson

We're at a production meeting for *The Walking Dead* (2010–22), working through a script and making notes. We get to a featured walker called Winslow and Greg [Nicotero] goes, "Gino's playing that."

Greg picks me for a lot of stuff. He knows I'm always game. Later, he showed me the design from KNB. He says, "Here's the suit you'll be wearing."

It was spectacular. I'm looking at it, thinking, "This is more than just a make-up."

When the suit showed up in Georgia, we did a few test fittings and I'm glad we did, because I wasn't in LA when they built it and a lot of adjustments had to be made. Like, the chest piece had to be let out so I could breathe. Also I added a jock strap with a cup just in case Andy Lincoln accidentally kicked or punched me in the balls during our fight scene. And I drilled little holes into the helmet, so I could detect Andy approaching and react, though I was still pretty much blind in that thing.

There were a lot of parts to that suit. Fibreglass parts. Cosmetic parts. And then they wanted me taller, so they built me these cumbersome Frankenstein shoes. I had trouble walking in them, which maybe added to my performance.

The day we shot, I was in make-up by 4am. It was a three-and-a-half hour application by Kevin Wasner and Jake Garber. Once they put me into it, man, it was so great. When I walked on set, the crew's jaws dropped. Winslow was stunning.

We shot it in the Heaps, this huge trash dump. It was 95 degrees that day. Hot and humid as hell, and the set had no air. KNB sent down a cool suit, basically a vest with tubes that pumps ice water around your body. Without that I'd never have been able to make it through the day.

It was a long, tough day, but worth all the effort. Winslow's probably the most iconic walker in the whole series, and I'm proud I got to play him. You see him on all sorts of stuff. Everyone knows Winslow.

Gino Crognale

Opposite (top): Gino Crognale en route to playing a Lovecraftian horror for John Carpenter's *In the Mouth of Madness* (1994).

Opposite (bottom): Kerrin Jackson touches up the Alma Mobley Ghost Story (1981) make-up that she applied for *The Walking Dead* (2010-2022).

Above (left): Gino Crognale takes a well-earned breather between takes as the Winslow Zombie for *The Walking Dead* (2010-2022).

Above (right): Gino Crognale in all his gory glory as the Winslow Zombie, designed and created at KNB EFX under the supervision of Greg Nicotero for *The Walking Dead* (2010-2022).

A good walker has as much to do with the person underneath as it does the sculpted make-up. Of the thousands of walkers we made up over the years on *The Walking Dead* (2010–22), though they were all a joy to work with, Coleman Youmans was a real standout for me.

Soon after the show started, Kevin Wasner did a make-up on him that blew my mind. The appliances were perfectly suited to Coleman's facial structure, and together with his physique and performance, created a truly iconic character.

Kevin subtly referenced the production artwork in his painting and airbrushing, and I feel his work played an integral part in the re-invention of the modern-day zombie make-up.

That style has been copied, adapted and paid homage to, countless times. It's a testament to how beautiful his make-ups were on the show.

Kerrin Jackson

"EVENTUALLY OUR WALKERS WERE LIKE MR POTATO HEAD!"

I tried to figure out once how many walkers I applied for *The Walking Dead* (2010–22). I did the first nine seasons, then some of the last two. Most of the seasons were 16 episodes long and I averaged 10 to 15 make-ups per episode. So I reckon at least 1,500.

The first season, there were four of us sculpting, figuring out how to do things. Mainly we used transfers the first year, with little hollowed-out pieces, but it became a storage issue. Where do you keep transfers for 30 or 40 people every day? It was a pain.

There was a learning curve, and every season we'd drop some things and try others. We switched to foam and learned to cut corners. Eventually our walkers were like Mr Potato Head! Each appliance was named after whoever sculpted it, so we'd be like, "Let's use a Kevin face and a Mitch head with Norman cheeks and a Dave chin."

Nothing was more important than the performers themselves, as there's no point putting a good make-up on a bad actor. Back in the second season, we had 40 walkers lined up, and when they set off, every one of them dragged their right foot. They fed off each other and we had to break them of that.

Usually we'd cherry-pick guys whose body form gave us more to work with – big eyes, small nose and long necks – then we'd train the heck out of them. That said, there were a few guys who weren't the right proportions at all, but really good performers, so we used them all the time.

Kevin Wasner

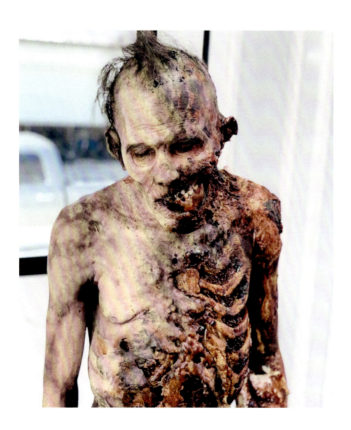

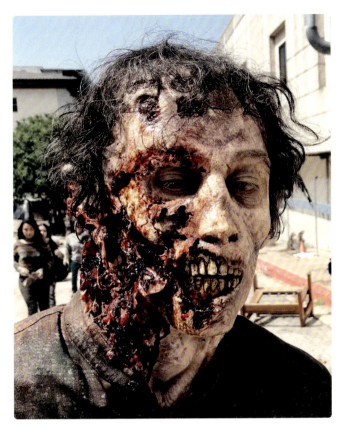

I've helped create countless walkers, but perhaps my favourites were ones that, at first, I really wasn't sure about. They were from an episode of Fear the Walking Dead (2015–23; S06, E07) that had a taxidermist, based on Ed Gein, clamping walkers down and sewing animal skins and horns on them.

I thought maybe it was too strange a concept, that people would find it laughable, but it turned out better and more effective than I ever expected. We created maybe six or eight of these custom walkers, and they were among the most difficult and time-consuming we've ever had to produce, as we had to hand-sew tufts of fur, alligator skin and horns onto all the usual prosthetic pieces.

When we finally got to set, though… They were so cool and unique, unlike anything I'd seen in a Romero film or really anywhere else. I fell in love with them.

John Wrightson

Opposite (left and right): There's never a shortage of zombies on *The Walking Dead* (2010-2022) thanks to Greg Nicotero and his incredible team.

All this page: A disparate trio of ghastly rotters in make-ups applied by John Wrightson for *The Walking Dead* (2010-2022).

It was easy suspending disbelief on the set of *The Walking Dead* (2010–22), because everything was so damn real. The level of commitment and expertise from the crew was off the charts. There were moments during filming, when I was being chased by walkers, or they were trying to bite me, or I was covered in blood, where it got so intense, the adrenaline kicked in and I was in danger of forgetting myself. Like, they'd say, "We love what you're doing, man, but maybe dial it back some, 'cos you don't wanna hurt anyone."

Then there'd be times when it was all just hilariously funny. Like at lunch, when you'd see a walker trying to decide which salad dressing to choose. Seeing them out of context like that, I'd just laugh my ass off.

Chad Coleman

Hafþór Júlíus Björnsson, who played the Mountain in *Game of Thrones* (2011–19) from Season 4, was a record-breaking strongman and absolutely enormous. We had to figure out how to paint him, and fast, because we never had a lot of time to do make-ups.

So it's 3am in a tent in Belfast, freezing cold, and there are three of us with rollers, painting him like he's a wall. Just going up and down his body, rolling this pale, undead flesh colour all over. More like decorating, really, but it worked!

Duncan Jarman

"THREE OF US WITH ROLLERS, PAINTING HIM LIKE HE'S A WALL."

Top: Chad Coleman and Sonequa Martin-Green as ill-fated siblings in *The Walking Dead* (2010-2022).

Right: Barrie Gower applies an early stage of deterioration make-up to Hafþór Júlíus Björnsson for his role as the Mountain in *Game of Thrones* (2011-2019).

Creepshow (2019–present) was such a fluke, the way it happened. I was at the airport, looking for something to download and read on my iPad, and I found this book called *Nights of the Living Dead* (2017). I'd never heard of it before, but I loved the idea. It's a collection of short stories, by a bunch of different authors, all set the same evening as *Night of the Living Dead* (1968).

One story, in particular, was right up my alley: 'A Dead Girl Named Sue', by Craig Engler. It was about the son of a local politician who's a paedophile and a murderer, but even after he's captured by the police, he acts like he's untouchable. So they drag a body bag into his cell – one of his victims, now a zombie – and she kills him.

I wanted the rights to the story, as I thought it would make a unique and interesting short film. It turned out the guy who wrote it was the head of Shudder. So I'm chatting with Craig, and he tells me, "It's funny you should reach out, because we want to make a *Creepshow* TV show, and need someone to be the creative force behind it."

I couldn't believe the synchronicity and jumped at the chance!

For me, the show was an opportunity to pay homage to my era of movie-making, when everything was practical. We told amazing stories with unique monsters, and yeah, we got to make *A Dead Girl Named Sue*. It turned out great!

Greg Nicotero

What I loved about the make-ups in *World War Z* (2013), which I worked on for Mark Coulier, is that there were three different groups that made up the infected masses. Bespoke hero prosthetics, generic mid-ground prosthetics, and for the background, old-school theatrical highlight and shadow using Aqua colours. I really enjoyed doing these the most, creating the illusion of cheekbones, sockets and wrinkles with paint.

I went to teach a load of Hungarian make-up artists how to do that, but they got so artistic about it! I was like, "No, no, no, just let yourself go! Look, there's the highlights in the brow. There's the highlights in the cheekbones. Bam! There's a different colour with a different brush, right next to you. Shadows! Step back and half-close your eyes. Go back in, do a bit of detail…"

You could get one out, literally, in five minutes. That was as enjoyable as anything else I've done.

Stephen Murphy

Above: One of a legion of infected victims from *World War Z* (2013), made up by artist Stephen Murphy.

Left: Stephen Murphy's sculpture of an infected victim, working under the supervision of make-up master Mark Coulier, for *World War Z* (2013).

CHAPTER 14 - TOO GHOUL FOR SCHOOL

The Alphas in *Army of the Dead* (2021) aren't your traditional zombies. They don't degrade. Whatever the disease is, it slowly dissolves their pigmentation until they become these translucent, ghostly, shrimp-like creatures.

For Zeus, we pushed Richard Cetrone's make-up to the extreme. It was like he'd walked out of Body Worlds. He's covered in silicone prosthetics from the waist up, with maybe 24 pieces on him: full chest piece, little oblique pieces, a full back piece, bicep, tricep, deltoid wraps, forearm, upper and lower, leaving spaces for joints and movement which we tied in with paint, and then a full, seamless neck piece. Then around eight pieces on the face, plus wigs.

The first time we did his make-up, it took four of us, five-and-a-half hours to achieve. Eventually we got it down to under three hours, and three people, as there's only so many bodies you could fit around him.

He was in that make-up close to 50 days. Not easy in the heat and humidity of New Mexico. They were long days for us too, maintaining that make-up during the monsoon. It was a tough shoot, but I'm happy with everything we did, and the movie's really fun.

Justin Raleigh

"WHATEVER THE DISEASE IS, IT SLOWLY DISSOLVES THEIR PIGMENTATION UNTIL THEY BECOME THESE TRANSLUCENT, GHOSTLY, SHRIMP-LIKE CREATURES."

Above: Justin Raleigh hid every trace of Athena Perample's beauty under her magnificent make-up as the Alpha Queen for Zack Snyder's *Army of the Dead* (2021).

Left: Justin Raleigh ensures his zombies are ready for their close-ups on the set of *Army of the Dead* (2021).

Opposite: Richard Cetrone is no stranger to wearing extensive prosthetic make-ups for his roles in films. For *Army of the Dead* (2021), he went full zombie to play Zeus the Alpha King.

I'd not yet played the game, but I was aware of the incredible creatures in *The Last of Us* (2013). Neil Druckmann and his team struck gold with all those strong, original, innovative designs. All those beautiful organic shapes and vibrant colours. Full disclosure, two seasons into the show, I've still not played the game, but I have held the controller on occasion and always died immediately. Honestly, I'm happier spending hours sitting behind my daughter Lottie as she plays it, telling her what to do, though it massively winds her up.

We got the gig as the showrunner on *The Last of Us* (2023–present), Craig Mazin, had worked with us before on *Chernobyl* (2019). He knew that even though we're not natural born gamers, we could definitely handle the make-up stuff.

Neil gave us access to all the designs Naughty Dog created for the games, but encouraged us to come up with concept art of our own. We spent a month working with Rob Bliss, Simon Webber and Howard Swindell, concepting variations of the clickers, bloaters, stalkers and other infected characters. And the guys came up with lots of gorgeous artwork, but eventually we said to Neil, "We could do this for the next six months, but we're not necessarily going to generate anything better or more original than what you've already done."

Ultimately, we combined the best of the Naughty Dog designs with subtle, organic ideas of our own, adding finishes, textures, glosses, mattes and fuzzes. None of which were required for the videogame, as you don't get close enough to the infected to require that level of detail, but they were essential to bring the infected into the 'real world' of live-action, high-definition television.

Again, being honest, I hate mushrooms. School dinners put me off them when I was a kid. Tinned and boiled, all those horrible, slimy, grey, snail-like fungal forms. Even the smell makes me want to retch. So of course we get a job requiring months of mushroom-themed research and development!

It's disturbing that the Cordyceps fungus that infects people in the game, and turns them into walking mushroom monsters, is a real thing. An actual parasite that burrows into insect brains, turns them into zombies, and makes them explode with infectious spores. The only reason Cordyceps can't survive in humans is our body temperatures are too high for them. But obviously in the game they evolve and 'shroom us, too.

Almost as horrifying, for me at least, was that for the second season, we started 3D-scanning mushrooms, so we could experiment with printing different sizes and combinations. We bought a ton of grow bags and dozens of mushroom varieties, all kinds of weird shapes and textures. We turned a warehouse round the corner from us into our own BGFX mushroom farm, and when the mushrooms were ripe and in full bloom, we scanned them. Then we left them to deteriorate. To rot and get mouldy, break down and liquefy into these horrible, meaty, glossy shapes. Then we scanned them again. It was a disgusting process, but worth the pain, as we were able to incorporate all that information into our sculptures for season two.

Barrie Gower

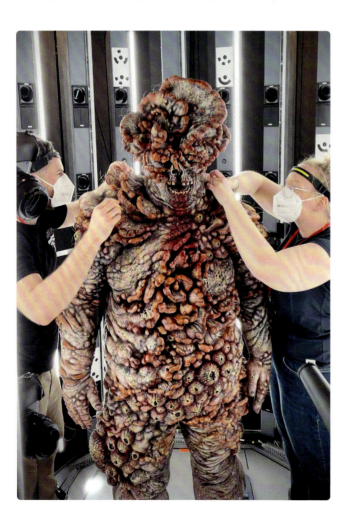

"I HAVE HELD THE CONTROLLER ON OCCASION AND ALWAYS DIED IMMEDIATELY."

Left: Barrie and Sarah Gower's crew suit up a full-body clicker for *The Last of Us* (2023–present).

Opposite: "Obviously the clickers from *The Last of Us* (2023–present) were based on Naughty Dog's character designs, but with enough of a BGFX twist to ground them in reality," said Duncan Jarman. "In the game they're animated and totally wild, so the challenge was to adapt them just enough to make them believable, if you saw them walking down the street."

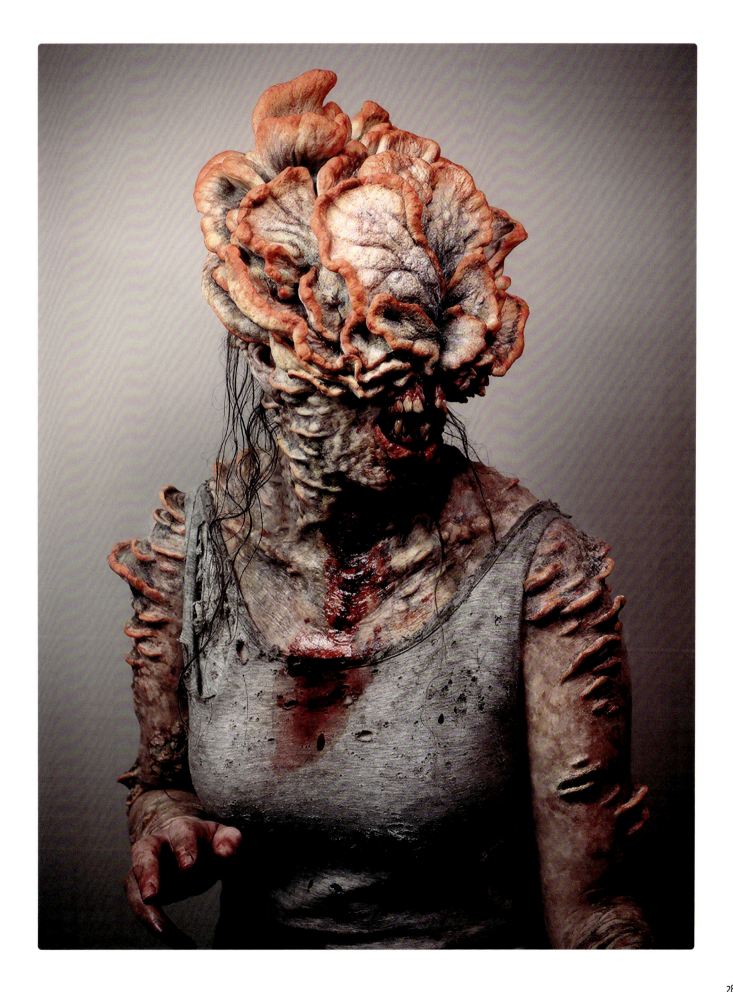

There's nothing quite like that moment when people see your creations up close and in person. On *Game of Thrones* (2011–19), the White Walkers didn't have too many shoot days. So whenever the six stunt guys were made up and had their uniforms on, particularly if the Night King [Richard Brake/Vladimir 'Furdo' Furdik] was there as well, everyone would just stop dead and stare. I'd get such a buzz from how excited they always got!

I remember when Neil [Druckmann] and Craig [Mazin] first saw our clicker make-up test for *The Last of Us* (2023–present). There was lots at stake as Barrie [Gower] and I are perfectionists. When you're creating something, it's all you do and all you think about. You put everything you have into it, because that's art, isn't it? Honestly we'd have been absolutely crushed if they weren't happy.

The stakes felt especially high with Neil, as they were his babies. When he wrote the original game I doubt he ever expected to see a clicker for real, let alone stand next to one. But he loved it! They both did. Even thinking about it now – how happy they were – I still get quite emotional.

Sarah Gower

Left: The team at Barrie and Sarah Gower's BGFX designed and created this gorgeous piece for *The Last of Us* (2023-present). Truly, an iconic wall decoration that any monster kid would be proud to hang in their home.

Below: Sarah Gower hangs out with a fun guy during production on *The Last of Us* (2023-present).

15

BOO STORIES

Have you ever felt like something's watching you? Heard a whisper from the shadows, or gotten goosebumps from a sudden chill? Have the hairs on the back of your neck ever jumped to attention, or an indiscernible blur caught the corner of your eye?

We don't mean to alarm you, but if you answered 'yes' to any of these questions, you are 100 per cent being haunted, so best snuggle with your shrieknificent smother as you cautiously tiptoe through the ghostliness ahead.

The *Ghostbusters* (1984) logo is known worldwide. Everyone can sing the song, even people who've never heard of the film. Back when he was making it, though, there's no way my dad could have predicted what a sensation it would become.

They just made it so quickly. The original *Ghostbusters* had a release date that was less than a year after their green light. They just went and made a movie, not knowing how the hell they were going to finish it. Just running and gunning. That's something my dad reminded me of any time I told him I didn't have enough time on something: "On *Ghostbusters*, we didn't even have time to think. We just made shit up as we went."

It's a nice reminder that you don't need all the time and money in the world to make a great film. You should just go with your gut, and have a good time.

I was at a DGA [Directors Guild of America] thing once, sitting next to Steven Spielberg, and he asked me, "What are you working on?"

I told him, "I'm going to make the next *Ghostbusters* movie."

He lit up and said: "Library Ghost. Top ten scares of all time."

My dad actually blushed when I told him that. I think Spielberg is right. Not because the library ghost is one of the best horror scenes of all time – it's just completely unexpected.

So you go in, knowing it's a comedy, right? It's got Bill. It's got Dan [Aykroyd]. But then the first major scare happens, and it's 1,000 per cent legit! It just comes with a knife. Most times if you're watching a comedy about ghosts, you know there'll be some scares, but you're kind of expecting B- scares at most. But with the Library Ghost, they come at you with an A+ scare right out of the gate. And you don't know what to expect from the movie any more, so it keeps you on your toes in a way no other comedy had ever done up until then.

Then it's ghost after ghost, each one more iconic than the last. A well-designed creature should be recognizable by silhouette, and what's crazy is, *Ghostbusters*, I'd argue, has three: Slimer, the Terror Dogs and the Stay Puft Marshmallow Man are all identifiable by silhouette, and that's a remarkable feat of design. The craziest part is, they weren't created by students of the form, but rather by comedy nerds who just had a feeling and ran with it.

Slimer is like that guy at the end of the bar who's had 20 drinks. He's funny to look at, but if he suddenly put his arm around you, you'd be terrified because you're not sure if he's going to belch in your face or stab you with a pen.

The Stay Puft Marshmallow Man is a cosmic piece of genius straight from the brain of Aykroyd. How does someone even come up with that? The grocery shelf smile, the chubby fingers... But somehow scary! It's inexplicable.

Above all else, the Terror Dog, I think, is perfect. His growl, his eyes, his reptilian skin... That was the ultimate horror creature of my youth. I remember thinking it was laying in wake under my bed every night and I was absolutely fucking terrified.

For *Ghostbusters: Afterlife* (2021), the one thing we wanted to improve about the Terror Dog was his run cycle. In the original, when you see the Claymation model run out of Rick Moranis's place, it kind of bunny hops across the street. For *Afterlife*, we wanted our heroes to feel as though they were being chased by a lion.

Brynn Metheney, our concept artist, widened the Terror Dog's hips so it could run rather than hop, but Arjen Tuiten, who designed and built the animatronics, fought to keep their humorously tiny hips, as that was more in keeping with the original design. Ultimately, we settled on a hybrid model that honoured that past and still got us to a gallop.

One feature I wanted Arjen to recreate exactly was the glassiness of the Terror Dogs' eyes. CG gives artists the infinite ability to keep adding details, but it can sometimes articulate too much and actually make things less scary. There was a simplicity to the original, practical design that made it much more horrifying and unsettling than any detail born from a computer.

Jason Reitman

"IT'S GHOST AFTER GHOST, EACH ONE MORE ICONIC THAN THE LAST."

The first movie I remember being frightened by was *Ghostbusters* (1984). The opening scene in the library where the old librarian unexpectedly turns into a monster: I was totally unprepared for that. It was the first time I felt unsafe during a movie and that intrigued me. I wanted to know what else was out there, and test the limits of what I could take.

Ti West

Slimer is pretty hard to beat. You know Dan Aykroyd based him on John Belushi?

Richard Edlund

Preceding Spread: A cagey Shayne Wyler as the Jackal in Dark Castle's *Thir13en Ghosts* (2001).

Opposite: Best not speak around Steve Johnson's iconic Library Ghost from Ivan Reitman's *Ghostbusters* (1984).

Below: Gozer's Terror Dog wants to go walkies in Jason Reitman's *Ghostbusters: Afterlife* (2021).

I loved working on *Thir13en Ghosts* (2001). Always looking for new and interesting ways to apply paint, and keep it on. Such a fun and creative set. And the laughs!

Norman Cabrera designed the Jackal and I helped Howard [Berger] apply the make-up for the camera test. After that, Howard's like, "You can do it from now on."

What an awesome job that was. Not one of those all-day make-ups that you do in the morning and it's locked. More like a long, involved process that took a lot of maintenance throughout the day. Besides applying the make-up on actor Shayne Wyler, I did the wig and helped wardrobe with the cage and gloves. I'd keep Shayne damp, gooey and gross all day, and if he needed a drink, I'd be there with a straw so he didn't wreck his make-up.

Shayne really brought that make-up to life. He was so scary! Honestly I had a little bit of a crush on him – not on Shayne, but the Jackal! It was almost a shame, at the end of every day, cleaning his make-up off.

I've had so many people come up to me saying how much they love the movie, and how the Jackal, in particular, is their favourite ghost. Between the make-up, the performance and the way they shot him, moving quickly, in short bursts, with his hair flying in the wind, he was terrifying. Iconic.

Thousands of people now have Jackal tattoos, and every one's like a mini-award for Norman, KNB and me. It's not like an award you get that just sits on a shelf. It's an award that someone wears forever, and that makes me feel great. It's honestly the greatest compliment. An honour.

Leanne Podavin

I was very young when I saw *Ghost Story* (1981). I was at my cousin's and my aunt put it on for us, not realizing it was scary, despite the title. It terrified me. For months I couldn't turn in bed for fear of Alice Krige lying dead behind me.

Dick Smith's make-ups are amazing in it, but so fleeting. I like to look at pictures of them, to properly appreciate how cool his work was.

Axelle Carolyn

Opposite (top left): John DeSantis as the Juggernaut, one of the *Thir13en Ghosts* (2001).
Opposite (top middle): Herbert Duncanson as the Hammer, eager to pulverise Matthew Lillard in *Thir13en Ghosts* (2001).
Opposite (top right): Shayne Wyler as the Jackal, probably the most popular phantom from *Thir13en Ghosts* (2001).
Opposite (bottom): The creepy cast of *Thir13en Ghosts* (2001) and the monster kids who made them.
Top: Make-up artist Leanne Podavin applies Shayne Wyler's Jackal make-up, for *Thir13en Ghosts* (2001).
Above: Howard Berger and Charles Porlier apply the Juggernaut make-up to actor John DeSantis, for *Thir13en Ghosts* (2001).

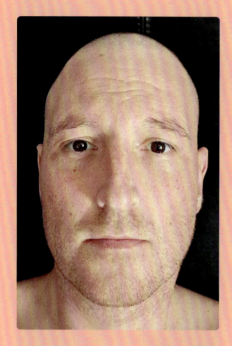

"IT'S LIKE I WAS SUDDENLY SOMEONE ELSE."

This page: Adam Lines lives his Halloween dream as he's made up as The Jackal from *Thir13en Ghosts* (2001) by make-up artist Rosie Doherty.

Opposite: Adam Lines is ready to go trick-or-treating as The Jackal from *Thir13en Ghosts* (2001).

I connected with Adam Lines through Matt Winston and the Stan Winston School via Make-A-Wish UK. Adam is a huge *Thir13en Ghosts* (2001) fan, and was asking how he could make himself up as the Jackal. So we ran a full set of appliances, pulled a wig and dentures, sent him a head cage and a straitjacket, and then a make-up artist friend of his applied it for Halloween.

He got to be the Jackal all night and had the best time ever. That's how powerful that character was.

Howard Berger

Thir13en Ghosts (2001) first caught my eye in a video shop, because while most movies have one monster, this had loads! The best and worst bit about the film is you can't see the ghosts until the characters in it wear special glasses. Most of the ghosts you only see for a moment, then, and the film's much scarier that way, but I always want to study them, so the amount of pausing I do on that movie is ridiculous. It's only 90 minutes long, but every time I watch it, it takes three hours!

The Hammer was an early favourite ghost – the big guy with the railroad spikes in him. But when I look at movie monsters and villains, I grade them by whether I could outrun them, beat them in a fight, reason with them, or if I'd be screwed. My favourite monsters are all ones I'd have no chance against. So while I reckon I could, at least, try to reason with the Hammer, I couldn't talk the Jackal round. And I certainly couldn't beat him in a fight. All he wants to do is kill you, and there's nothing you could do to prevent it. He's terrifying, and that's why he's my favourite ghost in the film.

All I wanted was a Jackal costume for Halloween. Because Halloween should be scary, and he's definitely that. So I emailed the Stan Winston School, just to see if maybe they could direct me to a website where I could buy a decent Jackal costume, but instead they connected me with Howard [Berger], who sent me a full set of prosthetics, and everything else I'd need to look exactly like the Jackal does in *Thir13en Ghosts*.

When everything arrived, my mum cried. It had been a tough twelve months for us, and she was just so elated that someone we didn't even know could be so kind.

I was expecting the application process to be a bit of a slog, but it was applied by a good friend of mine, Rosie Doherty, and she did a great job. Rosie's not a professional make-up artist, but in my opinion, she could be. As she applied the prosthetics in her mum's kitchen, I was getting more and more excited. I kept wanting to get up to look at myself in the mirror, but she made me sit still so she could get on with it. I was like a proper child!

After, in my car, I must have been a proper sight! Once I got home, I put in the contacts, put on the wig and cage, and looked in the mirror. It was so weird: I didn't look like me any more. It's like I was suddenly someone else and I felt invulnerable. Like I could take on the world.

I went to a Halloween party at my cousin's house and it was brilliant. It was all decked out, there was a smoke machine and UV lights that made my eyes glow. Everyone made an effort to come as something scary, but my Jackal costume was definitely the best on the night. I could feel everyone's eyes on me, like they didn't know what to make of me. I definitely made them nervous.

Lots of family was there, but not all of them recognized me. They'd come up to me and be all polite, saying, "Hi, nice to see you."

And I'd be like, "I'm your fucking nephew!"

Later, when I got home, I managed to take off the whole make-up in one go. There was no way I was going to rip it apart. What's disgusting is how much sweat was underneath. It just poured out! I found out later they were silicone pieces, and don't absorb sweat like foam rubber.

I'm going to set everything up on a mannequin – the make-up, cage and costume – and have it out at home. I'm a bit nervous about waking up in the middle of the night and seeing the Jackal staring at me, but I think mainly it'll be a wonderful memory of a brilliant day.

Adam Lines

MAKING A MONSTER

Congratulations on surviving our book so far. We didn't pull any punches. There were wall-to-wall monsters. It was all very scary. But still, you pressed on. How brave you are!

Is it possible you now feel sufficiently inspired to unleash your inner Dr Frankenstein and go fashion your own scary something? If so, we wholeheartedly encourage your efforts, and hope the advice-packed pages ahead prove somehow useful in your quest.

I've changed my mind a lot, over the years, as to what I consider the most important aspect of creature design. I used to say line. Then negative space. After that, I was obsessed with detail. Then it was all about the silhouette. My new thing is the flow of form.

When I'm doing commercial work, serving a film, I can't control the camera angle or the director's taste, but I can design what's coming to set. So what I'm trying to do is sculpt a 'dolly shot', in action, in my character. So even if the DP has one lens and the director is pooped, if that actor moves, you're gonna get something interesting. You're gonna see something that pulls you in.

I may change my opinion in a year.

Gabe Bartalos

If you want to make a good monster movie, get yourself a good story. Do that and you're halfway home. Make sure your monster moves like a real, living thing, and put it in half-light. Put it in backlight. Keep it dark. Really, though, you never know what's gonna work. The secret is, you just gotta be lucky.

John Carpenter

Bill: Nothing's more important than design. Even if a suit or make-up is poorly executed, strong design will save it. Though some of the earliest movie monsters are pretty crude by today's standards, they've remained iconic because their designs were so strong.

Take Lyle Conway's Mad Hatter from *Dreamchild* (1985). It's awesome, but crude. The finished sculpture has raked lines on it and that's how it was cast. It's not tightly detailed, it's loose, but the design is so strong, and looks so cool, it works.

Howard: Dick Smith's sculptures were all about form, too. He never did any hand tooling. Just stamped everything. There's barely any texture, but it didn't matter. His designs were incredible, and always looked perfect on screen.

Bill: At Joe Blasco's school, they taught you to stand three feet away from your make-up or the mirror, then close one eye and squint the other. Just blur it out, because that's what you'll see on screen. So punch up the basics and forget all the other stuff.

Things have changed, of course, now everything's digital. Now everyone can see every tiny detail. But still, nothing trumps design.

Bill Corso and Howard Berger

Flexibility is key to designing an effective creature suit. If an actor's going to wear it, how much movement will it allow? Will he be able to communicate emotion through it? The last thing you want is for him to be lumbering around like a giant water heater.

Stephan Dupuis

Preceding Spread: Tom Savini's Wall of Amazements in his Monster Kid Dungeon. How many creatures do you recognize?
Left (above): A characteristically cracked Gabe Bartalos creation. No one sees the world quite like Gabe!
Left (below): That magnificent man and his monster machine: Gabe Bartalos tinkers away on an idiosyncratic art piece.
Opposite (top): Bill Corso airbrushes a gremlin at Rick Baker's Cinovation for *Gremlins 2: The New Batch* (1990).
Opposite (bottom): Master of Horror Stephen King has a grand old time while Bill Corso tries to focus on making up Cynthia Garris as the Old Woman in the Bathtub for Mick Garris's King-scripted version of *The Shining* (1997).

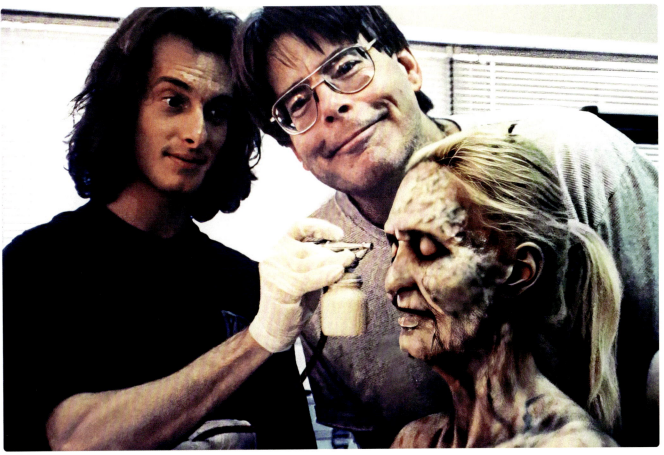

Obviously, the script gives us a cursory understanding of what we're supposed to create. The other pieces of the puzzle fall into place once we've picked the director's brain and understand what it is they want to achieve with the character. What is its reason for being? We take it from there.

Mike Elizalde

Designing a memorable monster takes clarity of vision. Too many things were destroyed because they were designed by committee. Like, I doubt the studio ever gave Ray Harryhausen notes, and he delivered a succession of iconic characters.

Alien (1980) is a perfect example of how to do things properly. The original xenomorph is still the best version of the monster because Ridley Scott, who's an artist himself, understood that Giger had a unique vision, so he let him get on with it. I'm sure there were some notes in terms of practicality, but artistically speaking, if you're going to go looking for someone as unique and amazing as Giger, you'd best respect and honour their work.

Next, start as early as you can with performance. Find the best suit performer you can and build it around them. Too many times I've seen people put their heart and soul into building something, only for some wooden top to wear it and it's dead.

We love the Doug Joneses of this world because they bring our creations to life. They give them heart. There's nothing more exciting, after building and painting a suit on a form, than when someone great puts it on and starts doing something interesting. So always make sure they can move, too. It's worth compromising a bit on the design if it means the performer can actually perform.

A good choreographer, too, is worth their weight in gold. Someone who'll help you cast the perfect performer, then work with them to build a body language and perfect their movement. When they're in a suit, often a performer can barely see, so it makes a world of difference to be on an earpiece with someone on the outside. A coach who'll be able to add more nuance to their performance than a director could inspire by telling them to just go a little more to the left next time, or do it faster.

Neill Gorton

Below (left): Mr. Wink from *Hellboy II: The Golden Army* (2008) stands guard at Mike Elizalde's Spectral Motion.

Below (right): Norman Cabrera was instrumental in the design and creation of the ethereally beautiful Angel of Death from *Hellboy II: The Golden Army* (2008), strikingly displayed here at Spectral Motion.

Opposite (top): Robert Kurtzman readies a Deadite for Sam Raimi's *Army of Darkness* (1992).

Opposite (middle): "Humans are such easy prey..." Robert Kurtzman co-designed Ted Sorel's Dr. Pretorius make-up under the supervision of Mark Shostrum for Stuart Gordon's *From Beyond* (1986).

Opposite (bottom): Richard Domeier waves hello as Robert Kurtzman transforms him into Evil Ed – designed by Shannon Shea under the supervision of Mark Shostrum – for *Evil Dead II* (1987).

For me, creature design comes down to one thing: it has to look cool.

Duncan Jarman

Producers always want something fresh. Something new. A creature no one's seen before, but at the same time, something that maybe hints at monsters we've all dug in the past. The line we've heard a million times is, "Give us *Alien*, but different."

So give them *Alien*, but different.

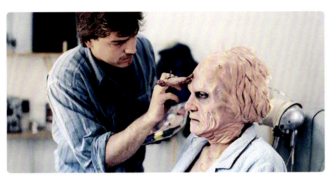

Also, if you're building a creature suit, don't forget that someone has to go in it. Consider mobility, and make sure they're able to deliver the performance that's expected of them.

Finally, after spending weeks or months building a creature, of course you want audiences to see it. Often though, less is more, so don't be precious about your creations. Usually, if they're shot more sparingly, they're scarier that way, and will make a bigger impression in the long run.

Robert Kurtzman

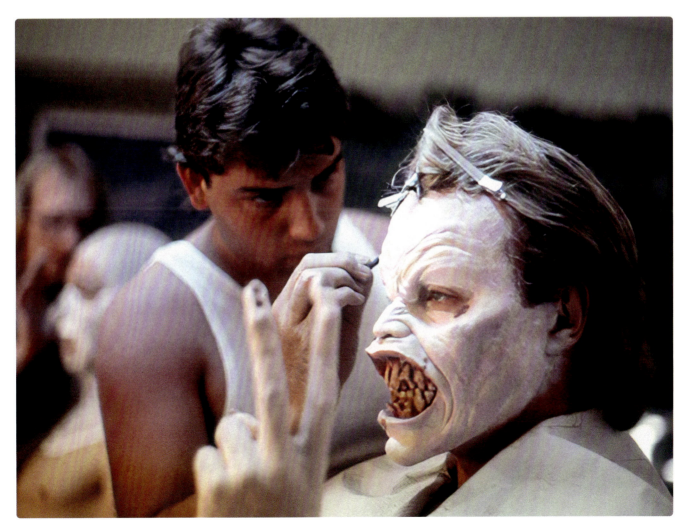

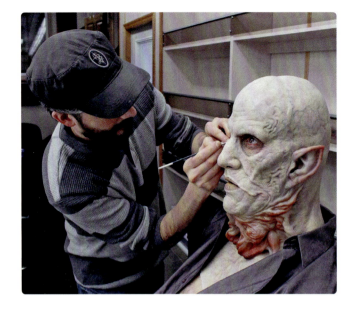

Filmmakers get a lot of notes from studios about clarifying things, as though the goal for an audience is to understand something completely, but that's not always the most important element. To this day, there are parts of *Alien* (1979) that I still don't quite understand. Like, I can't comprehend what I'm looking at when I see the Space Jockey. It's an unsolvable puzzle, but that's what makes it scary, interesting and perfect.

Jason Reitman

A good creature has to make sense. Its anatomy should reflect its environment. If it's aquatic, don't give it horns. If it's terrestrial, don't give it fins. Extraneous details stick out like a sore thumb and serve no purpose.

Sean Sansom

When we were doing *Face Off* (2011–18), a lot of times the boys would dismiss a monster for being unrealistic.

I'd be like, "Guys, it's a monster. It doesn't have to be realistic."

They'd say, "Why would it look like that? It's unbelievable."

I'd tell them, "It doesn't have to make sense. It's a goddamn monster."

"Yeah, but how does it move? It's got no legs."

"It doesn't need legs. It just shows up."

"Yeah, but..."

"IT'S A MONSTER! It can have eyeballs on its chest. It can have a tongue on the side of its head. How does it talk? Telepathy. Whatever. It doesn't matter. It's a monster. FUCK YOU. IT'S A MONSTER."

Ve Neill

Beyond a classic creature, a great story and strong characters are key. The reason I believe *Dog Soldiers* (2002) has sustained its popularity is not only the werewolves, but also the characters and their relationships.

What matters most is to first build a foundation of reality. If the audience believes in your characters, story and setting, the fantasy elements you layer on top will seem all the more authentic.

Neil Marshall

Nothing affects an audience's perception of a monster more than the reactions of the people in the scene. Without a doubt, if you were to reshoot the werewolf transformation in *The Howling* (1981), only instead of being terrified, Dee Wallace was on the 'phone or filing her nails, there's no way anyone watching would be afraid. Without an appropriately terrified reaction, you take the teeth out of the monster. It might as well be Bumble from *Rudolph the Red-Nosed Reindeer* (1964).

Greg Nicotero

For an audience to engage with a monster, they have to be able to relate to it. For that, it needs a sense of organic realism. As alien as, say, the Predator is, it has amphibian aspects that make it feel real and tangible.

Function is also key. I hate building make-ups or suits that are cumbersome, time-consuming and suck the life out of the performer and production. So I try to design with a sense of efficiency, always considering how quickly we'll be able to put it together every day.

Justin Raleigh

I saw *Creature From The Black Lagoon* (1954) at the theatre when I was eight. I didn't know about special effects yet, so I was scared, as I believed the monster was real. Dracula and Frankenstein were real too, and they all scared the fuck out of me.

The only two horror movies I've seen since I was a kid that felt real and scared me enough not to think about make-up effects, were *The Exorcist* (1973) and *Alien* (1979). The secret of *Alien*, and its almost unbearable suspense, is you hardly see the monster till the very end, when it blows away from the ship.

It reminds me of the time George [A. Romero] called me into his office after we'd finished making *Creepshow* (1982). He told me he had bad news, that Paul Hirsch, who edited *Star Wars* (1977) and also 'The Crate' sequence, had not put a lot of Fluffy in. He thought I'd be upset but actually it was great news.

As soon as you get a good look at the monster, it's over. You get used to it and feel you can deal with it. You're not scared any more. But if all you see are glimpses, it's much more frightening, especially if the movie focuses more on people reacting to the creature.

George was surprised I took it so well, but I was happy Fluffy wasn't in it a lot.

Tom Savini

Opposite (top): Sean Sansom transforms Doug Jones into The Master for Guillermo del Toro and Chuck Hogan's *The Strain* (2014-2017).

Opposite (bottom): Justin Raleigh applies one of many make-ups for Zack Snyder's *Rebel Moon – Part Two: The Scargiver* (2024).

Top: This is what happens when you take pictures at Tom Savini's house during a full moon.

Above: Tom Savini's daughter Lia enjoys a playdate with Lizzie from Tom Savini's episode of *Tales from the Darkside* (1983-1988), *Inside the Closet* (S01E07, 1984).

Simplicity in design is often, unfortunately, overlooked nowadays. Everyone wants to design everything to the Nth degree. Everything's got to have a million horns and spikes and scales and mouths and eyes. Despite being so busy, none of it convinces the audience that what they're seeing is real.

There has to be something I call an 'area of rest'. All great creature designs have this. The xenomorph from *Alien* (1979) has all this crazy shit going on, but then by contrast, a clean, smooth, phallic, glass-like dome with nothing on it at all.

It's a design element that nature uses all the time. An area of rest that will add a vital touch of authenticity to your creatures.

Jordu Schell

For a good design to be believable, for it to have life, it has to come from life. The pattern, texture, colouration – really, everything has to be in some way familiar to audiences, or they won't buy it.

I didn't learn that from a traditional make-up school. I studied anatomy, portraiture and sculpture at the Pennsylvania Academy of the Fine Arts in Philadelphia, and everything I learned there, I brought into the film world.

From Stan Winston I learned it's also vital for a design to look aesthetically cool. I remember once we were discussing a blinking eyeball. The mechanic wasn't happy because my design wasn't symmetrical, but Stan goes, "Function always follows form. If it doesn't look cool, I don't care what it can do."

The mechanic hated me, but I was like, "Hey, this comes from the boss."

Scott Stoddard

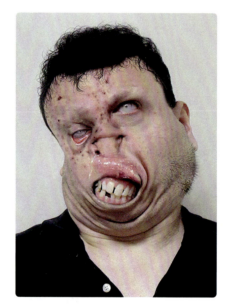

A good monster has to be believable, so realism comes first. You don't want audiences taken out of the movie by a phony rubber thing, or a make-up that, even if it's great, still looks like a make-up. It's a rare skill to be able to make an utterly fantastic, crazy-looking creature that feels real. Then you just have to hope it's shot well. Honestly a good DP is worth their weight in gold.

Wayne Toth

Imagination, first and foremost. Function's important, but it has to follow form. And when you're designing a creature, there have to be at least some aspects of its physical structure that are relatable to an audience. It doesn't have to be a human form, but there should be something there they can recognize.

Mark Tavares

Opposite (all): A selection of brilliant and beautifully warped latex masks from master of the art Jordu Schell.

Left: Wayne Toth gets batty with David Gale in Dr Hill's afterlife make-up for *Bride of Re-Animator* (1990). On set, David was referred to as Batty Batty Bat Bat!

Below: From the Poison Pen of Mark Tavares, his twisted take on the make-up effects crew for *Little Nicky* (2000). Mark played a demon in the movie and never wandered far from his pen and sketch pad.

For me, the two most important aspects of creature design are readability and relatability.

Within three seconds of looking at a design, you should know what it is. That's readability. What drives me crazy are people who do incredibly cool designs, but they don't belong in a movie, more like in a museum where they can be studied. In a film, a creature has to be understood very quickly.

Once you understand the physical reality of the creature, relatability is next, meaning the audience have to know how they're supposed to respond to the creature emotionally or intellectually.

Those aspects of design were critical on *Gremlins* (1984), as they helped set the film's reality. As we were aiming for a throwback, *It's a Wonderful Life* (1947) sort of environment, the creatures couldn't be modern or horrific as that would have ruined the tone of the film.

What we wanted for the Mogwai was for the audience to think, "Oh, cute!"

And for the Gremlins, something like, "Wow! Weird, fun."

You must design that stuff into it.

Chris Walas

Avoid over-designing. A monster doesn't need a million wrinkles. I have a pull of the E.T. head and the sculpture's a little broad, but it's a brilliant design and looks great.

Kevin Wasner

To create a truly memorable monster, you have to understand how it became a monster and incorporate that into the design. Also it has to have a personality that goes beyond it being just some angry, feral thing, and you have to work that personality into the face.

Without those things, you end up with what I call "Monster Salad": a beak from this, some eyes from that, and lots of growling and aggression. The sort of thing we've seen a million times before.

What you're aiming for is Harryhausen's Cyclops from *The 7th Voyage of Sinbad* (1958). As a kid, I'd never seen anything like it. The delight with which it cooked that guy on the spit... It was a truly singular, unforgettable creation.

Jeff Yagher

Left: Chris Walas eyeballs a beastly personal project. Prolifically creating creatures in his home studio, Chris inspires generations new and old with his weird and wonderful fabrications.

Opposite (top two rows, clockwise from top left): From the da Vinci of model kit makers, Jeff Yagher, come these lovingly crafted, detailed dioramas inspired by *Bride of Frankenstein* (1935), *Fright Night* (1985), *The Thing* (1982), *Dracula* (1931) and *The Mummy* (1932).

Opposite (bottom left): Jeff Yagher (left) shares a smile with the bastard son of a hundred maniacs and his brother Kevin.

Opposite (bottom left): Jeff Yagher's home office is the happiest place on Earth.

307

AFTERWORD

by Alex Winter

As an actor who has worked many times under full prosthetics and a filmmaker who has overseen elaborate productions with all manner of monsters and make-up creations, I've been lucky enough to perform in the make-ups of some of the great masters in this book.

I spent most of my childhood in St. Louis, Missouri, where my mother taught dance at a university, and my father ran a dance company. While my parents worked, I was either parked in the college campus cinema watching old movies or thrown on the stage in their drama department's plays. By the end of elementary school, I was an obsessive cinephile and also working professionally as an actor in TV and theatre. My love and respect for the magic of monsters and make-up effects began in those early years, being spellbound by the creatures of Ray Harryhausen and the work of actors like Lon Chaney.

When *The Exorcist* shook the world in 1973, suddenly everyone thought make-up effects were cool, and the artist behind that film, Dick Smith, became a kind of celebrity. I was eight and already experimenting with latex, spirit gum and nose putty, creating DIY monsters and wild characters for the Super-8 movies I made with my friends. When the Dick Smith Horror Make-up Toy Kit came out a year later, I graduated to more elaborate experimentation and creations, and my hobby was on its way to becoming a career.

I didn't have the skill or the calling to become a make-up effects artist. My heart was in acting and directing, and I came up in the age of analogue, long before digital effects overtook the medium. While I truly appreciate the talent required to do quality work with computers, my experience with the challenges of making real-world creature effects afforded me a deep understanding and appreciation for this craft in performance and narrative storytelling. I immediately began working with these artists in my acting and films.

At NYU Film School, my directing partner Tom Stern and I made student films with ambitious make-up effects that stretched our meagre financial resources. One of our films, *Aisles of Doom* (1985), in which I play an ogre who terrorizes children at a suburban toy store, required me to have scalding hot gelatine poured over my head daily to create the base mould for my creature. The result was pretty awesome, but the process was excruciating. I didn't care, I was suffering for my art, like Lon Chaney! While at NYU, I auditioned to work as an actor with director Joel Schumacher and MUFX geniuses Greg Cannom and Ve Neill in the movie, *The Lost Boys* (1987). It was a role I could only accept if I agreed to drop out of film school a year before I was due to graduate – I didn't hesitate for a second.

No more hot gelatine! I was working with the masters and getting a full body cast, fangs, facial appliances, and extremely painful, old-school contact lenses, so I was still suffering for my art. The pinnacle was a trip to the hospital with a scratched cornea when those rascally Coreys kicked a pile of dirt into my contact lenses (after I was ignominiously staked). The success of my next film, *Bill & Ted's Excellent Adventure* (1989), helped Tom Stern and I launch our MTV sketch-comedy, *The Idiot Box* (1991), which saw many of us in full make-ups. So when *Bill & Ted's Bogus Journey* (1991) was greenlit, the producers knew I had this 'creature kink' and let me play Bill's monstrous granny under a masterful design and application by Kevin Yagher.

Tom and I parlayed the popularity of *The Idiot Box* into the feature film *Freaked* (1993). To paraphrase the great Francis Ford Coppola, we had access to too much money and equipment and went insane. We knew the studio was bold to greenlight our movie and that we'd probably never get another chance to do something this audacious (we did not), so we crammed all our influences into one shot at the moon: Harryhausen, Chaney, Big Daddy Roth, *Mad* Magazine, EC Comics and Monty Python, to start.

To realize this insane vision, we employed not one but three separate armies of creature effects artists under the supervision of Steve Johnson and Bill Corso, Screaming Mad George and Tony Gardner. We were in our mid-twenties and had never shot 35mm before. And it wasn't enough that I was co-directing this behemoth. I was also starring under full prosthetics – the most visionary, elaborate and painful make-up I'd ever experienced. Five hours in, three hours out, every day. Bill Corso, who did the applications and supervision, dubbed it the "house of pain". I thought maybe I was ready to stop suffering for my art.

What makes us want to do this, and why do people respond to it? Ultimately, what audiences love about the performing arts is their transformative and transporting power. To work as an actor in creature make-up is to *live* in that power, fully immersed in another being with an expanded view of the world. Something happens to me when I'm performing in full prosthetics; it's the spark that drew me to this work as a young boy, that I felt in my first crude latex applications and later

in shows on stage and in film. It's liberating and cathartic, allowing me the freedom and imaginative inspiration to hurl myself into emotions and physicality that I wouldn't think to attempt with a more naturalistic character.

It's why, despite being primarily behind the camera for many years, I jumped back into the make-up chair the first chance I got. I was grateful to get into full prosthetics for Kevin Yagher in *Bill & Ted Face the Music* (2020), and then to embody a living monster, working with a brilliant design by Gabe Bartalos and applications and paint by my dear friend, the maestro Bill Corso, in the movie, *Destroy All Neighbors* (2024).

Not every actor responds to this work. Sitting for hours while an artist slowly applies cold glue and paint to the deepest crevices of one's face and body is hell for many people. For me, though, the reward not only outweighs the pain, but the pain is integral. There is no transformation without the discomfort, the labour, and the tactile. It's not hyperbole to say that my work in full prosthetics is among the most intense and rewarding experiences of my life.

Whether you're in the industry, love these movies as a fan, or simply appreciate superb craftsmanship, this book beautifully illustrates how creature effects are a profound and living art. I hold these talented wizards in the highest regard and am grateful to call many of them my friends.

January, 2025

Above: Co-writer, co-director and star Alex Winter was radically transformed by Bill Corso for *Freaked* (1993).

FILMOGRAPHIES

Audiences need a safe place to deal with their monsters. Real life rarely gives
them the chance, but movies do.

Charles Bernstein

Allan Apone *Evil Speak* (1981), *Friday the 13th: Part 3* (1982), *Frankenweenie* (1984), *The Return of the Living Dead* (1985), *Invaders From Mars* (1986), *Unbreakable* (2000), *The Prophecy* (1995), *Battleship* (2012), *Captain America: The Winter Soldier* (2014), *Westworld* (2016-2022; E).

Gary Archer *Interview with the Vampire* (1994), *Mars Attacks!* (1996), *Austin Powers: International Man of Mystery* (1997), *Blade* (1998), *The Green Mile* (1999), *X-Men* (2000), *Spider-Man* (2002), *Drag Me to Hell* (2009), *Watchmen* (2019), *Interview with the Vampire* (2022-Present).

David Arquette Star of *Buffy the Vampire Slayer* (1992), *Scream* (1996), *Scream 2* (1997), *Ravenous* (1999), *Scream 3* (2000), *Eight Legged Freaks* (2002), *Scream 4* (2011), *Bone Tomahawk* (2015), *Creepshow* (2019-Present), *Scream* (2022).

Rick Baker *The Autobiography of Miss Jane Pittman* (1974; E), *An American Werewolf in London* (1981; AA), *Greystoke: The Legend of Tarzan, Lord of the Apes* (1984), *Harry and the Hendersons* (1988; AA), *Coming to America* (1989), *Ed Wood* (1994; AA), *The Nutty Professor* (1996; AA), *Men in Black* (1998; AA), *How the Grinch Stole Christmas* (2000; AA), *The Wolfman* (2011; AA).

Gabe Bartalos *Friday the 13th: Jason Lives* (1986), *Gremlins 2: The New Batch* (1990), *Basket Case 2* (1990), *Frankenhooker* (1990), *Leprechaun* (1993), *Cremaster 3* (2002); Director of *Skinned Deep* (2004), *Saint Bernard* (2013); *Army of the Dead* (2021), *Destroy All Neighbours* (2024).

Peter Berg Star of *Shocker* (1989), *Fire in the Sky* (1993), *The Last Seduction* (1994), *Chicago Hope* (1994-2000); Director of *Very Bad Things* (1998), *Friday Night Lights* (2004), *Hancock* (2008), *Battleship* (2012), *Lone Survivor* (2013), *American Primeval* (2025).

Howard Berger (Co-founder of KNB EFX Group) *Day of the Dead* (1985), *Aliens* (1986), *Predator* (1986), *Casino* (1995), *Boogie Nights* (1997), *Kill Bill Vol. 1 & 2* (2003/04), *The Chronicles of Narnia: The Lion, the Witch and the Wardrobe* (2005; AA), *Hitchcock* (2012), *Oz the Great and Powerful* (2013), *Lone Survivor* (2013), *The Orville* (2017-Present), *American Primeval* (2025).

Charles Bernstein Composer of *Invasion of the Bee Girls* (1973), *Mr. Majestyk* (1974), *Gator* (1976), *CBS Schoolbreak Special: Little Miss Perfect* (1987; E), *Love at First Bite* (1979), *The Entity* (1982), *Cujo* (1983), *A Nightmare on Elm Street* (1984), *April Fool's Day* (1986), *Deadly Friend* (1986).

Axelle Carolyn Star of *Centurion* (2010); Director of *Soulmate* (2013), *Tales of Halloween* (2015), *The Haunting of Bly Manor* (2020), *The Manor* (2021), *Creepshow* (2019-Present), *American Horror Story* (2011-Present), *The Midnight Club* (2022), *Mayfair Witches* (2023-Present), *Them* (2021-Present).

John Carpenter Director of *Assault on Precinct 13* (1976), *Halloween* (1978), *The Fog* (1980), *Escape From New York* (1981), *The Thing* (1982), *Christine* (1983), *Big Trouble in Little China* (1986), *Prince of Darkness* (1987), *They Live* (1988), *In the Mouth of Madness* (1994).

Chad Coleman Star of *The Wire* (2002-2008), *The Walking Dead* (2010-2022), *Roots* (2016), *Freakish* (2016-2018), *Arrow* (2012-2020), *It's Always Sunny in Philadelphia* (2005-Present), *The Expanse* (2015-2022), *Copshop* (2021), *The Orville* (2017-Present), *The Angry Black Girl and Her Monster* (2023).

Randy Cook *Caveman* (1981), *The Thing* (1982), *Q: The Winged Serpent* (1982), *Ghostbusters* (1984), *Fright Night* (1985), *The Gate* (1987), *I, Madman* (1989), *The Lord of the Rings: The Fellowship of the Ring* (2001; AA), *The Lord of the Rings: The Two Towers* (2002; AA), *The Lord of the Rings: The Return of the King* (2003; AA).

Bill Corso *The Stand* (1994; E), *The Shining* (1997; E), *Galaxy Quest* (1999), *A Series of Unfortunate Events* (2004; AA), *Click* (2006), *Grey Gardens* (2009; E), *42* (2013), *Foxcatcher* (2014), *Deadpool* (2016), *Destroy All Neighbors* (2024).

Barbara Crampton Star of *Re-Animator* (1985), *Chopping Mall* (1986), *From Beyond* (1986), *Castle Freak* (1995), *You're Next* (2011), *The Lords of Salem* (2012), *House Mother* (2017), *Jakob's Wife* (2021), *Creepshow* (2019-Present), *Suitable Flesh* (2023).

Wes Craven Director of *The Last House on the Left* (1972), *The Hills Have Eyes* (1977), *Deadly Blessing* (1981), *A Nightmare on Elm Street* (1984), *The Serpent and the Rainbow* (1988), *Shocker* (1989), *The People Under the Stairs* (1991), *Vampire in Brooklyn* (1995), *Scream* (1996), *Red Eye* (2005).

Gino Crognale *Frankenhooker* (1990), *The Dark Half* (1993), *From Dusk Till Dawn* (1996), *Wishmaster* (1997), *Scream 2* (1997), *The Haunting* (1999), *Land of the Dead* (2005), *The Mist* (2007), *Halloween II* (2009), *The Walking Dead* (2010-2022; E).

Joe Dante Director of *Piranha* (1978), *The Howling* (1981), *Twilight Zone: The Movie* (1983), *Gremlins* (1984), *Explorers* (1985), *Innerspace* (1987), *The 'Burbs* (1989), *Gremlins 2: The New Batch* (1990), *Matinee* (1993), *Looney Tunes: Back in Action* (2003).

David Dastmalchian Star of *The Dark Knight* (2008), *Ant-Man* (2015), *The Belko Experiment* (2016), *Blade Runner 2049* (2017), *The Suicide Squad* (2021), *Dune: Part One* (2021), *The Boogeyman* (2023), *Oppenheimer* (2023), *Late Night with the Devil* (2023), *The Last Voyage of the Demeter* (2023).

Russell T Davies Writer of *Queer as Folk* (1999-2000), *Casanova* (2005), *Doctor Who* (2005-Present), *Torchwood* (2006-2011), *The Sarah Jane Adventures* (2007-2011), *Wizards vs. Aliens* (2012-2014), *A Very English Scandal* (2018), *Years and Years* (2019), *It's a Sin* (2021), *Nolly* (2023).

Stephan Dupuis *Scanners* (1981), *The Fly* (1986; AA), *RoboCop* (1987), *Tales from the Crypt* (1989-1996), *Cape Fear* (1991), *Deep Rising* (1998), *eXistenZ* (1999), *Jason X* (2001), *300* (2006), *Contagion* (2011).

Richard Edlund *Star Wars* (1977; AA), *Battlestar Galactica* (1978), *The Empire Strikes Back* (1980), *Raiders of the Lost Ark* (1981; AA), *Poltergeist* (1982), *Return of the Jedi* (1983), *Ghostbusters* (1984), *Fright Night* (1985), *Big Trouble in Little China* (1986), *The Monster Squad* (1987).

Robert Englund Star of *V* (1983-1985), *A Nightmare on Elm Street* (1984), *A Nightmare on Elm Street Part 2: Freddy's Revenge* (1985), *A Nightmare on Elm Street 3: Dream Warriors* (1987), *The Phantom of the Opera* (1989), *Wes Craven's New Nightmare* (1994), *The Mangler* (1995), *2001 Maniacs* (2005).

Mike Elizalde *A Nightmare on Elm Street 3: Dream Warriors* (1987), *Gremlins 2: The New Batch* (1990), *Darkman* (1990), *Addams Family Values* (1993), *Men in Black* (1997), *Blade II* (2002), *Hellboy II: The Golden Army* (2008), *Pacific Rim* (2013), *Scary Stories to Tell in the Dark* (2019), *Malignant* (2021).

Michael Giacchino Composer of *Lost* (2004-2010; E), *Star Trek* (2009), *Up* (2010; AA), *Fringe* (2008-2013), *Dawn of the Planet of the Apes* (2014), *Jurassic World* (2015), *Doctor Strange* (2016), *Rogue One: A Star Wars Story* (2016); Director of *Monster Challenge* (2018), *Werewolf by Night* (2022).

Neill Gorton *The Unholy* (1988), *Nightbreed* (1990), *Judge Dredd* (1995), *Little Britain* (2003-2006), *Doctor Who* (2005-Present), *Torchwood* (2006-2011), *Thor* (2011), *Cobweb* (2023), *The Toxic Avenger* (2023), *Dune: Prophecy* (2024).

Dana Gould Writer of *The Simpsons* (1989-Present; E 2003 & 2006), *Dana Gould: Let Me Put My Thoughts in You* (2009), *Dana Gould: I Know It's Wrong* (2013), *Stan Against Evil* (2016-2018), *Mystery Science Theater 3000* (2017-2022), *Creepshow* (2019-Present), *Toys of Terror* (2020); Star of *Hanging with Dr. Z* (2021-Present); *Ted* (2024-Present), *Dana Gould: Perfectly Normal* (2025).

Barrie Gower *28 Days Later* (2002), *Shaun of the Dead* (2004), *Game of Thrones* (2011-2019; E 2014, 2016 & 2018), *Life of Pi* (2012), *Stranger Things* (2016-2025, E), *Chernobyl* (2019), *The Witcher* (2019-Present), *Last Night in Soho* (2021), *House of the Dragon* (2022-Present), *The Last of Us* (2023-Present; E).

Sarah Gower *Dinotopia* (2002-2003), *Underworld* (2003), *Troy* (2004), *The League of Gentlemen's Apocalypse* (2005), *Nanny McPhee* (2005), *X-Men: First Class* (2011), *Game of Thrones* (2011-2019; E), *Chernobyl* (2019), *Last Night in Soho* (2021), *The Last of Us* (2023-Present; E).

Ray Harryhausen *Mighty Joe Young* (1949), *The Beast From 20,000 Fathoms* (1953), *It Came from Beneath the Sea* (1955), *The 7th Voyage of Sinbad* (1958), *Jason and the Argonauts* (1963), *One Million Years B.C.* (1966), *The Valley of Gwangi* (1969), *The Golden Voyage of Sinbad* (1973), *Sinbad and the Eye of the Tiger* (1977), *Clash of the Titans* (1981).

Tom Holland Writer of *The Beast Within* (1982), *Psycho II* (1983), *Cloak & Dagger* (1984); Director of *Fright Night* (1985), *Amazing Stories* (1985-1987), *Child's Play* (1988), *Tales from the Crypt* (1989-1996), *The Temp* (1993), *The Langoliers* (1995), *Thinner* (1996).

Del Howison Star of *Lord of Illusions* (1995), *Horrorvision* (2001), *The Vampire Hunter's Club* (2001), *The Erotic Rights of Countess Dracula* (2001), *Countess Dracula's Orgy of Blood* (2004), *The Mummy's Kiss: 2nd Dynasty* (2006), *Blood Scarab* (2008), *Ghost Hoax* (2010); Author of *When Werewolves Attack* (2010), *The Survival of Margaret Thomas* (2019).

Graham Humphreys *Hardware* (1990), *Dust Devil* (1992), *The Island of Dr. Moreau* (1996), *Killer Tongue* (1996), *Mean Machine* (2001); Author of *Drawing Blood: 30 Years of Horror Art* (2015), *Hung, Drawn and Executed: The Horror Art of Graham Humphreys* (2019), *Nightmare on One Sheet: The Horror Art of Graham Humphreys* (2023).

Kerrin Jackson *The Matrix* (1999), *The Chronicles of Narnia: The Lion, the Witch and the Wardrobe* (2005), *The Chronicles of Narnia: Prince Caspian* (2008), *Piranha 3D* (2010), *The Ward* (2010), *The United Monster Talent Agency* (2010), *The Hobbit: An Unexpected Journey* (2012), *American Horror Story* (2011-Present), *The Walking Dead* (2010-Present), *Jupiter's Legacy* (2021).

Duncan Jarman *Alice in Wonderland* (1999; E), *Arabian Nights* (2000; E), *Resident Evil* (2002), *World War Z* (2013), *The Revenant* (2015), *Stranger Things* (2016-2025, E), *Chernobyl* (2019), *The Witcher* (2019-Present), *House of the Dragon* (2022-Present), *The Lord of the Rings: The Rings of Power* (2022-Present).

Adam Johansen (Co-founder of Odd Studio) *Farscape* (1999-2003), *Superman Returns* (2006), *X-Men Origins: Wolverine* (2009), *Where the Wild Things Are* (2009), *Mad Max: Fury Road* (2015), *Alien: Covenant* (2017), *Possum* (2018), *I F*cked a Mermaid and No One Believes Me* (2018), *Thor: Love and Thunder* (2022), *Evil Dead Rise* (2023).

Larry Karaszewski Co-writer (with Scott Alexander) of *Problem Child* (1990), *Ed Wood* (1994), *The People vs. Larry Flynt* (1996), *Man on the Moon* (1999), *Screwed* (2000), *1408* (2007), *Big Eyes* (2014), *Goosebumps* (2015), *American Crime Story* (2016-Present; E 2016 & 2018), *Dolemite Is My Name* (2019).

Richard Kiel Star of *The Twilight Zone* (1959-1964), *Eegah* (1962), *Kolchak: The Night Stalker* (1974-1975), *Land of the Lost* (1974-1977), *Silver Streak* (1976), *The Spy Who Loved Me* (1977), *Force 10 From Navarone* (1978), *The Humanoid* (1979), *Moonraker* (1979), *Happy Gilmore* (1996).

Silvi Knight *Ticks* (1993), *Necronomicon* (1993), *Grindhouse* (2007), *Halloween* (2007), *Vampires Suck* (2010), *Hail, Caesar!* (2016), *American Horror Story* (2011-Present; E), *American Crime Story* (2016-Present; E), *Bright* (2017), *Star Trek: Picard* (2020-2023).

Robert Kurtzman (Co-founder of KNB EFX Group) *Evil Dead II* (1987), *Phantasm II* (1988), *A Nightmare on Elm Street: The Dream Child* (1989), *Misery* (1990), *Army of Darkness* (1992), *In the Mouth of Madness* (1994), *From Dusk Till Dawn* (1996), *Scream* (1996), *Men in Black* (1997); Director of *Wishmaster* (1997).

Tami Lane *The Lord of the Rings: The Fellowship of the Ring* (2001), *The Chronicles of Narnia: The Lion, the Witch and the Wardrobe* (2005; AA), *The Chronicles of Narnia: Prince Caspian* (2008), *The Hobbit: An Unexpected Journey* (2012), *Ted 2* (2015), *The Shallows* (2016), *Legion* (2017-2019), *The Orville* (2017-Present), *Jupiter's Legacy* (2021), *Interview with the Vampire* (2022-Present).

Damien Leone Director of *The 9th Circle* (2008), *Terrifier* (2011), *All Hallows' Eve* (2013), *Frankenstein vs. the Mummy* (2015), *Terrifier* (2016), *Terrifier 2* (2022), *Terrifier 3* (2024), *Terrifier 4* (2026).

Karl Walter Lindenlaub Cinematographer of *Ghost Chase* (1987), *Moon 44* (1990), *Universal Soldier* (1992), *Stargate* (1994), *Independence Day* (1996), *The Haunting* (1999), *The Chronicles of Narnia: Prince Caspian* (2008), *Houdini* (2014), *For All Mankind* (2019-Present), *Halo* (2022-2024).

Göran Lundström *The Chronicles of Narnia: Prince Caspian* (2008), *Doctor Who* (2005-Present), *Pandorum* (2009), *The Wolfman* (2010), *Harry Potter and the Deathly Hallows: Part 2* (2011), *Hansel & Gretel: Witch Hunters* (2013), *Beauty and the Beast* (2017), *Border* (2018), *The Batman* (2022), *The Last Voyage of the Demeter* (2023).

Tyler Mane Star of *X-Men* (2000), *How to Make a Monster* (2001), *Troy* (2004), *The Devil's Rejects* (2005), *Halloween* (2007), *Halloween II* (2009), *Devil May Call* (2013), *Victor Crowley* (2017), *Jupiter's Legacy* (2021), *Deadpool & Wolverine* (2024).

Neil Marshall Director of *Dog Soldiers* (2002), *The Descent* (2005), *Doomsday* (2008), *Centurion* (2010), *Game of Thrones* (2011-2019), *Tales of Halloween* (2015), *Hellboy* (2019), *The Reckoning* (2020), *The Lair* (2022), *Duchess* (2024).

Derek Mears Star of *Cursed* (2005), *Masters of Horror* (2005-2007), *The Hills Have Eyes 2* (2007), *Friday the 13th* (2009), *Predators* (2010), *The United Talent Monster Agency* (2010), *The Orville* (2017-Present), *Swamp Thing* (2019), *Rebel Moon – Part One: A Child of Fire* (2023), *Salem's Lot* (2024).

Eryn Krueger Mekash *Sabrina, the Teenage Witch* (1996-2003), *Nip/Tuck* (2003-2010), *Alpha Dog* (2006), *Glee* (2009-2015), *Eat Pray Love* (2010), *American Horror Story* (2011-Present; E 2015 x2, 2016 & 2017), *The Normal Heart* (2014; E), *American Crime Story* (2016-Present; E x2), *Feud: Bette and Joan* (2017; E), *The Fabelmans* (2022).

Mike Mekash *Prom Night* (2008), *American Horror Story* (2011-Present; E 2015 x2, 2016 & 2017), *John Carter* (2012), *The Normal Heart* (2014; E), *Teenage Mutant Ninja Turtles* (2014), *Mad Max: Fury Road* (2015), *Scream Queens* (2015-2016), *Stranger Things* (2016-2025, E), *Avengers: Infinity War* (2018), *Maestro* (2023).

Mike Mendez Director of *Killers* (1996), *Bimbo Movie Bash* (1997), *The Convent* (2000), *The Gravedancers* (2006), *Big Ass Spider!* (2013), *Tales of Halloween* (2015), *Lavalantula* (2015), *The Last Heist* (2016), *Don't Kill It* (2016), *Satanic Hispanics* (2022).

Jim Mitchell *Jurassic Park* (1993), *The Mask* (1994), *Jumanji* (1995), *Mars Attacks!* (1996), *Mighty Joe Young* (1998), *Sleepy Hollow* (1999), *Jurassic Park III* (2001), *Harry Potter and the Chamber of Secrets* (2002), *Harry Potter and the Goblet of Fire* (2005), *Jupiter's Legacy* (2021).

Donald Mowat *The Fly* (1986), *Mark Twain and Me* (1991; E), *In the Mouth of Madness* (1994), *Planet of the Apes* (2001), *Cowboys & Aliens* (2011), *Skyfall* (2012), *Nightcrawler* (2014), *Blade Runner 2049* (2017), *Dune: Part One* (2012), *Moon Knight* (2022).

Caroline Munro Star of *The Abominable Dr. Phibes* (1971), *Dracula A.D. 1972* (1972), *The Golden Voyage of Sinbad* (1973), *Captain Kronos: Vampire Hunter* (1973), *At the Earth's Core* (1976), *The Spy Who Loved Me* (1977), *Starcrash* (1978), *Maniac* (1980), *The Last Horror Film* (1982), *Slaughter High* (1986).

Stephen Murphy *Hellboy II: The Golden Army* (2008), *Kick-Ass* (2010), *Harry Potter and the Deathly Hallows: Part 2* (2011), *The Iron Lady* (2011), *World War Z* (2013), *Dracula Untold* (2014), *Suspiria* (2018), *Last Night in Soho* (2021), *The Witcher* (2019-Present), *Wicked* (2024).

Ve Neill *Pee-Wee's Playhouse* (1986-1991; E), *The Lost Boys* (1987), *Beetlejuice* (1988; AA), *Edward Scissorhands* (1990), *Mrs. Doubtfire* (1993; AA), *Ed Wood* (1994; AA), *Mars Attacks!* (1996), *The Shining* (1997; E), *Galaxy Quest* (1999), *Pirates of the Caribbean: The Curse of the Black Pearl* (2003).

Christopher Nelson *Men in Black* (1997), *Little Nicky* (2000), *Kill Bill: Vol 1* (2003), *Constantine* (2005), *Land of the Dead* (2005), *American Horror Story* (2011-Present; E x2), *World War Z* (2013), *Suicide Squad* (2016; AA), *Halloween* (2018), *The Exorcist: Believer* (2023).

Greg Nicotero (Co-founder of KNB EFX Group) *Day of the Dead* (1985), *Army of Darkness* (1992), *From Dusk Till Dawn* (1996), *Dune* (2000; E), *Death Proof* (2007), *Inglourious Basterds* (2009), *The Pacific* (2010; E), *The Walking Dead* (2010-2022; E 2011 & 2012), *Fear the Walking Dead* (2015-2023), *Creepshow* (2019-Present).

Simon Pegg Star of *Spaced* (1999-2001), *Shaun of the Dead* (2004), *Doctor Who* (2005-Present), *Land of the Dead* (2005), *Mission: Impossible III* (2006), *Hot Fuzz* (2007), *Star Trek* (2009), *Paul* (2011), *The World's End* (2013), *Star Wars: Episode VII – The Force Awakens* (2015).

Micheline Pitt Director of *Grummy* (2021).

Leanne Podavin *The X-Files* (1993-2018), *The Outer Limits* (1995-2002), *Poltergeist: The Legacy* (1996-1999), *Lake Placid* (1999), *Thir13en Ghosts* (2001), *X2: X-Men United* (2003), *Ginger Snaps Back: The Beginning* (2004), *Masters of Horror* (2005-2007), *A Series of Unfortunate Events* (2017-2019), *Chilling Adventures of Sabrina* (2018-2020).

Gerry Quist *Re-Animator* (1985), *Critters* (1986), *Star Trek: The Next Generation* (1987-1994; E 1988 & 1992), *Quantum Leap* (1989-1993; E), *Star Trek VI: The Undiscovered Country* (1991), *Addams Family Values* (1993), *Buffy the Vampire Slayer* (1997-2003; E), *Tropic Thunder* (2008), *The Sixth Sense* (1999), *Westworld* (2016-2022).

Justin Raleigh *Insidious* (2010), *True Blood* (2008-2014), *American Horror Story* (2011-Present; E), *The Conjuring* (2013), *Outcast* (2016-2017), *Swamp Thing* (2019), *Army of the Dead* (2021), *Malignant* (2021), *The Eyes of Tammy Faye* (2022; AA), *MaXXXine* (2024).

Jason Reitman Director of *Thank You For Smoking* (2005), *Juno* (2007), *Up in the Air* (2009), *Young Adult* (2011), *Labor Day* (2013), *Men, Women & Children* (2014), *Tully* (2018), *The Front Runner* (2018), *Ghostbusters: Afterlife* (2021), *Saturday Night* (2024).

Dirk Rogers Star of *Faust* (2000), *Zombie Strippers* (2008), *Legion* (2017-2019), *Nightmare Cinema* (2018), *The Lucky Southern Star* (2018), *There's One Inside the House* (2018), *Them* (2021-Present), *The Orville* (2017-Present), *The Santa Clauses* (2022-2023), *Interview with the Vampire* (2022-Present).

George A. Romero Director of *Night of the Living Dead* (1968), *The Crazies* (1973), *Martin* (1977), *Dawn of the Dead* (1978), *Knightriders* (1981), *Creepshow* (1982), *Day of the Dead* (1985), *Monkey Shines* (1988), *The Dark Half* (1993), *Land of the Dead* (2005).

Tom Savini *Dawn of the Dead* (1978), *Friday the 13th* (1980), *The Burning* (1981), *Creepshow* (1982), *Day of the Dead* (1985), *Invasion U.S.A.* (1985), *Monkey Shines* (1988). Actor in *Knightriders* (1981), *Creepshow 2* (1987), *From Dusk Till Dawn* (1996).

Sean Sansom *In the Mouth of Madness* (1994), *Jason X* (2001), *Wrong Turn* (2003), *Dawn of the Dead* (2004), *Land of the Dead* (2005), *Grey Gardens* (2009; E), *Carrie* (2013), *It* (2017), *Scary Stories to Tell in the Dark* (2019), *Guillermo del Toro's Cabinet of Curiosities* (2022).

Jordu Schell *Predator 2* (1990), *Galaxy Quest* (1999), *Planet of the Apes* (2001), *Dawn of the Dead* (2004), *Hellboy* (2004), *The Mist* (2007), *The Chronicles of Narnia: Prince Caspian* (2008), *Avatar* (2009), *The Thing* (2011), *The Cabin in the Woods* (2011).

Scott Stoddard *Body Snatchers* (1993), *The Texas Chainsaw Massacre* (2003), *Land of the Dead* (2005), *Serenity* (2005), *The Chronicles of Narnia: The Lion, The Witch and the Wardrobe* (2005), *Pirates of the Caribbean: Dead Man's Chest* (2006), *Friday the 13th* (2009), *Pandorum* (2009), *The Orville* (2017-Present), *The Mandalorian* (2019-Present; E).

Douglas Tait Star of *Zathura: A Space Adventure* (2005), *Star Trek* (2009), *Land of the Lost* (2009), *Thor* (2011), *Teen Wolf* (2011-2017), *Grimm* (2011-2017), *Hellboy* (2019), *Annabelle Comes Home* (2019), *Star Trek: Picard* (2020-2023), *Rebel Moon – Part One: A Child of Fire* (2023).

Mark Tavares *Tales from the Darkside: The Movie* (1990), *Child's Play 3* (1991), *Xena: Warrior Princess* (1995-2001), *Vampire in Brooklyn* (1995), *From Dusk Till Dawn* (1996), *Wishmaster* (1997), *Phantoms* (1998), *Little Nicky* (2000), *Thir13en Ghosts* (2001), *Land of the Dead* (2005).

Kirk Thatcher *Poltergeist* (1982), *Return of the Jedi* (1983), *Gremlins* (1984), *Star Trek III: The Search For Spock* (1984), *Cat's Eye* (1985), *House* (1985), *Dinosaurs* (1991-1994), *Muppets Tonight* (1996; E); Director of *Muppets Haunted Mansion* (2021); Star of *Werewolf by Night* (2022).

Phil Tippett *Star Wars* (1977), *Piranha* (1978), *The Empire Strikes Back* (1980), *Dragonslayer* (1981), *Return of the Jedi* (1983), *The Ewok Adventure* (1984; E), *Dinosaur!* (1985; E), *RoboCop* (1987), *Willow* (1988), *Jurassic Park* (1993; AA).

Wayne Toth *Halloween 4: The Return of Michael Myers* (1988), *Tales from the Darkside: The Movie* (1990), *Freddy's Dead: The Final Nightmare* (1991), *Pulp Fiction* (1994), *From Dusk Till Dawn* (1996), *Wishmaster* (1997), *The Haunting* (1999), *House of 1000 Corpses* (2003), *Halloween* (2007), *Planet Terror* (2007).

Christopher Tucker *I, Claudius* (1976-1976), *Star Wars* (1977), *The Boys From Brazil* (1978), *The Elephant Man* (1980), *Quest for Fire* (1981), *The Meaning of Life* (1983), *The Company of Wolves* (1984), *High Spirits* (1988).

Josh Turi *Saturday Night Live* (1975-Present; E 2010, 2011 & 2013), *Sgt. Kabukiman N.Y.P.D.* (1990), *Monsters* (1988-1990), *I Am Legend* (2007), *The Amazing Spider-Man 2* (2014), *John Wick* (2014), *The Tick* (2016-2019), *Mr Robot* (2015-2019), *Knock at the Cabin* (2023), *Jules* (2023).

Chris Walas *Piranha* (1978), *Dragonslayer* (1981), *Scanners* (1981), *Raiders of the Lost Ark* (1981), *Return of the Jedi* (1983), *Gremlins* (1984), *Enemy Mine* (1985), *The Fly* (1986; AA), *The Fly II* (1989), *Arachnophobia* (1990).

Kevin Wasner *Men in Black II* (2002), *The League of Extraordinary Gentlemen* (2003), *Hostel* (2005), *The Mist* (2007), *The Chronicles of Narnia: Prince Caspian* (2008), *Jennifer's Body* (2009), *Splice* (2009), *The Walking Dead* (2010-2022; E), *Oz the Great and Powerful* (2013), *Halloween* (2018), *X* (2022).

Ti West Director of *The Roost* (2005), *Trigger Man* (2007), *The House of the Devil* (2009), *Cabin Fever 2: Spring Fever* (2009), *The Innkeepers* (2011), *The Sacrament* (2013), *In a Valley of Violence* (2016), *X* (2022), *Pearl* (2022), *MaXXXine* (2024).

Mike Westmore *Trilogy of Terror* (1975), *Eleanor and Franklin* (1976; E), *Why Me?* (1984; E), *The Three Wishes of Billy Grier* (1984; E), *Mask* (1985; AA), *Amazing Stories* (1985-1987; E), *Star Trek: The Next Generation* (1987-1994; E 1988 & 1992), *Star Trek: Deep Space Nine* (1993-1999; E 1993 & 1995), *Star Trek: Voyager* (1995-2001; E), *Star Trek: Enterprise* (2001-2005).

Alex Winter Star of *The Lost Boys* (1987), *Bill & Ted's Excellent Adventure* (1989), *Bill & Ted's Bogus Journey* (1991), Director and Star of *Freaked* (1993), Director of *Downloaded* (2013), *Deep Web* (2015), *Zappa* (2020), Star of *Bill & Ted Face the Music* (2020), *Full Circle* (2023), *Destroy All Neighbors* (2024).

Terry Wolfinger *Frosty Returns* (1993), *The Lost World: Jurassic Park* (1997), *Terminator 3: Rise of the Machines* (2003), *Clifford the Big Red Dog* (2021).

John Wrightson *Star Trek: Beyond* (2016), *Underworld: Blood Wars* (2016), *Alita: Battle Angel* (2019), *Captive State* (2019), *The Walking Dead* (2010-2022), *Sleepy Hollow* (2013-2017), *The Maze Runner* (2014), *Patina* (2019), *Fear the Walking Dead* (2015-2023), *Tales of the Walking Dead* (2022).

Jeff Yagher Star of *V* (1984-1985), *The Twilight Zone* (1985-1989), *Bionic Showdown: The Six Million Dollar Man and the Bionic Woman* (1989), *Freddy's Nightmares* (1988-1990), *Tales from the Crypt* (1989-1996), *Murder, She Wrote* (1984-1996), *Seinfeld* (1989-1998), *Millennium* (1996-1999), *Star Trek: Voyager* (1995-2001), *Angel* (1999-2004).

Takashi Yamazaki Director of *Juvenile* (2000), *Returner* (2002), *Always: Sunset on Third Street 2* (2007), *Space Battleship Yamato* (2010), *Friends: Naki on the Monster Island* (2011), *The Fighter Pilot* (2013), *Stand by Me Doraemon* (2014), *Parasyte: Part 1* (2014), *Ghost Book* (2022), *Godzilla Minus One* (2023; AA).

Key: Academy Award (AA), Emmy (E).

INDEX

28 Days Later 270
9th Circle, The 156

A

A Dead Girl Named Sue 281
A Man for All Seasons 133
A Nightmare on Elm Street 29, 62, 148-149, 160
Abbasi, Ali 191
Abbott and Costello (movie series) 17, 43, 226
Abominable Dr Phibes, The 70
Abrams, J. J. 208-209
Ackerman, Forry 14-15
Alexander, Scott 190, 212-213
Alien (movie series) 28, 56, 60, 106, 134, 211, 218, 300-304
Alvarez, Ozzy 249
Always: Sunset on Third Street 2 92
Amazing Colossal Man, The 54
American Horror Story 119, 159, 194
An American Werewolf in London 31, 50, 169-171, 175, 176
Anderson, Barbara 188
Antal, Nimród 217
Apone, Allan 16, 110, 256-257, 258
Archer, Gary 24, 55, 96, 100, 101
Army of Darkness 35, 111, 300
Army of the Dead 282
Arquette, David 29, 100, 152
Ashton, Roy 15, 168, 262
Assault on Precinct 13 100
At the Earth's Core 230
Attack of the Killer Tomatoes! 126
Aykroyd, Dan 290-291

B

Baker, Rick 17, 24, 31, 64, 78, 80, 82, 169, 171, 175, 176, 179, 190, 226, 236 241, 265, 298
Bale, Christian 106
Bama, James 23
Bancroft, Victoria 62, 122
Barney, Matthew 274
Barron, Bebe and Louis 21, 138
Bartalos, Gabe 20, 31, 52, 53, 112, 122, 155, 241, 272, 274, 298
Basset, Angela 119
Batman 156
Battleship 217
Bearse, Amanda 96-97
Beast from 20,000 Fathoms, The 126-127
Beast with Five Fingers, The 51
Beetlejuice 114
Belushi, John 291
Ben Stiller Show, The 253
Berg, John 80, 202
Berg, Peter 28, 29, 217
Berger, Howard 6, 7, 20, 28, 31, 37, 41, 62, 70,87, 88, 102, 111, 114, 116, 132, 135,150,162, 168, 171, 172, 179, 211, 215, 220,228, 266, 267, 271, 293, 295, 298, 320
Bernal, Gael García 180
Bernstein, Charles 68, 148, 255, 258
Big Ass Spider! 88-89
Bishara, Joseph 116-117
Bisson, John 89, 114
Björnsson, Hafþór Júlíus 280
Black Sabbath 42
Black, Karen 25
Blaisdell, Paul 20, 21
Blasco, Joe 298
Bliss, Rob 284
Blob, The 23, 25
Bloch, Robert 188
Bobroczkyi, Robert 218
Bonneywell, Dave 176
Book of Lists, The: Horror 14
Border 191
Born, Agnes 122
Botet, Javier 106-107
Bottin, Rob 31, 168, 169, 171, 172, 208, 209
Bradbury, Ray 14
Bradley, Doug 113
Brain Death 74
Brain That Wouldn't Die, The 54
Bride of Frankenstein 18, 262, 265, 306
Bride of Re-Animator 64, 305
Broccoli, Cubby 186
Browning, Ricou 20, 228
Bryan, Billy 111
Bryniarski, Andrew 152
Buffy the Vampire Slayer 100
Burke and Hare 176
Burke, Michèle 100
Burnett, Michael 72
Burns, Bob 21
Burrell, Everett 210-211, 271
Burton, Tim 114, 190, 212, 213, 214, 258, 274
Butler, Bill 150

C

Cabrera, Norman 73, 120, 241, 293, 300
Cameron, James 28, 211, 217
Campbell Bower, Jamie 160-163
Campbell, Bruce 111, 211
Campbell, Evan 100
Candyman 113
Cannom, Greg 98, 99, 107, 172
Captain Kronos: Vampire Hunter 133
Carolyn, Axelle 33, 149, 192, 262, 265, 293
Carpenter, John 21, 24, 138-139, 142, 162, 208-209, 276-277, 298
Carrey, Jim 156
Carrie 143
Carson, Dave 202, 205
Castle, Nick 142
Cetrone, Richard 282
Chambers, John 212, 252
Chaney, Lon 14, 159, 273
Chaney, Lon Jr 46, 179, 262, 267
Charlton, Jac 101
Chernobyl 160, 284
Child's Play 150
Clark, Eugene 270-271
Clash of the Titans 134
Clements, Brian 133
Cloak & Dagger 96
Clooney, George 101
Close Encounters of the Third Kind 58
Coleman, Chad 24, 42, 280
Columbus, Chris 232, 236
Company of Wolves, The 175
Conjuring, The 117
Considine, Tim 73
Conway, Lyle 298
Cook, Randy 97
Coppola, Francis Ford 107
Corman, Roger 20, 42
Corso, Bill 35, 43, 75, 122, 298
Coscarelli, Don 119
Coulier, Mark 281
Count Crowley: Reluctant Midnight Monster Hunter 42, 98
Crampton, Barbara 25, 119, 272
Craven, Wes 29, 70, 71, 148-150
Crawford, Joan 194
Creature from the Black Lagoon 20, 226-228, 230, 303
Creepshow 134, 174, 188, 258, 281, 303
Cremaster 3 274
Critters 34
Crognale, Gino 168, 210-211, 270, 274-277
Cronenberg, David 32-33, 242-245
Cruise, Tom 100
Cujo 141, 258
Cundey, Dean 208
Cunningham, Sean 71, 143
Curse of Frankenstein, The 262
Curse of the Werewolf, The 15, 25, 168
Curtis, Jamie Lee 139, 142
Cushing, Peter 96, 230
Czapsky, Stefan 190

D

Danse Macabre 208
Dante, Joe 20, 32, 162, 169, 171, 172, 232-239, 256
Dark Crystal, The 34
Dark Knight, The 106
Dastmalchian, David 37, 42, 98, 106
Davies, Russell T. 25, 198, 201
Davis, Warwick 112
Davison, Jon 85, 256
Day of the Triffids 230
De Laurentiis, Dino 80-82
Dead Ringers 33

Dead Zone, The 33
Deadly Eyes 258
DeKnight, Steven S. 220
Del Toro, Benicio 17, 122, 179
Del Toro, Guillermo 120, 303
Depp, Johnny 190, 274
Descent, The 192
Destroy All Neighbors 53, 120-122
Devil's Backbone, The 192
Dillman, Bradford 256
Docherty, Jason 193
Doctor Who (TV series) 198-201
Dog Soldiers 176-177, 192, 302
Doherty, Rosie 294-295
Dorn, Michael 212-213
Dr. Jekyll and Mr. Hyde 16
Dracula (movie series) 27, 40, 71, 106-107, 162, 306
Dragonslayer 31, 84
Dreamchild 298
Druckmann, Neil 284-287
Dudman, Nick 84-85
Duffer, Matt and Ross 160-162
Dupuis, Stephan 134, 144, 188, 242 245, 298
Durand, Kevin 248

E

Ebert, Roger 134
Ed Wood 190, 253
Edlund, Richard 87, 186, 187, 291
Edward Scissorhands 274
Elizalde, Mike 41, 73, 120, 173, 300
Elsey, Dave and Lou 179
Emge, David 266-267
Esposito, John 100
Evil Dead, The (movie series) 34, 110-112, 211, 300
Evil Speak 110
Exorcist, The 24, 56, 303
Explorers 172

F

Face Off 302
Faculty, The 215
Fear the Walking Dead 279
Feige, Kevin 180
Feud: Bette and Joan 194
Fields, Lisa 147
Finnell, Mike 232
Fly, The (movie series) 25, 32-33, 242-245
Forbidden Planet 21, 138
Forsch, Bill 173
Francis, Freddie 25
Franco, Larry 214
Frankenheimer, John 257
Frankenhooker 272
Frankenstein 40, 45, 107, 262-265
Frankenstein Meets the Wolf Man 46, 262
Frankenweenie 258

Franklin, Richard 150, 188
Fraser, Mat 194
Friday the 13th (series) 142-147
Fright Night 96-98, 306
From Beyond 272
From Dusk Till Dawn 100-101, 162, 267
Fuller, Brad 144, 152
Fuller, Bruce 119
Fullerton, Carl 144

G

Game of Thrones 160, 280, 287
Garber, Jake 277
Garris, Mick 35, 36, 37, 102, 298
Ghost Story 31, 107, 277, 293
Ghostbusters (movie series) 61, 111, 290-291
Ghosts of Mars 21
Giacchino, Michael 48, 78, 134, 180, 255
Giannelli, Mike 156
Giant Claw, The 23
Giger, H. R. 28, 300
Gillis, Alec 144, 210
Godzilla (movie series) 37, 53-54, 92-93, 126
Goldblum, Jeff 32-33, 242-245
Golden Seal, The 258
Golden, Kelly 117
Goldsmith, Jerry 28, 32, 254
Goodman, Dave 100
Gordon Green, David 142
Gordon, Stuart 272, 300
Gorton, Neill 25, 198, 201, 300
Goth, Mia 193, 258
Gould, Dana 14, 46, 89, 252-253
Gower, Barrie and Sarah 23, 62, 122, 134, 160, 162, 280, 284-287
Great Mysteries of the World 40
Gremlins (movie series) 33-34, 62, 226, 232-241, 298, 306
Guillermin, John 80

H

Halloween 59, 138-142
Halo 222
Haney, Kevin 128
Hanging With Doctor Z 253
Hanks, Tom 135
Harris, Roy 68
Harry and the Hendersons 72
Harry Potter and the Goblet of Fire 84, 85
Harryhausen, Ray 14, 15, 45, 68, 87,88, 125-135, 300, 306
Hatton, Rondo 184
Hayes, Craig 85
Hellboy (movie series) 120, 300
Hellraiser 112, 213
Herrmann, Bernard 138
Hessler, Gordon 133

Hills Have Eyes, The 29
Hirsch, Paul 303
Hodder, Kane 144
Holland, Tom 96-97, 150, 188
Honda, Ishiro 55
Hooper, Tobe 210-211
Hopkins, Anthony 179, 182-184, 192
Hora, John 169
Horror Express 42
House Mother 119
House of 1000 Corpses 276
House of Horrors 184
House on Haunted Hill 26-27
Howard Thornton, David 156
Howard, Sherman 266, 269
Howison, Del 14, 23, 228
Howling Harry 46
Howling, The (movie series) 50, 168 173, 176, 302
Huebner, Mentor 80
Humphreys, Graham 23, 27, 110, 132,170-171, 180-181
Hunchback of Notre Dame, The 14, 122, 184, 273
Huston, John 14

I

In Search Of... 40, 180
In the Mouth of Madness 276
Independence Day 214
Insidious 117
Interview with the Vampire 61, 100 101, 104-105
Invaders from Mars 210-211
Invasion of the Saucer Men 21
Irons, Jeremy 33
It Came from Outer Space 21
It Conquered the World 21
It's a Wonderful Life 306
It's Alive 24

J

Jackson, Cheyenne 119
Jackson, Kerrin 31, 40, 102, 142, 259, 276-278
Jackson, Peter 75
Jakob's Wife 119
Jarman, Duncan 57, 62, 122, 162, 274, 280, 284, 301
Jason and the Argonauts 25, 128, 130-131, 135, 256
Jason X 144
Jaws 27, 57, 64, 148, 184, 252, 255
Johansen, Adam 112, 218
John Dies at the End 119
Johnson, Steve 35, 99, 173, 291
Johnson, Tor 190
Johnston, Joe 179, 204
Jones, Carey 48, 180
Jones, Doug 300, 302-303
Jordan, Neil 101, 175
Jovovich, Milla 120

Julius, Marshall 8, 9, 126, 165, 186, 320
Jupiter's Legacy 220-221
Jurassic Park (movie series) 45, 86, 87, 214

K

Karanouh, Nesrin 274
Karloff, Boris 14, 17, 18, 72, 107, 141, 184, 262, 265
Kaufman, Lloyd 73
Keaton, Michael 114
Keen, Bob 177
Ketner, Lukas 98
Kiel, Richard 186
King Kong 14, 20, 21, 45, 68, 78-83, 132
King, Stephen 35,174, 188, 208, 298
Kirkpatrick, Kevin 249
Knight, Silvi 34, 58, 114, 141, 194
Krige, Alice 31, 293
Kurtzman, Robert 31, 34, 100, 101, 111, 114, 119, 211, 301

L

Lanchester, Elsa 18, 265
Land of the Lost 73
Landau, Martin 190
Landis, John 35, 80, 169, 176
Lane, Tami 18, 61, 73, 105, 114, 139, 149
Lang, Colin 176-177
Lang, Fritz 106
Lange, Jessica 194
LaPorte, Steve 114, 171
Last House on the Left, The 71
Last Man on Earth, The 42
Last of Us, The 62, 284-287
Last Voyage of the Demeter, The 106-107
Laughton, Charles 143, 184
Lee, Christopher 23, 45, 71, 99, 262
Legend 191
Legend of the Werewolf 25
Legion 102, 246-247
Leone, Damien 15, 27, 33, 64, 130, 156
Leprechaun 112
Lindenlaub, Karl Walter 62, 214, 222
Lines, Adam 294-295
Little House on the Prairie 202
Little Nicky 111, 116, 305
Little Shop of Horrors 34, 42
Living Dead, The (movie series) 56, 100, 266-271, 281
Lone Survivor 28, 217
Lost 255
Lost Boys, The 34, 99
Lost World, The 14
Love at First Bite 50, 96
Lucas, George 186, 202, 205
Lugosi, Bela 16, 23, 45, 190, 253, 262
Lundström, Göran 107, 179, 191, 218

Lynch, John Carroll 159

M

Man Who Laughs, The 17
Mane, Tyler 64, 75, 139, 141, 220-221
Maniac 188
March, Fredric 16
Mars Attacks! 212-214
Marsan, Eddie 191
Marshall, E. G. 258
Marshall, Neil 74, 120, 176-177, 192, 302
Matango 55
Matthews, Kerwin 128
MaXXXine 188
Mazin, Craig 284, 287
Mbatha-Raw, Gugu 201
McCarthy, Frank 27
McCarthy, Kevin 256
McDowall, Roddy 96, 98, 252, 254
McVey, Tony 205
Mears, Derek 41, 146-147, 217, 248-249
Mekash, Eryn Krueger and Mike 59, 119, 159, 194, 212
Mendez, Mike 31, 34, 58, 88, 211
Metheney, Brynn 291
Metropolis 106
Mighty Joe Young 21
Million Dollar Movie, The 51
Milonoff, Eero 191
Mitchell, Jim 84, 87, 214
Moby Dick 14
Mole People, The 226
Mombrun, Dominic 101
Monster Challenge 180
Moonraker 186
Moore, Alan 248
Moore, Roger 186
Moore, Ted 133
Morricone, Ennio 139
Mowat, Donald 244
Mummy, The 14, 18, 21, 27, 265, 267, 306
Munro, Caroline 70, 133, 162, 230
Munsters, The 23, 168
Muren, Dennis 84, 87, 187, 202, 205
Murphy, Stephen 45, 281
Murphy, Ryan 194

N

Nakajima, Haruo 104
Natural Born Killers 100
Naughton, David 171
Necronomicon 114
Neill, Ve 18, 51, 98, 99, 114, 162, 190, 192, 274, 302
Nelson, Christopher 56-59, 171
Nelson, Dave 210-211
Nemolato, Luca 248
Neumeier, Ed 85
Nicotero, Greg 20, 21, 46, 134, 135,

166-168, 215, 217, 230, 268 271, 277-279, 281, 302
Nightmare Cinema 37, 102
Nimoy, Leonard 180
Nispel, Marcus 144, 147, 152
Nosferatu 40, 107
Nyby, Christian 208
Nye, Ben 64

O
O'Brien, Willis 14, 20-21
Oldman, Gary 122
Omen, The 45
Ormsby, Alan 43
Oswalt, Patton 180
Øvredal, André 106

P
Patric, Jason 34
Patrick, Butch 168
Patrick, Milicent 226
Patriots Day 217
Paulson, Sarah 119
Paxton, Bill 211
Pegg, Simon 93, 135, 162, 198, 208, 269
Percy, Lee 272
Peters, Evan 119
Phantom of the Opera, The 14-15
Picardo, Robert 50, 171, 172
Pierce, Jack 18, 46, 48, 169, 179, 265
Piranha 256-257
Pitt, Micheline 226, 265
Planet of the Apes (movie series) 33, 252-255
Podavin, Leanne 50, 174, 175, 293
Poltergeist (movie series) 61, 174-175
Popeye 31
Predators 217
Prentice, Margaret 244
Price, Vincent 27, 29, 70, 96
Prophecy 256-257
Psycho (movie series) 150, 188

Q
Quatermass and the Pit 24
Quist, Gerry 128, 184

R
Rabid 33
Raiders of the Lost Ark 186-187
Raimi, Sam 34, 35, 75, 111, 211, 300
Raleigh, Justin 16, 24, 117, 248, 282, 302
Rambaldi, Carlo 80-82
Raponi, Carlo and Isidoro 82
Re-Animator 272
Rear Window 96
Reed, Oliver 15, 25, 168
Reeves, Matt 254
Reign of Fire 84
Reitman, Ivan 61, 291
Reitman, Jason 60, 149, 290-291, 302
Reservoir Dogs 100
Resident Evil 270, 274
Rice, Anne 105
Richards, Emil 255
RoboCop (movie series) 84-85

Roddenberry, Gene 213
Rodriguez, Robert 101, 215
Rogers, Dirk 36, 53, 61, 91, 102-105, 246
Romero, George A. 40, 258, 266-270, 279, 303
Rosengrant, John 87, 100
Roth, Ed "Big Daddy" 36
Rubano, Sarah 193
Rudolph the Red-Nosed Reindeer 302
Ruffalo, Mark 122

S
Salem's Lot 41, 192
Sansom, Sean 32, 262, 270, 302-303
Savini, Tom 56, 101, 135, 143, 144, 162, 174, 188, 258, 266-268, 271, 298, 303
Scanners 188
Schell, Jordu 28, 33, 54, 56, 304-305
Schneer, Charles H. 133
Schoneberg, Andy 252-253
Schumacher, Joel 99
Schwartz, Ben 180
Scorsese, Martin 33
Scott, Ridley 24, 28, 218, 300
Sgt Kabukiman N.Y.P.D. 73
Shaun of the Dead 162, 268-270
She-Creature, The 21
Shelley, Mary 262-265
Shining, The 35, 298
Shocker 29
Short, Bob 257
Silence of the Lambs, The 184, 192
Simpsons, The 253
Sims, Aaron 117, 155
Sinbad (movie series) 45, 128-129, 132-133, 134, 306
Singer, Bryan 75
Siodmak, Curt 46, 262
Skinned Deep 155
Smith, Dick 24, 31, 46, 107, 174, 293, 298
Smith, Matthew 274
Smith, Tom 187
Spaced 269
Spielberg, Steven 86-87, 93, 186, 232, 236, 252, 290
Spy Who Loved Me, The 186
Squirm 80
Stan Against Evil 89
Stand, The 35
Star Trek (series) 68, 168, 212-213
Star Wars (movie series) 25, 28, 188, 202-209, 303
Steiner, Max 78
Stoddard, Scott 21, 52, 144, 146-147, 152, 304
Stoltz, Eric 244
Strange, Glenn 17
Stranger Things 160-162
Swamp Thing 248-249
Swindell, Howard 284

T
Tai, Kobe 217
Tait, Douglas 72-73, 120
Takeya, Takayuki 37

Talbot, Larry 46
Tales From the Crypt 272-273
Tarantino, Quentin 100
Tavares, Mark 28, 88, 111, 116, 130, 162, 305
Taylor, Rod 230
Terrifier (movie series) 64, 156
Texas Chainsaw Massacre, The 152
Thatcher, Kirk 48, 68, 130, 203, 205
Thing, The (series) 31, 139, 208-209, 306
Thir13en Ghosts 291-295
This Island Earth 226
Tierno, Mark 267
Time Machine, The 230
Tiomkin, Dimitri 138
Tippett, Phil 31, 45, 84-87, 135, 202, 205, 256
Todd, Tony 113
Torres, Mario Jr 120
Toth, Wayne 36, 52, 72, 100, 135, 139, 141, 276, 305
Trilogy of Terror 25
Tripper, The 29
Trog 194
True Romance 100
Tucker, Christopher 175
Tuiten, Arjen 291
Turi, Josh 31, 55, 73
Twilight Zone, The 156

U
Ure, Stephen 193

V
Valley of Gwangi, The 26-27, 132
Vampires 139
Van Dyke, Vincent 194
Varan 104
Varner, Steve 82
Veidt, Conrad 17
Verhoeven, Paul 85
Very Bad Things 217
Videodrome 33
Vining, Stephen 259
Vulich, John 266, 271

W
Walas, Chris 32, 53, 84, 130, 134, 187, 202, 232-240, 242-245, 257, 306
Walken, Christopher 33
Walker, Megan 98
Walking Dead, The 259, 262, 274-280
Wallace, Dee 141, 302
Wan, James 117, 248
Ward, Alexander 119
Warren, Lorraine 117
Wasner, Kevin 34, 138, 142, 193, 221, 259, 277, 278, 306
Wayne, John 144
Webber, Simon 284
Weintraub, Jerry 150
Welch, Raquel 133
Werewolf by Night 48, 180

West, Kit 205
West, Ti 75, 188, 193, 258, 291
Westmore, Bud 20, 226, 228
Westmore, Michael 18, 21, 168, 184, 212-213, 228
Where the Wild Things Are 55
White, Ted 144
Williams, John 68, 148, 255
Williams, Steve 'Spaz' 87
Winston, Matt 295
Winston, Stan 28, 87, 100, 211, 274, 295, 304
Winter, Alex 54, 98, 122
Wishmaster 114
Witcher, The 122
Witkin, Joel-Peter 152
Wolf Man, The 46
Wolfinger, Terry 23, 41, 50, 59, 113
Wolfman, The 17, 179
Woods, James 33
Woolley, Stephen 175
World War Z 281
Wray, Fay 14, 68
Wright, Edgar 269
Wrightson, Bernie 28, 98, 215, 248, 264-265
Wrightson, Bernie and Michelle 57, 59, 188
Wrightson, John 18, 28, 57, 64, 264 265, 279
Wyler, Shayne 291, 293

X
X 193, 258
Xena: Warrior Princess 88
X-Files, The 89
X-Men 75

Y
Yagher – Chris, Jeff and Kevin 272-273
Yagher, Jeff 48, 49, 168, 273, 306
Yagher, Kevin 48, 144, 150
Yamazaki, Takashi 37, 55, 84, 93, 131
Youmans, Coleman 278
Young Frankenstein 43

Z
Zeller, Gary 188
Zombie, Rob 36, 139, 141

ACKNOWLEDGEMENTS

Thanks, first, to our incredible cast of contributors, for their wonderful stories and fantastic photographs: Allan Apone, Gary Archer, David Arquette, Rick Baker, Gabe Bartalos, Peter Berg, Charles Bernstein, Axelle Carolyn, John Carpenter, Chad Coleman, Randy Cook, Bill Corso, Barbara Crampton, Wes Craven, Gino Crognale, Joe Dante, David Dastmalchian, Russell T Davies, Stephan Dupuis, Richard Edlund, Jason Edmiston, Mike Elizalde, Robert Englund, Michael Giacchino, Neill Gorton, Dana Gould, Barrie Gower, Sarah Gower, Ray Harryhausen, Tom Holland, Del Howison, Graham Humphreys, Kerrin Jackson, Duncan Jarman, Adam Johansen, Larry Karaszewski, Richard Kiel, Silvi Knight, Robert Kurtzman, Tami Lane, Damien Leone, Karl Walter Lindenlaub, Adam Lines, Göran Lundström, Tyler Mane, Neil Marshall, Derek Mears, Eryn Krueger Mekash, Mike Mekash, Mike Mendez, Jim Mitchell, Donald Mowat, Caroline Munro, Stephen Murphy, Ve Neill, Christopher Nelson, Greg Nicotero, Simon Pegg, Micheline Pitt, Leanne Podavin, Gerry Quist, Justin Raleigh, Jason Reitman, Dirk Rogers, George A. Romero, Tom Savini, Sean Sansom, Jordu Schell, Scott Stoddard, Douglas Tait, Mark Tavares, Kirk Thatcher, Phil Tippett, Wayne Toth, Christopher Tucker, Josh Turi, Chris Walas, Kevin Wasner, Ti West, Mike Westmore, Alex Winter, Terry Wolfinger, John Wrightson, Jeff Yagher and Takashi Yamazaki.

Thanks to our editor Ross Hamilton, our designer Russell Knowles, to Joe Cottington and everyone else who helped us along the way: Heidi Berger, Holly Berger, Emma Cammack, Robert Carrelli, Regina Castruita, Mary Challman, Scott Chesebrough, Sam Clements, Andrew and Debbie Doubleday, Aran Doyle, Branan Edgens, Joshua Evans, Stacie and Josh Finesilver, Pete Fletzer, Ronald Fogelman, David P. Geister, James Hancock, John and Lisa Hernandez, Amy Homma, Russell Julius, Jessica and Michael Kolence, Bill Kramer, Heather and Allan Kruse, Wendy and Oliver Laws, Jaime Leigh, Scott Marquette, Mitch Matthews, Craig McFarland, Naimie, Mark and Lauren Noble, Jeannie and Sonny Raffle, Joe Russo, Emma Rutherford, Alfonso Salazar, Patrick Savage, Matt Serverson, Meredith Shea, Robert Skidmore, Penny and Anthony Smith, Kimberly Stephens, Thiago Nishimoto, Sean Sobczak, Sal Stella, Bill Strauss, Joshua Thomas, Dax Thorup, Veronica Torres, Johnny Villanueva and Mary and Alan Wanbon. Also our kids, Kelsey, Travis and Jacob, Martyna, Maia and Phoebe, and our parents, Susan and Kenneth Berger, and Myrna and Morris Julius.

Thanks to Forrest J. Ackerman, James Bama, Terence Fisher, Jerry Goldsmith, Boris Karloff, Stephen King, Christopher Lee, Edgar Allan Poe, James Whale, John Williams and Bernie Wrightson for a lifetime of inspiration.

The authors would also like to thank the following people, without whose help and artistry this book would not have been possible: Ali Abbasi, J.J. Abrams, Scott Alexander, Roy Ashton, Matthew Barney, Tom Baker, Bebe and Louis Barron, Amanda Bearse, John Berg, Joseph Bishara, Karen Black, Paul Blaisdell, Robert Bobroczkyi, Agnes Born, Javier Botet, Rob Bottin, Jamie Campbell Bower, Ray Bradbury, Doug Bradley, Mel Brooks, Ricou Browning, Billy Bryan, Michael Burnett, Bob Burns, Tim Burton, Bill Butler, Norman Cabrera, James Cameron, Bruce Campbell, Dave Carson, John Chambers, Lon Chaney, Lon Chaney Jr, Lyle Conway, Roger Corman, Don Coscarelli, Mark Coulier, David Cronenberg, Tom Cruise, Dean Cundey, Sean Cunningham, Jamie Lee Curtis, Peter Cushing, Warwick Davis, Jon Davison, Dino De Laurentiis, Benicio Del Toro, Guillermo del Toro, Steven S. DeKnight, Jason Docherty, Richard Donner, Neil Druckmann, Nick Dudman, The Duffer Brothers, Jay Dugré, Griffin Dunne, Stephan Dupuis, Ed Edmunds, David Emge, Freddie Francis, Stuart Freeborn, Carl Fullerton, Mick Garris, H. R. Giger, Basil Gogos, Jeff Goldblum, Stuart Gordon, Mia Goth, David Gordon Green, John Guillermin, Roy Harris, Rondo Hatton, Craig Hayes, Frank Henenlotter, Jim Henson, Bernard Herrmann, Alfred Hitchcock, Kane Hodder, Ishirō Honda, Tobe Hooper, Anthony Hopkins, John Hora, Sherman Howard, Peter Jackson, Joe Johnston, Carey Jones, Doug Jones, Nesrin Karanouh, Roger Kastel, Lloyd Kaufman, Bob Keen, Lukas Ketner, Rich Koz, Elsa Lanchester, Martin Landau, John Landis, Colin Lang, Jessica Lange, George Lucas, Bela Lugosi, John Carroll Lynch, Leanne Mabberley, Kerwin Matthews, Gugu Mbatha-Raw, Roddy McDowall, Fredric March, Frank McCarthy, Dominic Mombrun, Ennio Morricone, Dennis Muren, Haruo Nakajima, David Naughton, Marcus Nispel, Maila Nurmi, Willis O'Brien, Gary Oldman, Alan Ormsby, André Øvredal, Milicent Patrick, Cassandra Peterson, Robert Picardo, Jack Pierce, Mitch Pileggi, Vincent Price, Sam Raimi, Carlo Rambaldi, Oliver Reed, Matt Reeves, Sam Reid, Ivan Reitman, Gene Roddenberry, Robert Rodriguez, Sue Roy, Sarah Rubano, Joel Schumacher, Ridley Scott, Rod Serling, Mary Shelley, Curt Siodmak, Dick Smith, Roberta Solomon, Steven Spielberg, Max Steiner, Bram Stoker, Glenn Strange, Daniel Striepeke, Drew Struzan, Takayuki Takeya, Quentin Tarantino, Al Taylor, David Howard Thornton, Tony Todd, William Tuttle, John Vulich, Megan Walker, James Wan, Alexander Ward, Perc Westmore, Ted White, Steve 'Spaz' Williams, Stan Winston, Alex Winter, Fay Wray, Edgar Wright, Meg Wyllie, Kevin Yagher, Gary Zeller and Rob Zombie.

Thanks also to ABC Television, The Academy Museum of Motion Pictures, The Academy of Motion Picture Arts and Sciences, Altered States FX, Alterian Inc, Amazon Studios, Amblin Entertainment, AMC, Aurora Monster Models, Autonomous FX, Bad Robot, BBC, CBS, Cinefex, Cinovation, Columbia Studios, DDT, Disney Studios, Don Post Studios, Dreamworks Pictures, Empire Pictures, *Famous Monsters of Filmland*, *Fangoria*, Fractured FX, Frends Beauty Supplies, Funky Monkey Designs, Hammer Studios, HBO, Henson Productions, ILM, KNB EFX Group, Inc, Legacy Effects, Lucasfilm, Makeup Effects Lab, Margaret Herrick Library, Marvel Studios, MGM Studios, National Galleries Scotland, NBC, Netflix, New Line Cinema, Optic Nerve, Paramount Pictures, Point Grey, Pronrenfx, Saturday Night Live, Searchlight Films, Sony Studios, Stan Winston Studios, Starlog Publications, StudioADI, 20th Century Fox, Toho Co., Ltd., United Artists, Universal Studios, Warner Bros. Studios, WETA Workshop and Wingnut Films.

Finally, boundless thanks to our wives, Mirjam and Ruta, for all their help, encouragement, patience and love. We couldn't have done it without them.

FILM CREDITS

20 Million Miles to Earth (1957), Morning Side Productions 127

Abbott & Costello Meet Frankenstein (1948), Universal International Pictures 43

Alien (1979), 20th Century Fox / Brandywine Productions / Scott Free Productions 28

Alien: Covenant (2017), 20th Century Fox / TSG Entertainment / Scott Free Productions 218 219

American Horror Story (2011–present), 20TH Television / Ryan Murphy Television / Brad Falchuk Teley-Vision 118, 158-159

An American Werewolf in London (1981), PolyGram Pictures / The Guber-Peters Company 170

A Nightmare on Elm Street (1984), New Line Cinema / Heron Communications / Smart Egg Pictures 148-149

Army of Darkness (1991), Dino De Laurentiis Company / Renaissance Pictures / Introvision International 34, 111, 301

Army of the Dead (2021), The Stone Quarry / Netflix 282-283

Aurora Model Kits, The Aurora Plastics Corp / Monogram Models 23

Battleship (2012), Universal Pictures / Hasbro/ Bluegrass Films 217

Beetlejuice (1988), The Geffen Company 114

Big Ass Spider! (2013), Epic Pictures Group / Film Entertainment Services / ICE Animations 89

Blade (1998), New Line Cinema / Amen Ra Films / Imaginary Forces 94-95

Border (2018), Meta Film Stockholm / Black Spark Film & TV / Karnfilm 191

Brain Death (1992), Neil Marshall & John Slater, 74

Bride of Frankenstein (1935), Universal Pictures 19, 263, 307

Bride of Re-Animator (1990), Wild Street Pictures / Re-Animator II Productions 305

Candyman (1992), Polygram Entertainment / Propaganda Films / Candyman Films 113

Child's Play (1988), United Artists 151

Count Crowley: Reluctant Midnight Monster Hunter (2019-present), Image Comics, 42, 98

Countdown (2019), STX Films / Wrigley Pictures / Two Grown Men 102

Creature from the Black Lagoon (1954), Universal Pictures 20, 226-229

Creepshow (1982), United Film Distribution Company / Laurel Show, Inc 174, 188

Dawn of the Planet of the Apes (2014), 20th Century Fox / Chernin Entertainment / Ingenious Media 254-255

Dawn of the Dead (1978), Laurel Group 267

Day of the Dead (1985), Laurel Entertainment 266-268

Deadpool & Wolverine (2024), Marvel Studios / 20th Century Studios/ Maximum Effort 75

Destroy All Monsters (1968), Toho Studios 90

Destroy All Neighbors (2024), Counterpart Pictures / RLJE Films / Shudder 52, 123

Doctor Who (2005-Present), BBC Wales / BBC Studios 196-201

Dog Soldiers (2002), Centurion / Kismet Entertainment / The Noel Gay Motion Picture Company 176-177

Dracula (1931), Universal Pictures 16, 307

Dracula 73 (1972), Hammer Films 26

Dracula A.D. 1972 (1972), Hammer Films 70

Dragonslayer (1981), Paramount Pictures / Walt Disney Productions 31, 84

Dr. Jekyll and Mr. Hyde (1931), Paramount Pictures 16

Edward Scissorhands (1990), 20th Century Fox / Tim Burton Productions 274

Ed Wood (1992), Touchstone Pictures / Tim Burton Productions / DiNova Pictures 190

Evil Dead II (1987), Renaissance Pictures 211, 301

Evil Dead Rise (2023), Department of Post / Ghost House Films / New Line Cinema 112

Famous Monsters Magazine, Warren Publishing 17

Feud (2017–24), Plan B Entertainment / Ryan Murphy Productions / Fox 21 Television Studios 194-195

Frankenhooker (1990), Levins-Henenlotter / Shapiro-Glickenhaus Entertainment 272

Frankenstein (1983), Universal Pictures 264

Frankenstein Meets the Wolf Man (1943), Universal Pictures 262

Freaked (1993), Chiodo Brothers Production / Tommy / Ufland Productions 309

Friday the 13th (1980), Paramount Pictures / Georgetown Productions Inc. / Sean S. Cunningham Films 143

Friday the 13th (2009), new Line Cinema / Paramount Pictures / Platinum Dunes 145, 146-147

Friday the 13th: The Final Chapter (1984), Paramount Pictures / Georgetown Productions Inc. / Sean S. Cunningham Films 144

Fright Night (1985), Columbia Pictures / Vistar Films 96-97, 307

From Beyond (1986), Empire Pictures / Taryn Prov 301

From Dusk Till Dawn (1996), Dimension Films / A Band Apart / Los Hooligans Productions / Miramax 100-101

Game of Thrones (2011-2019), HBO Entertainment / Television 360 / Grok! Television / Generator Entertainment / Startling Television / Bighead Littlehead 280

Ghostbusters (1984), Columbia Pictures / Delphi Films / Black Rhino Productions 290

Ghostbusters: Afterlife (2021), Columbia Pictures / BRON Studios / Ghostcorps 60, 291

Ghost Story (1981), Universal Pictures 30

Ginger Snaps 3 (2004), 49 Films / Combustion / Lions Gate Films 50

Godzilla Minus One (2023), Robot Communications / Toho Studios / Toho 37, 55

Godzilla Vs. The Thing (1964), Toho Studios 92

Gremlins (1984), Amblin Entertainment 233-238

Gremlins 2: The New Batch (1990), Amblin Entertainment 224-225, 238-241, 299

Halloween (1978), Compass International Pictures / Falcon International Pictures 139

Halloween (2007), Dimension Films / Nightfall productions / Spectacle Entertainment Group 136-137, 140-141

Halloween (2018), Blumhouse Productions / Miramax / Night Blade Holdings 58, 142

Halo (2022-2024), 343 Industries / Amblin Television / Chapter Eleven 22-223

Hanging With Doctor Z (2012-present), Dana Gould & Robert Cohen, 252-253

Harry Potter and the Goblet of Fire (2005), Warner Bros. Pictures / Heyday Films 85

Hellboy (2019), Columbia Pictures / Revolution Studios / Lawrence Gordon/Lloyd Levin Productions 121

Hellboy II: The Golden Army (2008), Relativity Media / Lawrence Gordon/Lloyd Levin Productions / Dark Horse Entertainment 120, 300

Hellraiser (1987), Film Futures / New World Pictures 113

He Who Gets Slapped (1924), MGM 159

House on Haunted Hill (1959), Allied Artists Pictures / William Castle Productions 26

Howling V: The Rebirth (1989), Allied Vision / Lane Pringle Productions / Mafilm 173

Insidious (2010), FilmDistrict / Stage 6 Films / Alliance 117

Interview with the Vampire (2022-present), AMC Studios / anonymous Content / Dwight Street Book Club 61, 101, 104-105

In the Mouth of Madness (1994), New Line Cinema 276

Invaders From Mars (1986), Cannon Pictures 210-211

It's Alive (1974), Warner Bros. / Larco Productions 24

Jason and the Argonauts (1963), Charles H. Schneer Productions 128, 130-131

Jaws (1975), Zanuck/Brown Productions / Universal Pictures 27, 250-251, 255

John Dies at the End (2012), M3 Alliance / M3 Creative / Midnight Alliance 119

Jupiter's Legacy (2021), DeKnight Productions / Di Bonaventura Pictures / Image Comics 220-221

Jurassic Park (1993), Universal Pictures / Amblin Entertainment 45, 86-87

Jurassic Park III (2001), Universal Pictures / Amblin Entertainment 87

King Kong (1933), RKO Radio Pictures 21, 68-69, 78-79

King Kong (1976), Dino0 De Laurentiis Company 76-77, 81-83

Land of the Dead (2005), Universal Pictures / Atmosphere Entertainment MM / Romero-Grunwald 269-271

Land of the Lost (2009), Universal Pictures / Relativity Media / Sid & Marty Krofft Pictures 72

Laserblast (1978), Irwin Yablans Company / Charles Band Productions 51

Legion (2017-2019), FX Productions / Marvel Television 102-103, 246-247

Leprechaun (1992), Trimark Pictures 112

Little Nicky (2000), New Line Cinema 108-109, 116, 305

Mars Attacks! (1996), Warner Bros. / Tim Burton Productions 213-214

Mondo, Funco / Alamo Drafthouse Cinemas 90

Movie Monsters (1975), Scholastic Book Services 43

Nightmare Cinema (2018), Cinelou Films / Cranked Up Films / Good Deal Entertainment 36, 102

Night of the Living Dead (1990), 21st Century Film Corp. / Columbia Pictures 271

Nosferatu (1922), Prana Film 40

Piranha (1978), new World Pictures / Chako Film Company 256-257

Planet of the Apes (1968), APJAC Productions 252, 254

Poltergeist: The Legacy (1996–99), PMP Legacy Productions / Showtime Networks / Trilogy Entertainment Group 175

Predators (2010), Davis Entertainment Company / Dune Entertainment / Ingenious Media / Troublemaker Studios 216-217

Prophecy (1979), Paramount Pictures 257

Raiders of the Lost Ark (1981), Paramount Pictures / Lucasfilm 187

Rebel Moon - Part Two: The Scargiver (2024), Grand Electric / The Stone Quarry 303

Return of the Jedi (1983), Lucasfilm Ltd 202-207

RoboCop (1987), Orion Pictures 85

Scanners (1981), Canadian Film Development Corp. / Filmplan International 189

Scream (1996), Dimension Films / Woods Entertainment 71, 150

Shocker (1989), Alive Films / Universal City Studios / Carolco International 29

Sinbad and the Eye of the Tiger (1977), Columbia Pictures / Charles H. Schneer Productions / Andor Films 129

Skinned Deep (2004), Center Ring Entertainment 154-155

Stan Against Evil (2016–18), Radical Media 89

Star Trek III: The Search for Spock (1984), Paramount Pictures 66-67

Star Trek: Deep Space Nine (1993–1999), Paramount Pictures 213

Star Trek: The Next Generation (1987-1994), Paramount Pictures 212

Star Wars (1977), Lucasfilm / 20TH Century Fox 203

Stranger Things (2016-25), 21 Laps Entertainment / Monkey Massacre / Netflix 160-163

Swamp Thing (2019), Big Shoe Productions / Atomic Monster / DC Universe 248-249

Svengoolie (1970-present), WCIU 42

Tales From the Crypt (1989-1996), HBO 273

Tales From the Darkside (1983-1988), Paramount Pictures / Laurel Entertainment

Terrifier 2 (2022), Dark Age Cinema / Fuzz on the Lens Productions 157

Terrifier 3 (2024), Dark Age Cinema / Bloody Disgusting / Fuzz on the Lens Productions 64-65

The 7th Voyage of Sinbad (1958), Columbia Pictures / Morningside Productions 128-129

The Amazing Spider-Man 2 (2014), Columbia Pictures / Marvel Entertainment 73

The Beast From 20,000 Fathoms (1953), Jack Dietz Productions / Mutual Pictures of California 127

The Chronicles of Narnia: Prince Caspian (2008), Walt Disney Pictures / Walden Media 62-63

The Company of Wolves (1984), Incorporated Television Company / Palace Pictures 175

The Curse of Frankenstein (1957), Hammer Films 262

The Curse of the Werewolf (1961) Hammer Films 12-13, 25, 168

The Descent (2005), Celador Films / Northman Productions / Pathe UK 192

The Evil Dead (1981), Renaissance Pictures 110

The Exorcist (1973), Hoya Productions 24

The Faculty (1998), Dimension Films / Los Hooligans Productions 215

The Fly (1986), SLM Productions Group / Brooksfilms 32, 33, 242-245

The Force Awakens (2015), Lucasfilm / Bad Robot 208

The Golden Voyage of Sinbad (1973), Columbia Pictures / Charles H. Schneer Productions /Andor Films 129, 133

The Haunting of Bly Manor (2020), Amblin Television / Intrepid Pictures / Paramount Television Studios 149

The Howling (1981), AVCO Embassy Pictures / Wescom Productions 166-167, 169, 171-172

The Hunchback of Notre Dame (1939), RKO Radio Pictures 184

The Last of Us (2023-present), Naughty Dog 63, 284-287

The Last Voyage of the Demeter (2023), Universal Pictures 106-107

The Lost Boys (1987), Richard Donner Production 99

The Mummy (1932), Universal Pictures 18, 26, 265, 307

The Munsters (1964-66), CBS 23

The Phantom of the Opera (1925), Jewel Productions 15

The Punisher (2017-2019), ABC Signature / Disney-ABC Domestic Television / Marvel Entertainment 73

The Shining (1997), Warner Bros. / Hawk Films / Peregrine 299

The Silence of the Lambs (1991), Strong Heart Productions 182-183

The Spy Who Loved Me (1977), Eon Productions 34

The Strain (2014-2017), Double Dare You / Mirada Studio 302

The Texas Chainsaw Massacre (2003), New Line Cinema / Focus Films / Radar Pictures 152-153

The Thing (1982), Universal Pictures / Turman-Foster Company 209, 307

The Thing from Another World (1951), Winchester Pictures Corp.

The Thing with Two Heads (1972), AIP

The Time Machine (1960), George Pal Productions / Galaxy Films Inc. 230-231

The United Monster Talent Agency (2010), UMTA Productions 46-47

The Valley of Gwangi (1969), Charles H. Schneer Productions 26, 124-125, 132

The Walking Dead (2010-2022), Idiot Box Productions / Circle of Confusion / Skybound Entertainment / Valhalla Entertainment / AMC Studios 260-261, 275-280

The Ward (2010), FilmNation Entertainment / Premiere Pictures / Echo Lake Entertainment 142

The Witcher (2019 – present), Cinesite / Hivemind / Netflix 122

The Wolfman (2010), Universal Pictures / Relativity Meda / Bluegrass Films 178-179

Thir13en Ghosts (2001), Warner Bros. Pictures / Columbia Pictures / Dark Castle Entertainment 288-289, 292-295 Topps, Fantastic Collectibles 149

Trog (1970), Herman Cohen Production 195

Werewolf by Night (2022), Marvel Studios 48, 180

Wishmaster (1997), Image Organization / Pierre David 114-115

World War Z (2013), Paramount Pictures / Skydance Media / Hemisphere Media Capital 281

X (2022), A24 / Little Lamb / Mad Solar Productions 193

Xena: Warrior Princess (1995–2001), Universal Television 88

Young Frankenstein (1974), Gruskoff/Venture Films / Crossbow Productions, Inc. / Jouer Limited 43

PHOTO CREDITS

The publishers would like to thank the following sources for their kind permission to reproduce the pictures in this book:

Academy Museum of Motion Pictures: 135BR, 209T
Alamy Stock Photo: 12, 13, 15, 16 (ALL), 17, 18 (ALL), 19, 20 (ALL), 21B, 23 (ALL), 25, 28, 29, 30 (ALL), 32 (ALL), 37, 40, 68, 69, 70, 71, 78 (ALL), 79 (ALL), 84T, 89B, 90, 94, 95, 97 (ALL), 124, 125, 127 (ALL), 128 (ALL), 129, 130, 131, 132T, 133 (ALL), 158B, 161T, 182, 183, 184 (ALL), 185, 189 (ALL), 195 (ALL), 210, 211TL, 211BL, 217B, 226 (ALL), 230, 231, 250, 251, 252T, 255(sheet Music), 257B, 262 (ALL), 265B, 290, 291
Rick Baker: 24B, 76, 77, 81 (ALL), 82 (ALL), 83 (ALL), 178 (ALL), 179, 199, 209B, 224, 225, 240 (ALL), 241 (ALL)
Gabe Bartalos: 52 (ALL), 112B, 154, 155, 272T, 298 (ALL)
Howard Berger: 34, 46, 47, 73T, 88, 100, 101 (ALL), 102 (ALL), 108, 266T, 263, 109, 111, 116 (ALL), 135BL, 150, 166, 180R, 211R, 215 (ALL), 220 (ALL), 221 (ALL), 228, 263, 267B, 292 (ALL), 293 (ALL), 296, 297, 303T, 319
Charles Bernstein: 148 (ALL)
Axelle Carolyn: 149L
Cinema Makeup School: 9 (lower), 320
Chad Coleman: 280T
Randy Cook: 132
Bill Corso: 35 both, 43 (ALL), 123 (ALL), 299 (ALL)
Barbara Crampton: 272B
Leigh Cresswell: 9, 126
Gino Crognale: 270, 275, 276T, 277 (ALL)
Phil d'Angelo: 139
Joe Dante: 169 (ALL), 171 (ALL), 172 (ALL), 238, 239
David Dastmalchian: 42 (ALL), 98 (ALL), 106
Russell T. Davies: 198, 200 (ALL)
Stephan Dupuis: 242, 244 (ALL)
Robert Englund: 11

Mike Elizalde: 41L, 120 (ALL), 173, 300 (ALL)
Michael Giacchino: 180L, 254 (ALL), 255T
Neill Gorton: 196, 197, 201
Dana Gould: 89TR, 89MR, 252 (Dr. Z), 253 (ALL)
Barrie Gower: 63, 160 (ALL), 161BL, 161BR, 280B, 284, 285, 286, 287
Mike Hill: 135T
Tom Holland: 96 (ALL), 151 (ALL)
Del Howison: 15B
Graham Humphreys - 22, 26 (ALL), 27 (ALL), 110, 170, 181
Kerrin Jackson: 36T, 259 (ALL), 276B
Duncan Jarman: 57L, 122 (ALL), 162, 163
Adam Johansen: 112T, 218 (ALL), 219
Marshall Julius: 92, 93, 186 (ALL), 229
Larry Karaszsewski: 190T, 213BR
Silvi Knight: 58B
KNB Archives: 216, 217T, 247 (ALL)
Robert Kurtzman: 114T, 115, 119, 301 (ALL)
LA Times: 14T
Damien Leone: 65, 157
Adam Lines: 294 (ALL), 295
Justin Lubin: 7
Karl Walter Lindenlaub: 62T, 222, 223 (ALL)
Göran Lundström: 107 (ALL), 191 (ALL)
Tyler Mane: 75
Paul Mann: 94
Neil Marshall: 74 (ALL), 176, 177 (ALL), 192
Derek Mears: 41T, 146TL, 146TR
Eryn Krueger-Mekash: 118
Mike Mekash: 158, 159T, 194 (ALL)
Mike Mendez: 58T
Jim Mitchell: 87T, 214 (ALL)
Donald Mowat: 245 (ALL)
Stephen Murphy: 44, 281 (ALL)
Ve Neill: 51, 99 (ALL), 114B, 190B, 274
Christopher Nelson: 56
Greg Nicotero: 21T, 271T
Simon Pegg: 208 (ALL), 269
Micheline Pitt: 227, 265T
Leanne Podavin: 50, 175B, 288, 289
Justin Raleigh: 117, 248, 249 (ALL), 282 (ALL), 283, 302B
Jason Reitman: 60
Dirk Rogers: 53, 61, 91, 103 (ALL), 104, 105 (ALL)
Sarah Rubano: 193
Tom Savini: 134T, 143, 144, 174 (ALL), 258, 266B, 267T, 268 (ALL), 271B, 303B
Sean Sansom: 302T
Jordu Schell: 54, 304 (ALL)
Dick Smith: 24T
Scott Stoddard: 145 (ALL), 146B, 147, 152 (ALL), 153
Douglas Tait: 72R, 121 (ALL)
Mark Tavares: 164, 165, 305B
Kirk Thatcher: 48, 66, 67
Phil Tippett: 21, 45 (ALL), 85 (ALL), 86, 87B, 134B, 202 (ALL), 203 (ALL), 204 (ALL), 205, 206, 207, 256 (ALL), 257TL, 257TR
Wayne Toth: 36B, 52B, 72L, 136, 137, 140 (ALL), 141 (ALL), 305T
Christopher Tucker: 175TL, 175TR
Josh Turi: 73B
Kimberly Gottlieb-Walker: 138
Chris Walas: 33, 84B, 187 (ALL), 233 (ALL), 234, 235, 236, 237 (ALL), 243 (ALL), 306
Kevin Wasner: 142 (ALL), 260, 261, 278 (ALL)
Michael Westmore: 168TL, 168TR, 212, 213TL, 213ML
Alex Winter: 309
Terry Wolfinger: 4, 38, 39, 59, 113 (ALL)
John Wrightson: 57L, 188, 264 (ALL), 279 (ALL)
Jeff Yagher: 49 (ALL), 168B, 273, 307 (ALL)
Takashi Yamazaki: 55 (ALL)

AUTHOR BIOGRAPHIES

Special Make-up Effects Artist **Howard Berger** has over 800 feature film credits that span four decades. Over the course of Howard's career, he has worked on projects such as *Dances With Wolves* (1990), *Casino* (1995), *From Dusk Till Dawn* (1996), *The Green Mile* (1999), *Kill Bill 1 & 2* (2003), *Oz the Great and Powerful* (2012), *Lone Survivor* (2013), *The Amazing Spider-Man 2* (2014), *The Orville* (2017-Present) and *American Primeval* (2025). In recognition for his work on *The Chronicles of Narnia: The Lion, The Witch and the Wardrobe* (2004) Howard won the Academy Award for Best Make-Up as well as a British Academy Award for Best Achievement in Make-Up. In 2012 Howard was again nominated for an Academy Award for designing and creating Sir Anthony Hopkins' portrait make-up for the FOX Searchlight feature *Hitchcock* (2012). In 1988 Howard co-founded KNB EFX Group, Inc. For the past 37 years KNB has garnered a reputation as the most prolific special effects make-up studio in Hollywood. He resides in Sherman Oaks, CA, with his artist wife, Mirjam.

A veteran nerd with boundless enthusiasm for everything you love, **Marshall Julius** is a film critic, blogger, broadcaster, quizmaster and collector of colourful plastic things. He's also the author of *Action! The Action Movie A-Z* (Batsford Film Books, 1996), *Vintage Geek* (September Publishing, 2019) and, with Howard Berger, *Masters of Make-Up Effects* (Welbeck Publishing, 2022). Marshall lives in Norfolk, England, with his wife Ruta and their hounds Merlin and Morgan.

Also by Howard Berger and Marshall Julius from Welbeck Publishing:
Masters of Make-Up Effects: A Century of Practical Magic (2022)